# Photojournalism

# Photojournalism

## Principles and Practices

## Clifton C. Edom

Professor Emeritus
University of Missouri, Columbia

wcb

**WM. C. BROWN COMPANY PUBLISHERS**
Dubuque, Iowa

Consulting Editor

Curtis MacDougall
Northwestern University

*Dedicated*
*to*
*Vi*

# Contents

Contents

# Preface

Persons reading this book presumably know much about lenses, filters, and film—that is, about the mechanics of a camera. Now, hopefully, they are ready to probe inquiringly and honestly into the very heart and soul of photocommunication.

With regard to the print media, there are those who have said, "Photojournalism is dead," . . . that, with the death of so many large newspapers and the demise of the picture magazine giants *Life* and *Look,* "there is little or no opportunity for the young man or woman who would dedicate his life to the field of Photojournalism."

Don't you believe it!

The challenge is greater, to be sure, and the person who succeeds must know more and work harder than did his predecessor. But—if he or she is willing to pay the price, willing to work hard at the learning process—the opportunity is greater today than ever before.

This book will among other things, hopefully point an aspiring photographer the way thirty years of teaching and close contact with the profession indicate he or she should go. The book is for the photojournalist of tomorrow . . . the photojournalist of twenty years hence.

*Photojournalism: Principles and Practices* is the work of more than one writer. It is a collection of comments brought together under one cover. Rather than "pick the brains" of these experts and translate their message for you, it has been my privilege to stand aside and let the words you read come from the experts themselves. In so doing, I sincerely believe that I have avoided dilution and have strengthened and thereby have increased the value of this book.

All of the contributors are co-workers or students in the School of Journalism, in the Missouri Photo Workshop, or in picture competitions. I am happy, indeed, to share the platform with this illustrious group.

Clifton C. Edom

# Acknowledgments

Grateful acknowledgment is made for the guidance, encouragement, and help given by the following persons: J. Bruce Baumann, Illustrations Department, *National Geographic* magazine; Hal G. Buell, Executive Newsphoto Editor, The Associated Press; Howard Chapnick, President, Black Star Publishing Company; Rich Clarkson, Photo Director, *Topeka Capital-Journal;* W. E. (Bill) Garrett, Senior Assistant Editor, *National Geographic* magazine; Robert E. Gilka, Director of Photography, *National Geographic* magazine; special thanks to Gilbert M. Grosvenor, Editor of *National Geographic* magazine, who gave so much cooperation and who was very generous in permitting use of *National Geographic* photos; Gifford D. Hampshire, Director of Documerica; Wayne V. Harsha, Executive Editor of the *Inland Printer.* and *American Lithographer;* Jack Kenward, Farmland Industries, Inc.; H. Edward Kim, Chief, Layout and Production, *National Geographic* magazine; Bill Kuykendall, free-lance photographer; Brian Lanker, formerly with photo department, *Topeka Capital-Journal;* Ed Lehr, Picture Editor, *Jackson Citizen Patriot;* David Lipman, Assistant Managing Editor, *St. Louis Post-Dispatch;* Giorgio Lotti, *Epoca Magazine,* Milan, Italy; F. W. Lyon, Vice President for Newspictures, United Press International; Prof. Angus McDougall, Director, Photojournalism, School of Journalism, University of Missouri; Tom Riordan, Managing Editor, *Jackson Citizen Patriot;* Dr. Keith P. Sanders, Professor, Communication Research, School of Journalism, University of Missouri; Verna Mae Edom Smith, Teacher, researcher, and consultant in sociology; Dale R. Spencer, Professor of Journalism, University of Missouri; Dr. William Stephenson, Distinguished Research Professor, School of Journalism, University of Missouri; William H. (Bill) Strode III, Assistant Director of Photography for the *Courier-Journal* and the *Louisville Times;* Jerry Umehara, Foreign Picture Editor, United Press International; Arthur L. Witman, St. Louis. A special thanks is due all former students, co-workers, and friends who gave permission to use their photographs.

# Introduction

In 1951 a book titled *Picture Editing*, directed to photojournalism students, free-lance photographers, and newspaper and magazine workers—to all concerned with pictures as a communications tool—was published. The principles set forth in the foreword, written by Frank Luther Mott, Dean of the Missouri University School of Journalism, are as applicable today as they were a quarter of a century ago.

Photojournalism is growing up. It seems only yesterday that the news photographer was looked upon as a queer fellow —half artist and more than half roughneck—and his product was referred to as the "embellishment" of a story or feature. But now, having had an opportunity to observe pictures supplied in rich profusion, and having studied the function of pictures in a world full of them, we who are concerned with producing newspapers and magazines have been forced to take a different attitude. To put it colloquially, we've got a different slant on the whole business. We know that pictures are just as definitely reporting as the written story is. Whether pictures are better reporting than words depends on many factors in individual cases, and is a purely academic question anyway. The point is that they are a necessary part of reporting today.

And if they are reporting, they must lend themselves to the requirements of reporting—timeliness, accuracy, honesty, and so on. Further, they must submit to the techniques of editing just as news stories and features must. Pictures are today an extremely important part of journalism, and we must increasingly regard them as integral with all of journalism. They are, indeed, integral with all of modern communication, not only in newspapers and magazines, but in books, in motion pictures, in television, in advertising, in education . . .

The authors of this book [*Picture Editing*] are committed to this principle of integration. They are striving to apply to pictures the best editing techniques that have been developed in the wide field of communications . . .

The literature of photography is growing: and that is an especially good sign because it indicates that photographers are thinking about their craft. Too long the camera has been a plaything and a gadget. It will always have something of that appeal, but serious cameramen are now realizing that their craft has some of the elements of a profession: it has to be studied, and its use brings responsibilities. There should be a reason for every picture. We have only begun to explore the possibilities of *significance* in photography. It takes thinkers and scholars to lead us in this direction, and books and serious articles and professional associations and schools and seminars. These phenomena of an expanding field and a new profession we are now witnessing . . .

Present-day leaders must be more versatile, must know a great deal about many things. Today the job market is tougher. Competition is keener. If one makes good in photojournalism today and in the future, he must have greater all-around knowledge than was necessary twenty-five to fifty years ago.

To make sure that all of us are on the same wavelength, let's define the term *photojournalism.*

In either the print or electronic media, persons who record a news event with a camera are photo reporters, photo communicators, photojournalists, if you will. But in either television or newspapers, trade journals, and magazines, the photographer is not one whit more a photojournalist than is the picture editor or photo director who sends him on assignment. After the cameraman has returned, the editor must select the picture or pictures which are to appear before the public, and may also do the picture layouts and plan how they are to be presented.

Some modern newspapers have gone beyond this. To ensure the best use of pictures, words, and type, they employ an art director or a director of graphics. The workers who fill these positions work in the field of photojournalism and are, therefore, photojournalists.

They, like photographers, are specialists.

Wilson Hicks emphasized the belief that photojournalism is a partnership affair. Among Mr. Hicks important conclusions, gleaned from many sources are the following:

"An *idea* can come from copy or art. No difference. They both deal with images, either words or pictures . . . copy and art ought to fall in love with each other."

"A clear, concise presentation of the principles of creative advertising [should be] based on the premise that copy, layout, and typography must combine to achieve a simple effect."

"What holds for advertising holds for non-advertising matter . . . Layout and graphic display play an important part in joining visual images. Typography, when used in the spirit of the story, can become a transitional element uniting words and pictures."

# Photojournalism

Two of the most important keys to photojournalism as we know it today were the invention of the halftone screen and the coming of documentary photography. (Photo courtesy New York Public Library.)

# 1

# In the Beginning

Recording history with pictures began thousands of years ago on the cave walls of ancient man.

Ours is a visual age. Pictures are important whether we see them on television, in books, in newspapers, or in magazines. The camera stops a bullet in flight . . . permits us to see man's first step on the moon . . . even lets us examine the miracle of life itself.

To better realize this age of pictures and to savor more fully the "visuality of our time," let us glimpse into the past. Nearly a hundred years ago, Mason Jackson, a perceptive and observant Englishman, wrote:

> The inherent love of pictorial representation in all races of men and in every age is manifest by the frequent attempts made to depict natural objects, under the most unfavourable circumstances and with the slenderest means. The rude drawing scratched on the smooth bone of an animal by the cave-dweller of prehistoric times, the painted rocks of the Mexican forests, and the cave paintings of the Bushmen, are all evidences of this deeply-rooted passion. The child of civilized life looks with delight on his picture book long before he can make out the letters of the alphabet, and the untutored Esquimaux treasures up the stray number of an illustrated newspaper left in his hut by the crew of some whaling ship, though he cannot understand one word of the printed page. But the pictures speak a universal language, which requires no teaching to comprehend.[1]

Predating the alphabet by thousands of years are the paintings and carvings on the walls of the caves of ancient man. In remote areas of Spain, France, Italy, and India remain crude "pictographic records." Hunts, battles and skirmishes, births, deaths—events which took place centuries ago—are, thanks to the fact that they were recorded, subject to visual review.

The story of the illustrated press is long. The illuminated manuscripts of ancient Egypt are thought by some authorities to be the first chapter of that story, and the second chapter, which followed closely, to be the use of woodblocks in the manufacture of playing cards. Soon after came newssheets—one-page, one-shot illustrated publications which recorded the story of a flood, war, famine, or other disaster.

---

1. Mason Jackson, *The Pictorial Press: Its Origin and Progress* (London: Hurst and Blackett, Publishers, 1885).

The sketch artist in the mid-1800s followed a genteel profession. Dressed in top hat and frock coat, John W. Barber, well-known sketch artist–historian, made many trips throughout the nation prior to the Civil War. This engraving from a photograph appeared in the book *A Panorama and Encyclopaedia of the U.S.* by John W. Barber and Henry Howe.

In the hazardous journey from the early crude engravings to the fine wood-cuts of Thomas Bewick (1753–1828) wood engraving as an art form many times stumbled and fell, even after reaching its peak. The illustrations that appeared in the early press made this fact abundantly apparent. However, once the quality of wood engraving had stabilized and the form had become an accepted commodity, illustrated publications gained an important rung on the ladder of mass communications. The wedding of words and pictures did much to enhance the printed page aesthetically and communicatively.

Although both the camera and an embryonic form of photographic reporting were known in the 1840s and 1850s, illustrations then and for many years afterward were, for the most part, the work of sketch artists. True, in 1855

In the Beginning

photographs of the Crimean War by Roger Fenton appeared as woodcuts in the *London Illustrated News,* and photographs of the Civil War by Mathew Brady and his staff appeared in the same manner in United States publications. Nevertheless, the main source of illustrations remained the sketch artists who with pad and pencil recorded the scenes before them.

The outbreak of the Civil War in the United States was propitious for the publishing industry and served as a stimulant, especially to the growth of the illustrated press. In the June 1, 1861 *Leslie's Illustrated Newspaper,* we find the following words:

> OUR ARTISTS IN THE FIELD: Long before the commencement of hostilities, we made arrangements for thoroughly illustrating every event that might arise out of the national difficulties.
>
> We enjoyed the services of first class artists and photographers in all cities and towns within the circle of probable hostilities. We also sent out several artists at a very heavy cost on special missions to the South and West . . .
>
> From these gentlemen we receive 20 to 40 sketches per day . . . From this immense mass of authentic matter we select the most striking, and transferring them to our columns, present them in *Frank Leslie's Illustrated Newspaper,* the only correct and authentic illustrations of the war.[2]

Equally enthusiastic were spokesmen for *Harper's Weekly.* In an advertisement in the March 15, 1862 issue, we read:

> The crisis which the war has reached imparts fresh interest to the war pictures which are appearing in every number of *Harper's Weekly.* We have now regular Artist Correspondents, to wit: Mr. A. R. Waud, with the army of the Potomac; Mr. Alexander Simplot, with Gen. Grant's army; Mr. Henry Mosler, with Gen. Buell's army; Mr. Theo. R. Davis, with Gen. Sherman's army; Mr. Angelo Wiser, with Gen. Burnside's army, besides a large number of occasional and volunteer correspondents in the Army and Navy at various points. These gentlemen will furnish us faithful sketches of every battle which takes place, and every other event of interest, which will be reproduced in our pages in the best style. People who do not see *Harper's Weekly* will have but a limited comprehension of the momentous events which are occurring.[3]

By 1870, film and photographic equipment had improved, but even then "slow" film, lenses, and inadequate shutter mechanisms were incapable of stopping appreciable amounts of action. Furthermore, just as important to publishers at this juncture was the fact that the halftone and the photoengraving camera as adjuncts to the press were as yet in an experimental stage. It was impossible to reproduce the tonal range of a painting or a photograph. These accomplishments would come later.

In deference to the profession of photography which it represented and to its desire for good illustration, *The Philadelphia Photographer,* a monthly magazine, used actual photographs as frontispieces. The quantity was limited. Mass production of photographs was slow and expensive, and naturally such operations were restricted to small circulation publications. Illustrative material for the total press—for books, magazines, and newspapers—required thousands of sketches and wood engravings, with a sizable number of steel engravings and lithographs for good measure.

---

2. *Frank Leslie's Illustrated Newspaper,* 1 June, 1861.

3. *Harper's Weekly,* March 15, 1862.

# Student Participation

*Above,* A self-portrait showing sketch artist Mr. W. Waud appeared in *Frank Leslie's Illustrated Newspaper,* May 31, 1962. With shells exploding all around him, Waud nonchalantly goes about the business of sketching the battle.

Predating the alphabet by thousands of years, cave paintings are among the earliest records left by man. Illuminated manuscripts were next, and were followed by the use of crude woodcuts and the beginning of the illustrated press.

For many years sketch artists were the source of book, magazine, and newspaper illustrations. Human beings have always been interested in "visuals," and the United States citizen of the 1860s learned much about the Civil War by perusing woodcuts in *Leslie's Illustrated Newspaper, Harper's Weekly,* and other similar publications.

1. It has been said that ours is a visual age. Do you agree or disagree? Give reasons for your thinking.
2. Use an encyclopedia as a reference and prepare a brief report on early cave paintings.
3. Why was it impossible for Roger Fenton (Crimean War) and Mathew Brady (Civil War), using the cameras of their time, to stop appreciable amounts of action?
4. Judging from the pictures you have seen, would you agree with some authorities that Brady's photographic coverage of the Civil War was "the best" until David Douglas Duncan's pictures of the Korean War?
5. Brady used wet plates and cumbersome equipment. Compare his pictures with the informality of those made by Duncan with his fast film, fast lenses, and miniature equipment.

In the Beginning

# 2 Price of Progress

Progress, although of benefit to the masses, usually extracts a penalty from the few.

Technological changes, while important to progress, exact a toll. When the typesetting machine was invented, for example, it increased production of printed matter beyond the fondest dream. Even so, at some levels the change caused dissension and brought on genuine hardship. One mechanical typesetter could do the work of dozens of hand compositors—could do it much faster, easier, and at considerable saving. Describing the "encroachment," a Canadian newspaper publisher in 1950 told his readers:

> In the early '90s, people knew very little of the practical application of electricity; nothing of airplanes; nothing of automobiles or of motor boats. The telephone had been in practical use only a few years and was but little used, and the electric light was still a novelty . . .
>
> Editions of daily newspapers consisted of 8, 12, and 16 pages, and up to 100 hand compositors were quite frequently employed to get out big Sunday editions. The largest and fastest presses of the time could not print in a day as many copies as a modern press can turn out in a half-hour. Five of the fastest hand compositors in the world could not then produce as much type as a typesetting operator of equal comparative ability can produce today.
>
> The Linotype[1] came into practical use in daily newspaper offices when I was a small boy, but I can remember its advent caused a feeling of uneasiness, almost a feeling of consternation, among hand compositors of the day. At the time (1896), three or four of the straight-matter hand compositors employed by my father in the production of a small-city daily newspaper in the middle West made a visit to a nearby larger city to see the new Linotypes which had just been installed . . . One of them was so discouraged with the future prospects of the hand compositor in the printing business that he quit his work as a printer, and took up another occupation. In fact, the feeling was somewhat general among printers throughout the world that the day of the hand compositor was fast drawing to a close.[2]

## Genesis of the Illustrated Press

The genesis experienced by the picture portion of the illustrated press was just as painful. Like the hand compositors whose jobs were nearly obliterated

---

1. Trade name for the typesetting machine produced by the Mergenthaler Company. Intertype and Linograph were trade names for other typesetting machines soon on the market.
2. Frank M. Sherman, ed. and compiler. *The Genesis of Machine Typesetting* (Chicago: M & L Typesetting & Electroplating Company, publisher, 1950).

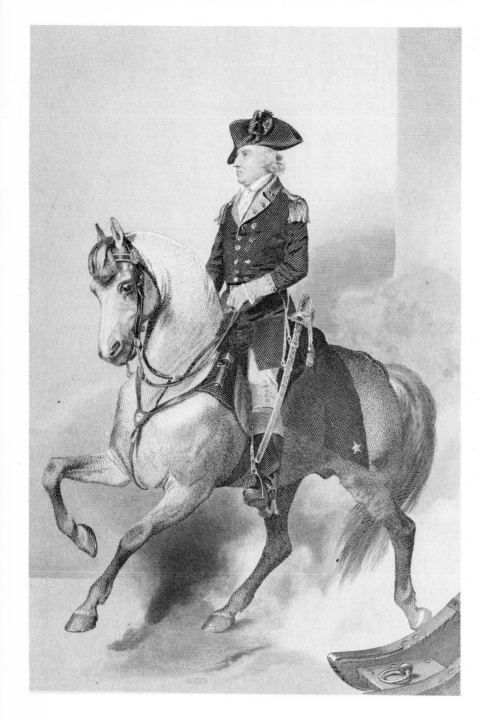

Soldiers of the Civil War (and many soldiers earlier) often complained that sketch artists were not truthful. Examples were cited where a battle was shown with the participants in full dress. The steel engraving of a painting by Alonza Chappel of Horatio Gates (*left*) is an example of over-romanticizing. It remained for photo-journalism, nearly a century later, to give the true story of combat.

by the typesetting machine, many sketch artists and wood engravers were adversely affected by the arrival of photoengraving. One example was the artist-engraver W. J. Linton who waged a bitter war against the publishers of his time. Battle lines were drawn in 1879 when *Century Magazine* made the claim that "from the moment our magazine began to avail itself of the art of photographing pictures upon the wood (in preparation for the engraver) a great development took place."

Linton, a fine artist and an excellent wood engraver, challenged the statement in his book *Wood Engraving, A Manual of Instruction*. In that little volume, Linton wrote:

This excellent illustration of Walt Whitman (*right*) is a fine example of what a "good engraver" could do. To produce this portrait, W. J. Linton drew it from a photograph and transferred the sketch, without the aid of photography, to a wood block. The image was then engraved. In his book *Wood-Engraving, a Manual of Instruction* printed in London in 1884, Mr. Linton used this portrait as an example of the type of work which would outdo those engravers who had come to depend so much on photography.

Gravure and tools

Photographing on wood will save the time of the draughtsman, when a reduction of a drawing or a picture is wanted. If you must have the lines of the larger facsimile drawing, you can only get them by photography. . . . Use it then! . . . But, if you would have the best copy of a picture, do not be content with a photograph! The "correctness" of photography is a mistake. It is never correct. It always alters colours, and more or less disturbs effect . . . The artist-copier translates the painting into black and white, so making a truer copy than the photographer's; and he puts on the block only what he knows can be engraved, helping the engraver by saving him the unpleasant and dangerous task of leaving out. Let the draughtsman economical of time have the picture—especially a portrait—photographed on the block, and then draw his translation over that. The engraver will be grateful to him.

It may not be uninteresting to give account of the origin and occasion of this photographic usage, which was certainly not invented for the benefit of engravers . . . It was invented by or for artists who could not draw on wood . . . From newspaper work, the new system spread to book-work; and following a long, cheap system of careless facsimile—fairly exemplified in early numbers of *Punch* . . . gave the death-blow to engraving as an art. . . .

For the mechanic-engraver, the days of engraving are numbered. Only the artist-engraver, while he upholds the dignity, can assure the future of engraving. Beware of photography![3]

In agreement was Linton's fellow countryman Mason Jackson of Britain who believed "Sir John Gilbert was the very foremost" in establishing the pictorial press. In his book, *Pictorial Press,* Jackson pointed out:

Other Royal academicians and eminent painters have drawn on wood for the illustrated press, but Gilbert stands out preeminently the great popular illustrator of the Victorian age. He it was who first gave a distinctive character to the illustration of news. He seemed to possess an inborn knowledge of the essentials of newspaper art, and could express by a few freely drawn lines and touches the hurried movement of street crowds or the state and dignity of Court ceremonies. Whether Gilbert had to draw a knight in armour or a gentleman in paletot, he did it in a way exactly suited to rapid engraving and printing.[4]

In March 1880, the same month and year in which a halftone engraving appeared in the daily press, *Scribner's Monthly* had a rather caustic report on Linton and his book:

The main difference between the old and the new schools, as they have been called, concerns the limits and the function of wood engraving. Here Mr. Linton's conservatism is apparent. He would have nothing called wood-engraving that is not done mainly in "pure line." And would permit no progressiveness. The new school, on the contrary, is intent upon experiments with new methods of a less conventional kind. Between the two, this magazine, though it originated the experiments, has never discriminated. It has never said "we will have no pure line," or "we will have nothing but pure line," but has left the engraver free from dictation, and has tried to judge his work on its merits. Where we have liked the new style, it has not been because of the technique, but of the results. . . The very men whose experiments Mr. Linton decries may yet prove that, even with his methods, better results are obtainable than his school has yet produced.

This difference of opinion, as to the limits of wood engraving, finds its battleground chiefly on the question on the use of photography—a question quite apart from the intrinsic value of the photograph as a work of art. The artists, and most of the engravers, prefer the results of its use while Mr. Linton will have none of it, and declines to engrave pictures so transferred to the block. . . .[5]

Five years later the question was still unsettled. In a "Word About Our Pictures," W. Lewis Fraser of *Century Magazine* wrote in the January 1885 issue:

Something more than twenty years ago, drawings were made on the wood block, and cut on the drawn surface. The designer of that period was happy if he saw given back to him the dry bones of his design with such alterations of

3. W. J. Linton, *Wood Engraving, A Manual of Instruction* (London: George Bell and Sons, 1884).

4. Mason Jackson, *The Pictorial Press, Its Origin and Progress* (London: Hurst and Blackett, Publishers, 1885).

5. *Scribner's Monthly,* editorial, March, 1880.

In his war against photography as a tool for the wood engraver, Mr. Linton singled out Timothy Cole of *Scribners* and later of *Century Magazine.* Cole made a trip to Europe where he learned a new style of engraving utilizing the photograph. The portrait of Abraham Lincoln which, engraved from a portrait done by Wyatt Eaton, shows Cole's earlier style. The portrait of Paul Potter (*above, right*) done for *Century Magazine* in the 1890s shows the new style of engraving done by Timothy Cole after he began to use photography.

light and shade as best suited the method of the particular engraving. Then came, fostered and encouraged and developed by this magazine, the new school of American wood engravers mainly induced by the return from Europe of many promising young artists who in foreign schools had learned new methods of art expression, and who the management of the magazine thought should have a hearing. Marvelous reproductions of these men's work were made by the engravers of this new school—notably by Timothy Cole and the late Frederick Juengling; but the fault of the school, with some individual exceptions, lay in the too slavish imitation of surfaces and textures, and the artists, who at first were delighted after a while complained that their forms, the expression of their faces, and their artistic intention, were not satisfactorily reproduced. Then came the half-tone process, which claimed to be able to reproduce the work of the artist by mechanical means, and without the intervention of the engraver. It was hailed with delight by the most serious of the artists because it was supposed, being a mechanical process, to be faithful to the original. But it was true, and still remains true, that this new process is largely what its name implies —a *half-tone;* that is, as the deepest darks cannot be rendered by it, nor the highest lights, only the middle of the scale of the drawing can be reproduced . . .

A year or two ago it seemed as though the noble art of wood engraving would be, through the popularity of half-tones, lost to the world. But the American engravers, realizing the situation, resolved, if they must die, to die game. Learning its deficiencies as perhaps they never could have done, had their art remained as popular as it was at one time, they have set themselves heroically at work to make the deficiencies good; and they are today, as may be seen from the wood engravings in this number of *The Century,* making a good fight. They have emancipated themselves largely from the slavish adherence to texture and meaningless detail and are engraving with definite reference to the artistic intention of their originals. This is evident in a more or less degree in all the

In the continuing battle of wood engraving versus halftone, *Century Magazine* in January 1895 conceded that the ultimate in illustration would probably be a combination of photoengraving and hand engraving. As an example editors cited the illustration (*left*) showing Napoleon on his way to Corsica with his sister Elsie. The drawing by Mr. Pape was first made into a halftone plate. Using his engraving tools, Mr. Pape then dropped out several of the highlight areas to add contrast and snap to the halftone. *Century* editors liked the combination very much and predicted that if any type of illustration was to replace the wood engraving this probably was it.

engravings printed in this number from the work of the veteran Timothy Cole to that of the youngest acquisition to the ranks of first class engravers.

Working in this manner, and with this impulse, there is little danger of the death of their beautiful art unless it should be brought about by the last movement shown in the reproduction of the drawing by Eric Pape . . . This is an entirely new development—a half-tone plate originally worked over by the wood engraver until about one-half of its surface has felt the touch of the engraver. Those portions of the reproduction where the mechanical process has been adequate have been left untouched; where the mechanical process failed to produce the effect of the original, the engraver has not merely supplemented it, but in many places replaced it entirely. For some time it has been the practice for engravers to retouch process plates by re-entering the lines, in order to lighten the tones, and by burnishing, to deepen the darks, but this new reproduction not only does that, but takes the bull by the horns, and frankly substitutes engraving where the mechanical process fails . . . First-class wood engraving is ten times dearer than good half-tone; engraved half-tone costs three or four times as much as unengraved or ordinary half-tones. *The Century* uses these various methods solely with reference to the fidelity with which they reproduce the difficult-to-be reproduced drawings of today.[6]

But in spite of all of the arguments, the photograph was destined to replace the sketch, and the halftone, because of its ability to reproduce a photograph "direct from nature," sooner or later was to replace the wood engraving.

For many years it was impossible to stop action with a camera. Then sketch artists such as Frederic Remington really came to the forefront. The Remington drawing shown here, used by *Century Magazine* in 1891 in the story of "Custer's last stand," shows a tremendous amount of realism and fidelity. Remington, unlike his contemporaries and many of the sketch artists who preceded him, did not romanticize his subjects. Perhaps that's the reason a few years later William Randolph Hearst gave him an assignment to sketch the Spanish-American War in Cuba.

# Some Sketch Artists

As incidental to the transition, let us briefly follow the careers of a few artists. Alfred A. Waud of *Harper's Weekly* was among the better-known Civil War sketchers. In 1866, two years after the war had ended, the *Harper's* management sent Mr. Waud on an extended tour of the South "to illustrate the rising of a new world from chaos."

Another increasingly famous artist was Thomas Nast. He first achieved prominence during the rough and tumble times of the Civil War and continued to grow in stature long after the struggle had ended. Nast is better remembered today as a caricaturist and satirist than as a combat artist, especially for introducing the donkey as the symbol of the Democratic party, the elephant as the symbol of the Republican party, and the tiger to symbolize Tammany Hall.

---

6. W. Lewis Fraser, "A Word About Our Pictures," *Century Magazine*, January, 1885.

# Appletons' Journal

### OF LITERATURE SCIENCE AND ART.

Entered, according to Act of Congress, in the year 1869, by D. APPLETON & CO., in the Clerk's Office of the District Court of the United States for the Southern District of New York.

No. 17.—WITH SUPPLEMENT.]      SATURDAY, JULY 24, 1869.      [PRICE TEN CENTS.

ON THE ROAD TO LAKE GEORGE. BY WINSLOW HOMER.

Nast's caricatures, more than any other factor, were credited with the breakup of the William M. (Boss) Tweed Ring.[7]

Winslow Homer was another Civil War artist who gained prestige after the end of the war. His skill and sensitivity as a young artist on the battlefield foretold the honors he later won as a painter of seascapes.[8]

Others, notably Frederic Remington and Charles Russell, "artists of the Old West," helped bridge the gap between sketch artist and photoreporter. Remington, who did many illustrations for publications of the 1870s and 1880s, was hired by the Hearst publications as a sketch artist to cover the Spanish American War in 1898.[9]

# Student Participation

Illustrations for magazines, books, and newspapers during the period 1850–1890 were for the most part produced by sketch artists and wood engravers.

1. Name three factors which prevented development of "an earlier photo-journalism."
2. Why in the newspaper, magazine, and book was the photographer destined to replace the sketch artist; why was the halftone photoengraving destined to replace the woodcut?

7. Frank Luther Mott, *American Journalism—A History of Newspapers in the United States Through 250 Years—1690–1940* (New York: Macmillan Co., 1942). (Hereafter cited as Mott: *American Journalism—A History of Newspapers*.)

8. Lloyd Goodrich, *Winslow Homer* (New York: Macmillan Co., 1944; published for the Whitney Museum of American Art).

9. Mott, *American Journalism—A History of Newspapers*.

Sketches by young Winslow Homer were often featured in *Appletons Journal of Literature, Science and Art* and in other contemporary publications. In this illustration for the cover of the July 24, 1869, issue we see the sensitivity and skill which before many years were to produce Winslow Homer the great painter of seascapes—a man whose paintings remain feature attractions in nationally known art museums.

# The Halftone Takes Over

# 3

T he halftone was so important to the development of photojournalism that it is well for us to probe the beginnings of photoengraving and use of halftones.

The first halftone, a scene in Shantytown, New York "Direct from Nature," appeared March 4, 1880 in the New York *Daily Graphic*.

The first halftone, A Scene in Shantytown, New York, "direct from nature," appeared March 4, 1880, in the New York *Daily Graphic.*

## The Halftone—Its Invention and Use

To share in this interesting historical event, and to put it in proper perspective, we turn to the booklet *The Beginnings of Halftone* by Lida Rose McCabe. Based on material in the notebook of Stephen H. Horgan, "Dean of Photo-Engravers," the story was originally written for *The Inland Printer,* also the publisher for Miss McCabe's *The Beginnings of Halftone.* In her foreword, Miss McCabe announced:

> Through the courtesy of the editor of *The Inland Printer* the writer has been permitted to revise the following important bit of history. This was first printed in *The Inland Printer* for March and April, 1924.[1]

Here are excerpts from Miss McCabe's *Inland Printer* articles and her booklet which followed:

> March 4, 1880, the day the New York *Daily Graphic* printed its first halftone [reproduction] of a picture (photograph) entitled 'Shantytown' marked the beginning of a new era in engraving and printing circles. It was on that day that photoengraving, [The first halftone reproduction, Horgan says, was in the March 4, 1880 *Daily Graphic,* and was produced using the lithographic, not letterpress, process.] as it is now known, first came into commercial use, and on that day and date were born the present revolution and evolution of the printing industry and the business world itself. In an illuminating article on "Photo-engraving, The Mainspring of Progress in the Graphic Arts," Louis Flader [Louis Flader was for many years Secretary of the Photo-Engravers Union and editor of the Photoengravers Bulletin] thus fixes the date of an epoch-making

**Halftone of the Late Seventies**
The screen used was made from perforated cardboard. The negative and screen are preserved among Mr. Horgan's notes.

---

1. Lida Rose McCabe, *The Beginnings of Halftone* (Chicago: The Inland Printer, 1924) Foreword.

From the booklet *The Beginnings of Halftone* by Lida Rose McCabe. (Courtesy of *The Inland Printer.*)

event. This comprehensive tribute to the importance of photoengraving appeared in the fortieth anniversary number of *The Inland Printer,* October, 1923. First reprinted in the *Photoengravers Bulletin,* October, 1923, the article since has been reprinted frequently both at home and abroad.

Mr. Flader's article substantiates not only the date of the first halftone printed, but dispels much misinformation on this vital subject. For a long time it has been the wont of writers and lecturers to attribute the invention of halftone to Meisenbach in 1882. Mr. Flader's statement that the New York *Daily Graphic* began the making of halftones two years before that date is amply verified. This first illustrated daily newspaper began publication on March 4, 1873, and for eighteen years, from 1873 to 1891 it did much to promote photo mechanical methods of illustration. For the first time in the history of the graphic arts, it proved that photography could be depended upon to produce illustrations with certainty, printing a newspaper daily through photography's aid.[2]

Years ago, while studying the history of halftone engraving, I visited Beaumont Newhall at the George Eastman House in Rochester, New York. Later, Mr. Newhall sent me a copy (see below) of an annotation by John A. Tennant of the passage on the alleged "first halftone" by Horgan of "Shantytown" in Newhall's book *The History of Photography:*

> The first halftone engravings (Leggo, 1871—in Canada; Leggo 1873 and Horgan 1880 in N.Y. *Daily Graphic*) were *not* "relief blocks" as we understand the term today—capable of being printed with or without type in a typographic press.
>
> Horgan's 1880 "Shantytown," the first halftone reproduction of a continuous *tone* original (photo) *made through a screen* was transferred to a lithoplate or stone and *printed on a lithographic press.* Today we would call it a half tone lithograph. The *Daily Graphic* was a demonstration house organ of the Graphic Co.—leading photolitho house of U.S. and all their work was printed lithographically on a litho press—not on a *typographic* press.
>
> Halftone photoengraving in the form of "relief blocks" for printing in an ordinary typographic press began with Ives, Moss, Mumler and others (1878–1885) by various stereotype methods—gelatine relief casts, etc. But halftone engraving through a screen began with Ives (1883–1885) although some say Meisenbach (1883), Petit (Paris 1875). These were all relief *blocks*—i.e. mounted type high on a wood or metal base for printing in a typographic press.
>
> The *point* in Horgan's invention with the *Tribune* was a method of handling a halftone plate so that it could be printed from the *curved stereotype plate in a web perfecting press.*[3]

Miss McCabe's article, however, goes on to say:

> The success of the *Daily Graphic* heartened capital and quickened experimenters throughout the world. Scientists, photographers, and experimenters in photomechanical methods at home and abroad subscribed to the *Graphic,* and studied its methods with the hope of improving them. . . .
>
> Born in February, 1854, among the slaves of a Norfolk, Virginia plantation, Stephen H. Horgan showed throughout his school days a bent for drawing and a love of pictures. It was quite natural, he asserts with a humorous twinkle, that his life work should begin at the age of 16 years with photography learned from a Methodist minister at Nyack on the Hudson, New York. Young Horgan, on the sudden death of the minister, bought the photograph gallery from the widow and at 18 was proprietor of a studio. The panic of 1873 put him out of business. A year later he was in the employ of Abraham Bogardus, described in

Stephen H. Horgan, the man credited with using the first halftone in a daily newspaper —the *Daily Graphic,* March 4, 1880. (Courtesy of *The Inland Printer.*)

---

2. McCabe, *The Beginnings of Halftone,* p. 1.

3. Beaumont Newhall, *The History of Photography* (New York: Museum of Modern Art, 1949), pp. 222–23.

the October 1871 issue of the *Philadelphia Photographer* as "one of nature's generous and genial noblemen," as a photographer—none started higher.

Shortly after, the New York *Daily Graphic* advertised for a photographer. Horgan applied for the position and got it. . . . Out of nearly thirty applicants he was selected and put under a $5,000 bond not to reveal the *Graphic's* methods. Within three years, Mr. Horgan invented an improvement of the *Graphic's* processes and was given charge of the department, which at that time included the largest photomechanical equipment on the American continent. This was a tremendous responsibility for so young a man, but not too great for his tireless energy. . . .

The notebook of the young Horgan of this period reveals that as early as 1875 he was formulating (mentally) a method by which the gradations in opacity and transparency in an ordinary photographic negative might be translated into lines after the manner of wood engravers. He contemplated a line screen with gradations from opacity to transparency, since called an "optical V," which screen inserted between the negative and the sensitized surface would by light action break the shadows in the negative into lines and dots. The only way to obtain such a screen . . . was to have a large drawing made of graded lines and photograph this drawing. The idea was carried out on October 25, 1876. . . .[4]

Mr. O. G. Mason, secretary of the American Institute, explained March 2, 1880, before the photographic section of that august body how Stephen H. Horgan made the first halftone ever to appear in a newspaper. Mason in a report which appeared in Anthony's Photographic Bulletin said:

---

4. McCabe, *The Beginnings of Halftone,* pp. 1–2.

# THE DAILY GRAPHIC

An Illustrated Evening Newspaper

39 & 41 PARK PLACE

VOL. XXII. | All the News, Four Editions Daily. | NEW YORK, THURSDAY, MARCH 4, 1880—TWELVE PAGES. | $12 Per Year in Advance. Single Copies, Five Cents. | NO. 2264.

A Combination Halftone and Line Plate of 1880

This reproduction of the front page of the New York *Daily Graphic* of March 4, 1880, shows what is now called a combination plate, a pen-and-ink drawing with a halftone inserted. The pictures on the easel are a reproduction in halftone of the double page in that issue. The woman's right hand covers the now famous halftone of "Shantytown." Processes of that day believed it impossible to print halftones made with a crossed line screen on a "steam press," consequently Mr. Horgan was compelled to make halftones with a single-line screen.

According to Stephen H. Horgan, who thus defined it in the January 1924 *Inland Printer,* the term *halftone* includes all pictures in which the lights and shades are defined by lines and dots of different surface areas made through a mechanically lined screen. The first halftone ever to appear in print was titled "A Scene in Shantytown, New York." Reproduced "direct from nature" (*see left*), only a single-line screen was used, not the crossline screen made famous by Levy.

I have here a print which might be called an advance copy of a supplement of the *New York Daily Graphic,* which will be issued two or three days hence. Knowing that I have taken a good deal of interest in the various printing processes which were founded on photography, the publishers, and Mr. Horgan, who has charge of the photographic work, took pains to send me this sheet. It is particularly interesting to *us* from the fact that it has in it a picture (Shantytown) made and printed in the power press directly from a negative by our chairman (Henry J. Newton). It is issued on this advance sheet and will be printed in the paper by the thousands, without the slightest touch of the hand on photographic work. The method of producing it may be described as follows:

A negative is made from a series of fine rulings slightly out of focus. The film of that negative is transferred by the use of collodian—or rather taken off and placed between the negative from nature and the bichromated gelatine film—a print made and treated as the ordinary photo lithographic prints are treated, the effect is to produce detail in the shadow parts, and where there is a light portion the ruling shows very slightly. . . .[5]

The important part of this report, and a point which Horgan, himself many times emphasized (and reiterated in the note sent me by Beaumont Newhall— see page 15), was that the print *was made and "treated as ordinary photo lithographic prints are treated."*

In a booklet titled "More About the Beginnings of Halftone" addressed to

---

5. O. G. Mason, "Report of the Photographic Section of the American Institute," *Anthony's Photographic Bulletin,* March 2, 1880. Reprinted in McCabe, *The Beginnings of Halftone,* p. 3.

members of the American Institute of Graphic Arts, Horgan, in reply to a pamphlet by Frederick Eugene Ives,[6] July 1925, said in part:

> Mr. Ives is peeved because the writer was honored "by the medal of a pretentious American society . . ." Mr. Ives thinks this award was due to articles on "The Beginnings of Halftone" by Miss Lida Rose McCabe, published in the *Inland Printer* for March and April 1924 . . . Mr. Ives is mistaken. The valued medal has engraved on it: "Presented to Stephen H. Horgan for photo mechanical achievements, 1874–1924."
>
> Some of these achievements were enumerated by Edmund G. Gross in the presentation address, and included: "His experiments of 1877 and his making of a single-line screen halftone in 1880; his making of the first halftone printed on a stereotyping web perfecting press; his invention in 1881 of a method of photo-intaglio engraving; his part in the introduction of pictures in country newspapers and the great metropolitan dailies; his part during the present year in the sending of a color photograph by telegraph, and his books and other contributions to the literature of photoengraving."—*American Printer,* December 5, 1924.[7]

Horgan quoted Mr. Ives as saying in his July 1925 pamphlet:

> "The only newspaper halftone I ever saw, before I commenced supplying halftone plates commercially, was a single example in the . . . *New York Daily Graphic.*"[8]

To this statement, Mr. Horgan replied:

> If the only newspaper halftone Mr. Ives ever saw before he commenced supplying halftones commercially was a single example in the *lithographically printed New York Daily Graphic,* he would learn something even at this late date if he would look up the files of that paper, the first daily illustrated paper in the world, and see the issues which appeared after March 4, 1880.[9]

Horgan continued:

> Mr. Ives insinuates that a halftone must be a relief plate, and still in his letter, he says "I was the inventor and patentee of the *intaglio halftone* plate, etc," showing as everyone knows that a halftone can be printed by the intaglio, relief, or planographic methods.[10]

Further along in his booklet, Mr. Horgan corrected Mr. Charles W. Gamble of the Manchester (England) College of Technology when the latter stated, "It would appear that 'Shantytown' was the earliest dated halftone relief block used in the public press." Horgan once more pointed out in no uncertain terms that "Mr. Gamble is in error in calling it a relief block."

---

6. Frederick Eugene Ives, then at Cornell University, like Horgan, had done much experimenting with the halftone. Robert S. Kahan, University of Wisconsin, in a paper delivered at the AEJ convention in 1964, pointed out that magazines lagged behind in the use of photo-engravings but that the first magazine to use an Ives halftone was the *Philadelphia Photographer* in the June, 1881 issue. For more credit to Mr. Ives, as "inventor of the halftone" see W. E. (Bill) Garrett's article on the National Geographic magazine, pages 215–242.

7. Stephen H. Horgan, "More About the Beginnings of Halftone" (Speech delivered before The American Institute of Graphic Arts, July, 1925).

8. Horgan, *More About the Beginnings of Halftone.*

9. Ibid.

10. Ibid.

# The Photoengraving Process

Once the photoengraving process had been accepted, use of woodcuts was on the wane, and halftone engravings began to grow in stature. At the research session of the photojournalism division at the 1969 convention of the Association for Education in Journalism, Robert S. Kahan pointed out:

> Just how the halftone played an important role in the history of magazines is exemplified in the emergence of *Cosmopolitan, Munsey's,* and *McClure's.* These three magazines were harbingers of a new style in establishing themselves as major publications between 1890 and 1895. In taking their place, they also helped to establish photojournalism as a means of mass communication.[11]

The big problem with the application of photography to platemaking was not in reproducing the lines of a black-and-white drawing, but in reproducing the actual tones of a painting, a wash drawing, and more important at this juncture the tones of a photograph.

To capture the tonal range of a photograph and to transfer that gradation to the page of a newspaper or magazine, most of those experimenting with the photoengraving process in the 1870s realized that some sort of screen system was essential.

Preliminary to publishing the "Scene in Shantytown," Stephen Horgan evolved the theory that a negative made from a line drawing would show gradations "from opacity to transparency," and would, thus, break up the original pictures into different sized and shaped dots which on the printed page would give the illusion of highlights, middletones, and shadows.

The highlight dot in a relief printing plate (after etching) looks like a tiny toadstool; middletone dots vary in shapes and sizes. Shadow dots are tiny pinholes etched into the darkest portion of the plate. The tiny dots suggest a tone, which solid metal does not. The tiny wells also add to the printability of the engraving.

When he first began experimenting with halftone, Horgan used a perforated cardboard as a screen.

---

11. Robert S. Kahan, unpublished paper given at the 1969 AEJ convention, Berkeley, California.

A magnified portion of a reproduction made through a halftone screen—an eye—is an optical illusion. Highlight, middletone, and shadow dots are used to interpret the lighter and darker portions of the original and the tones in between.

Newspaper halftones made with a glass crosshatched screen were very popular for many years. The Levy Brothers perfected manufacture of the glass screen and in the early 1900s sold thousands of them to publications which had gone in for pictures.

To make a glass screen, glass is first coated with an acid resist and tiny marks are then cut through the coating to the glass. Furrows etched into the glass plate are carefully filled with an opaque substance. Two such pieces of glass, with the opaque lines facing inward and crossing each other at right angles, provide a crosshatched screen. The tiny apertures in a glass crosslined screen vary in size. Coarse ones, such as the 55-line screen, produce 55 dots per linear inch or 3,025 dots per square inch. In letterpress printing, coarse screens are best suited to newsprint, newspaper ink, etc. The finer the dot, generally speaking, the closer the reproduction represents the original picture. All relief printing plates are made from negatives which take into account the etching process. Letterpress newspapers require engravings with sufficient depth for stereotyping and for clean printing. Books and magazines, printed with better ink and on a better grade of paper, on the other hand, use finer screens than newspapers. Production of a book or magazine also requires more careful makeready on the halftones than does a short-lived newspaper.

Letterpress, offset, and gravure are the three types of printing in use today. The development and perfection of each has greatly influenced the growth of photojournalism.

The photogravure plate, the exact opposite in appearance to the plate (or cast) used in letterpress printing, was described as follows by Herbert Denison in 1892:

> . . . The gravure plate is one of metal, preferably of copper, which bears on its surface in intaglio an etched representation of the subject to be reproduced. In other words, the portions of the plate representing the shadows and halftones of the subject are sunk, instead of being the highest points—as in the case of half-tone and other blocks intended for use in ordinary letterpress printing— and the portions representing the highlights of the subject still retain the original level and surface of the plate.
> . . . The mechanical nature of photogravure is distinctly in its favour for reproductive purposes; there is no opportunity for the individuality of the engraver to leave an impress on the print antagonistic to that of the painter. It is the work of the painter in its entirety that the reproduction should portray—not a portion only of his work contaminated with the style of another . . .[12]

To better understand the gravure process, let us examine the old method used in making "engraved" (intaglio) calling cards. A metal plate (copper) is engraved, using acid or a cutting tool. The proper amount of ink is rolled onto the plate, after which the surface is rubbed clean, usually with the palm of the hand. During this phase, the engraved portion is undisturbed. Under pressure, ink from below the surface of the plate is forced onto the card. The deeper, wider portions yield the darker objects; the shallower, narrower portions of the engraving, on the other hand, transfer what appear to be the lighter portions of the symbol to the calling card.

No screen is needed in gravure printing, although a copper mesh (not half-

---

12. Herbert Denison, *A Treatise on Photogravure* (London: Iliffe and Son, 1892).

**The Principle of the Offset Press**

Photo-offset is a printing process based on the assumption that oil and water do not mix. On a press, the type and illustrations accept the ink. The whole printing plate is bathed in water–chemical solution, which is rejected by the printing area coated with the greasy ink. Bare zinc, on the other hand, which accepts the water solution rejects the ink. The type and illustrations do not print directly on the paper, as in the case of letterpress. They transfer to a rubber blanket which in turn offsets onto the paper as it runs through the press. The illustration *above* is from a brochure, *Lithography's Place in Printing Production,* issued by the Lithographers National Association, Inc.

The Halftone Takes Over

*Above,* a Civil War woodcut from a photograph by Alexander Gardner (then working for Brady) as it appeared in the July 16, 1864 *Frank Leslie's Illustrated Newspaper. Below,* the retouched photograph from a 1907 book published by Edward Baily Eaton, who owned a large collection of Brady photographs. Note how the photograph was "doctored" in the Eaton book, and how the illustration was drawn on the block before it appeared in *Leslie's.* The event was a council of war at Massaponax church in Virginia. Both the line cut and the halftone originally are examples of letterpress printing.

First Sunday rotogravure section in this country appeared in 1914 in the *New York Times*. A year earlier Adolph Ochs had brought equipment and workmen to this country from Germany. Originally intended as a means of "presenting masterpieces of art" to his readers, the Sunday roto section has become a magazine in every sense of the word. Most Sunday roto magazines today appear as tabloids, and good color reproduction is commonplace.

tone screen) covers the printing cylinder to hold the ink in place until pressure is applied. The squeeze of the press during the instant the cylinder comes in contact with the paper forces ink through the mesh. Dots thus formed are so fine that they hardly show in the finished product.

From the foregoing it would seem gravure has greater fidelity than do letterpress and offset printing. Generally speaking, this is true and this fact explains why many of the finest photographic books today are done by sheet-fed gravure.

In 1914, realizing the great potential of gravure printing, Adolph Ochs of the *New York Times* imported craftsmen and gravure printing equipment from Germany. Welcomed as the most faithful of reproductive mediums, the

**Over the Top.** This picture was taken in World War I by an unknown Canadian photographer. It shows warfare far different from that of the atomic age. Included in 50 Memorable Pictures exhibit. (Archives of U.S. Defense Department.)

**Spanish Soldier Dies** by Robert Capa for *Life*-Magnum. Unique in war coverage, this is one of the most dramatic exact-moment pictures of all time. The camera clicked just as a Loyalist soldier was shot through the head by a Falangist machine gunner. The incident took place in 1936 near Cordoba, Spain. Included in the 50 Memorable Pictures exhibit.

**Weeping Frenchman** by George Mejat, Fox Movietone News. This is one of the most emotional pictures to come out of World War II. A French civilian weeps as he watches historic battle flags being taken from Marseilles for protection from the Nazis. Included in 50 Memorable Pictures exhibit. (Wide World Photos.)

**Gestapo Informer** by Henri Cartier-Bresson for Magnum. Here's what happened when an informer was discovered in the midst of a German concentration camp during World War II. The make-believe refugee was denounced by camp inmates. Included in 50 Memorable Pictures exhibit.

*Times* "roto supplements capitalized on this fidelity to give its readers fine reproductions of the world's greatest art pieces."[13]

Stimulated by the need for pictures from faraway lands, camera reporting and gravure picture sections took on added importance during World War I. Photojournalism, then in its infancy, abandoned its swaddling clothes and began to grow up.

# Student Participation

In spite of the battle between the sketch artist and the wood engraver, the camera and the halftone were destined to take over by the turn of the century.

1. The three types of printing now in use are: Letterpress, photogravure, and photo-offset.
   a. Describe the characteristics of each.
   b. Which gives the most faithful reproduction of a photograph or painting?
2. Bring to class three examples of letterpress printing, of lithographic printing, and of photogravure printing. Use an encyclopedia or other source to learn the approximate date each came into use.
3. The key to invention of the typesetting machine was the spaceband. What was the key to development of the halftone and photoengraving?

---

13. Stanley E. Kalish and Clifton C. Edom, *Picture Editing* (New York: Rinehart & Co., Inc., 1951).

# 4 Photojournalism
## Is It One Word, Two Words, or Hyphenated?

Photojournalism becomes an important part of mass communication.

Frank Luther Mott succeeded Frank Martin in 1942 as the third dean of the School of Journalism, University of Missouri, Columbia. One of the first things Dr. Mott did upon taking over his new charge was to enlarge the school's photographic offerings. Not only did he establish a "sequence in the photography department" to take its place alongside the news-editorial department, the magazine division, the advertising division, etc., but he also gave the new sequence a one-word name for the first time in academic history. From that time, in the Missouri School of Journalism, and in many other places as well, the word designating photo reportage has not been two individual words nor hyphenated, but one word: *photojournalism.*

The important fact, however, is not that Mott coined a new word, but rather the recognition of pictures—photographs, if you please—as important to the field of communications (see discussion of photography as a language, starting on page 29).

Prior to this time, in most journalism schools, photography was at best considered a "craft," not worthy of academic consideration. More often than not, it was looked upon as something to be learned by on-the-job apprenticeship or at a vocational or technical school. Certainly, many people believed that photography had no place in a college or university curriculum.

Eventually the camera earned a place in journalism schools—an honorable one—and photographic reporting, too, slowly changed from a craft into a profession. Which, thanks to *Look, Life,* and a lot of great photographers, is where we find it today.

## Development of Photo Wire Services

One of the factors which upped the value of pictures and which helped the news and magazine photographer to find his place in the sun was invention of a system to transmit pictures by wire. Historians have told us how undeveloped

# 1935 Magic—News Pictures by Wire

## Tribune in Virephoto System

By WHITLEY NOBLE

ALADDIN with his magic lamp and ring and the two frightful genii, slaves thereto, in their best moments couldn't have done it. They lacked imagination and never operated that fast.

The flashing of pictorial matter by wire across a continent 3,000 miles wide in the brief space of one-sixtieth of a second is a miracle of today. Wirephoto, the new system of telephotography by which The Chicago Tribune collects pictures and photographs from far and wide in somewhat the same manner (though far more marvelously) as it collects news by telegraph, operates with a speed approximately the same as that of light.

Photographs scanned by an uncanny "electric eye" are borne by electrical impulses along wires to other "electric eyes" in far-away cities, picked up at an amazing rate of speed, and reproduced upon negatives to be made immediately into duplicate photographs, so that readers within the daily circulation range of newspapers participating in the Wirephoto service may see them in just a matter of minutes and hours after they are taken. No longer do

Diagrammatical layout of Wirephoto equipment, showing among the various units the sending and receiving machines, switchboard, and power plant. This equipment occupies 240 square feet of floor space.

In tests to ascertain the best type of film for reception of pictures by wire, ordinary film was exposed in seven stages varying from correct exposure to 70 per cent of correct. Above is the result, showing (left to right) loss of detail at successive stages of underexposure. A special Wirephoto film was evolved which at 70 per cent of correct exposure shows little detrimental effect.

---

film was sent out by pigeons during the siege of Paris (Franco-Prussian War, 1871) to let the rest of the world know what was going on. In the *Encyclopedia of Photography* David Eisendrath, at a much later date, told how *Chicago Times* photographers used carrier pigeons to rush exposed film back to the office to meet early deadlines.[1] In news photography speed and more speed were the order of the day. Pictures sent by wire provided speed never before dreamed of. Wirephoto, trade name of the Associated Press (AP) network, Telephoto, first owned by Acme and now by United Press International (UPI), and Sound Photo, originally the trade name for International News Photo and now a part of the UPI network, all had a part in bringing photojournalism into the spotlight.

The wire services made it possible to send and receive picture and word reports almost simultaneously. When techniques to transmit pictures by radio and satellite were perfected, global picture and word coverage became realities. Unfortunately, during the earlier years some people believed the quantity, rather than the quality, of the pictures was the objective. But with the passing of time the world has come to value meaningful, quality pictures.

At one time, within easy memory of many parents of present-day college students, newspaper photographs were looked upon as a "necessary evil," something tolerated only to meet competition. Some publishers also referred to the news photographer as a "reporter wth his brains knocked out."

Rapid transmission of pictures has always been a goal of newspapers and magazines. During the siege of Paris (Franco-Prussian War), for example, homing pigeons were used to transmit messages and pictures from the capital city to let the rest of the world know what was going on. As late as the 1940s, according to David B. Eisendrath, Jr., the *Chicago Times* used carrier pigeons to transmit exposed film back to the office where it was quickly processed to meet early deadlines. Better than carrier pigeons to ensure quick transmission of pictures was the system introduced in 1934–35 of sending pictures by telephone. Radio transmission of visual images soon followed.

---

1. *Encyclopedia of Photography,* 1st ed., s. v. "The Complete Photographer." New York, 1942.

The American Telephone and Telegraph Company was *the* earliest pioneer in the picture-by-wire business. Realizing the tremendous importance of the invention, the Associated Press began its own Wirephoto network in 1935. *Left,* an early AP Wirephoto transmitter.

In my mind, things were never quite that bad, but in the beginning the cameraman had a pretty poor image. In many cases news photographers had very little schooling and were almost illiterate, incapable of writing a story or even a caption to accompany the pictures taken. Fortunately, the scene has changed. Today's successful photojournalist can do many things. He can take the picture, crop it, and lay it out in picture story form if need be. More than that, if he is a photojournalist from many journalism schools, he is quite capable of taking the picture *and* writing the story. Today's photojournalist is a journalist, first of all and second, a photojournalist.

The story of "pictures by wire" surfaced August 29, 1924, when a memorandum was sent by the American Telephone and Telegraph Company (Bell System) to "all chief engineers." Titled "Notes on Phototelegraphy," the bulletin explained some amazing experimental work which had been done in the speedy transmission of pictures. H. P. Charlesworth, plant engineer, sent the bulletin from the New York office that August day. It explained:

> The first demonstration of this system was made a short time ago and during the Republican and Democratic conventions a large number of pictures transmitted between Cleveland and New York and between New York and Chicago were distributed to the press. It is expected that a further trial of this system will soon be made in order to determine the commercial possibilities of such a service. If, in the future, any specific cases come up in your territory where it is thought that a picture service might prove in, we shall be glad to furnish to you the latest information available.[2]

Even with such a successful start, pictures by wire required considerable selling before they were accepted. In 1927 in an annual book of printing

---

2. H. P. Charlesworth, "Notes on Phototelegraphy," 1924 (company bulletin, American Telephone and Telegraph Co.).

achievements published by the Photo-Engravers Union, we find an historic advertisement—a two-page presentation of the AT&T accomplishment. It reads:

> The ever-increasing use of Telephotographs in the business world is not surprising to those familiar with this method of picture transmission. It is obvious that if the Telephotograph can serve the daily newspapers by instantly reproducing pictures of big news events, it also can be of great value to commercial houses, industrial plants, and professional people. In the fashion field for instance, Telephotographs enable buyers for stores throughout the country to see and study the latest Parisian designs in hats, gowns, shoes, etc., within an hour or so of the arrival of such apparel in New York. The time of transmission is seven minutes.
>
> The almost perfect reproduction of layouts and printed forms of all kinds makes the Telephotograph invaluable to advertising agencies and bond and security companies. Such matter cannot be transmitted accurately by any other rapid means. Likewise, financial statements, legal documents, finger prints, and x-ray pictures are among the many transmissions made daily over the long distance wires of the Bell System. Lithographs and wash drawings also make excellent Telephotographs. Anything that can be photographed can be sent by wire to eight important cities in the United States and from these cities the train and air mails complete a rapid and accurate service to all of the principal cities of the country.[3]

Bell proved the worth of Telephotographs. In a short time the Associated Press, with the help of thirty-eight of its member newspapers, formed a 10,000 mile circuit—the world's first newsphoto network. This story appeared in the *Chicago Sunday Tribune,* December 23, 1934—a year before the network was announced to the world:

> The flashing of pictorial matter by wire across a continent 3,000 miles wide in the brief space of one-sixtieth of a second is a miracle of today. Wirephoto, the new system of telephotography by which the *Chicago Tribune* collects pictures and photographs from far and wide in somewhat the same manner (though far more marvelously) as it collects news by telegraph, operates with a speed approximately the same as that of light.
>
> Photographs scanned by an uncanny "electric eye" are borne by electrical impulses along wires to other "electric eyes" in far-away cities, picked up at an amazing rate of speed, and reproduced upon negatives to be made immediately into duplicate photographs, so that readers within the daily circulation range of newspapers participating in the Wirephoto service may see them in just a matter of minutes and hours after they are taken. No longer do obstacles of time and distance compel news photographs to trail hours and days behind the actual news. Side by side with the day's grist of news, important stories of eventful happenings, accounts of vital and startling occurrences, flash on parallel wires the last-minute photographs that illustrate the news. Speeding trains and specially chartered planes, photograph vehicles of yesterday, are snail-like by comparison.
>
> Wirephoto, materialization of a ten-year old dream and result of three or four years of careful planning, begins operating now, today, tomorrow, not later, according to schedule, than the new year. The *Tribune* and 37 other newspapers in 24 cities are joined in the 10,000 mile network of the Wirephoto circuit, which stretches from coast to coast and from as far north as Minneapolis to as far south as Miami, for the purpose of supplying each other with the important news pictures of the day.[4]

---

3. Louis Flader, ed., *Achievements in Photo-Engraving and Letter-Press Printing* (Chicago: Photo-Engraver's Union, 1927).

4. *Chicago Tribune,* 23 December, 1934.

# Development of Modern Photojournalism

Almost parallel with introduction of Wirephoto were other events which influenced the maturation of photojournalism. Among them without a doubt was the birth of the great picture magazines *Life* (1936) and *Look* (1937). These publications spotlighted a full-grown style of picture reporting and brought in what some authorities refer to as the Golden Age of Photojournalism.

Another factor which gave dignity and importance to photojournalism was the rebirth of the documentary picture. The documentary photograph and its use and purpose as exemplified by Roy Stryker and the Farm Security Administration in this country during the thirties, is discussed at length in Chapter 5.

"Modern photo reportage," says Tim N. Gidal "originated in Germany between 1928 and 1931. Three things which caused the breakthrough are development of the modern 35 mm. camera; the emergence of a new generation of photo reporters . . . and the attitude assumed by the editors of the illustrated magazines . . ."[5]

No one will contradict Gidal, who was himself a pioneer in the new photojournalism. Kurt Safranski, Alfred Eisenstaedt, and the great Dr. Erich Salomon all not only contributed enormously to documentary photography, but also gave distinction to photojournalism. Most of these pioneers were run out of Germany by Hitler and the pressures of World War II and came to the United States where they and the type of photographs they made greatly influenced the new photojournalism.

# Photography Is a Language

Many years ago John R. Whiting wrote a book titled *Photography Is a Language*.[6] In its function as language, not only do many blessings accrue to photography, but also many responsibilities.

Whether the photographer is working on a local scene or on a battlefield far from his homeland, he many times literally takes his life in hand to do the job. Robert Capa, Werner Bischof, Dickie Chappelle, Larry Burroughs, and many others died "in the line of duty." And deaths and injuries all too often have been the story of the photographer on the home front covering a shoot-out, an explosion, a fire, or other violent event. If he is to report a riot or a fire, the cameraman must be at the scene, and dangerously close to the heart of it. He cannot take a picture by making a quick telephone call. *He is the eyes of the world,* and those eyes must be close enough to see what is going on.

From 1839 when photography made its debut under the guidance of Daguerre to the present time there has been a steady movement toward *visual reporting*. Most artists felt the camera was an interloper—a competitor in the sketch and portrait fields. Laymen long had hoped for a means of artistic expression which did not require great skills or long periods of training. The

---

5. Tim N. Gidal, *Modern Photojournalism* (New York: Macmillan Co., 1973; Frankfurt: Verlag C. J. Bucher, 1972).

6. John R. Whiting, *Photography Is a Language* (Chicago: Ziff-Davis Publishing Co., 1946).

fellow who could not draw or paint found what he wanted in photography. From the start, he was a devotee of the "new art."

Once the camera appeared upon the scene, it was given many chores. Not only was it an ideal instrument to record informal family portraits, but it also was soon recognized as an instrument for education, information, and entertainment.

The earliest records of war photography were not impressive. A few daguerreotypes were made in 1846 and 1848 in Saltillo, Mexico, and some were made during the Crimean War. Oliver Wendell Holmes, who had a hand in developing and popularizing the three-dimensional stereoscope, reported that the Franco-Prussian War (1859) also had its photographer. Holmes predicted that "the next European conflict would send us stereographs."

Because they could not be reproduced as halftones, the photographs taken by Mathew Brady and co-workers during the Civil War had little or no market in newspapers and magazines. Brady hoped to make money from selling the stereoptican views direct to persons at home. With the three-dimensional system Brady believed his customers would be able to see the battles in all their realism.

It did not turn out exactly that way, but Brady, Alexander Gardner, Timothy O'Sullivan, and others of the Civil War photographic team did produce a priceless set of Civil War pictures now in the national archives. Brady took photographs of the first engagement of the Civil War—the Battle of Bull Run, July 21, 1861. More pictures—many more—followed.

The war photographs which Brady and his crew produced, although seldom used by publications of that day, were seen in exhibits and in home photo albums where (mostly as portraits) they appeared as *carte de visite* pictures, printed to a standard 2¼ by 4 inches in size.

Many of the war pictures "by Brady," as many Currier & Ives lithographs, were helpful in building and maintaining fighting morale in the North. Lincoln, who gave Brady permission to follow the Union armies, was well aware of the value of the pictures produced by the diminutive photographer and co-workers.

The chief reasons for his being elected president were credited by Lincoln to be his Cooper Union speech and a Brady photograph.[7]

Pictures of the Civil War (usually produced as line cuts) many times were used as propaganda. Jefferson Davis, president of the Confederacy, in speaking of the "atrocity photographs" taken of the Andersonville, Georgia, prison camp conceded that they "might have been genuine, but the way in which they were taken and the manner in which they were used were dishonest." Although the Andersonville pictures never appeared in Northern journals, they were given wide distribution. Roy Meredith claimed that they were distributed throughout the North and that copies of the pictures were shown to President Davis by his spies.[8]

Photography had an important role during the opening of the West. The work of Alexander Gardner, Captain A. J. Russell, and T. H. O'Sullivan (all of whom had photographically documented the Civil War) and the photo-

---

7. Robert Taft, *Photography and the American Scene* (New York: Macmillan Co., 1942), p. 224.
8. Roy Meredith, *Mr. Lincoln's Cameraman* (New York: Charles Scribner's Sons, 1946).

graphs of others, notably William Henry Jackson, had much influence on establishing our national park system and on inducing hordes of people to follow the railroads in their westward movement.

Coincident with the opening of the West, technological improvements gave a boost to photography and made it possible to do a better job. Better camera equipment, introduction of dry film as opposed to wet plates—plus invention of the halftone engraving—made it possible for magazines and newspapers to reproduce photographs "direct from nature."

As the Spanish-American War approached, tools for taking photographs under adverse lighting conditions and reproducing them in newspapers and magazines became available. "War passion was whipped to a frenzy by news stories, headlines, pictures and editorials."[9] Typical of the photographs which appeared in the press were those taken for *Collier's* magazine by Jimmy Hare. Cecil Carnes introduced us to this ubiquitous photographer with these words:

> He snapped the wreck of the Maine from every point of the compass. He caught divers still busy at the somber task of bringing up the drowned . . . With the aid of an interpreter, Jimmy prowled through reconcentrado camps. He photographed swollen bodies with bones breaking through the skin; he took pictures of the emaciated living, and of babies ravaged by disease. Every ship that passed Morro Castle enroute to New York carried a packet of snapshots. Their influence upon public opinion can hardly be overestimated.[10]

Photography reached a new level of importance in World War I when faked pictures became an important tool for propagandists. Many of the pictures released for publication during the years 1914 through 1917 have since been discredited.

In 1937 the *Des Moines Register and Tribune* published an article entitled "War Propaganda Exposed" which placed side-by-side identical pictures released by both the Allies and Germany. Sketches distributed in this country, showing German soldiers killing and mutilating French and Belgian children were in sharp contrast to the pictures made by German photographers showing German soldiers treating those children with kindness. In World War I, Kaiser Wilhelm, "the Beast of Berlin," did not cut off the hands of babies, as posters, newspapers, and even motion-picture strips sometimes led us to believe.

However, all World War I photographs were not fakes. Cameras, used on land and at sea, were first to reveal the use of camouflage. It was through photography that we became acquainted with and kept up with the exploits of Capt. Eddie Rickenbacker and other heroes.

For the record: Photographers in World War I were attached to combat units. Col. Edward Steichen, who went to France with the First American Air Corps, was made chief of the photographic section and was given command of all American photographic operations. Working with Gen. William (Billy) Mitchell, a man whom the colonel greatly admired, Steichen's photographers made daily reconnaissance and mapping flights over enemy territory.

Photography spoke loudly during World War II. One of the factors which made for efficient photographic coverage of this global conflict was the war photographic pool—a new concept in photographic reporting. World War II

---

9. Mott: *American Journalism—A History of Newspapers.*

10. Cecil Carnes, *Jimmy Hare, News Photographer* (New York: Macmillan Co., 1940), p. 15.

was far more complicated than preceding wars, and the demand for pictures was greater. The pool permitted everyone who wanted them to have pictures, even though all news and other organizations were not allowed to send photographers to the battlefronts.

For the first time during any war, pictures could be transmitted across the country by wire and across the oceans by radio. Not long after Pearl Harbor, the Navy Public Relations department asked Acme, Associated Press, International News, and *Life* to form a picture cooperative. When it heard of the arrangement, the Army asked that the pool cover land warfare as well. By 1943 the pool was spending $400,000 annually for war pictures. In April of that year, 28 pool photographers were on assignment, and the Army Signal Corps was transmitting pictures from North Africa to the United States.[11]

Stories told with pictures welded a strong bond of friendship between the United States and its allies and widened the gap between us and our adversaries. At home pictures helped fight fifth-column activities and made us eager to support patriotic drives. One exhibit, a great panorama of pictures entitled "Road to Victory," provided many emotional thrills. This exhibit was produced by the combined talents of the poet Carl Sandburg and his famous brother-in-law photographer Edward Steichen and was indeed a powerful bit of propaganda—a photographic masterpiece.

Many youngsters and their parents were thrilled by Joe Rosenthal's famous flag-raising picture "Marines on Mt. Suribachi." (See page 120.) Reproduced more than any other photograph up to that time, it must be one of the greatest propaganda pictures in history.

The wars which introduced the great work of Cartier-Bresson, Robert Capa, Larry Burroughs, Eddie Adams, Michael Rougier, and hundreds of others prove beyond a doubt that "photography is a language."

But photography has served eloquently in peace time, also. Long ago the *St. Louis Post-Dispatch* used its photographic guns to argue that a Missouri Valley Authority similar to the Tennessee Valley Authority would be a good thing and were proved to be right. Long before there was national interest in ecological problems, the *Post-Dispatch* was fighting the smoke evil and the rat menace in the St. Louis area. And during a sustained drive of many years the *Post-Dispatch* consistently used a powerful word-and-picture combination to hammer home the message that in the St. Louis area it was a matter of "Progress or Decay."

Editorial, crusading, propagandizing photographs are not new. Frank Luther Mott partially summed up the importance of photography as a language when he said: "The camera has a devastating effectiveness in portraying evils. It is the best crusader of our time. Think of any abuse—social, economic, political— and sound and honest pictures which will bring the evils to our eyes suggest themselves immediately."[12]

---

11. "Journalism in Wartime, a Symposium held by the School of Journalism, the University of Missouri." Published by the American Council of Public Affairs, 1943; see especially the chapter by Ralph H. Turner, "Photographers in Uniform."

12. Frank Luther Mott, Foreword, *University of Missouri Third Annual Fifty Print Bulletin,* January 1946.

# Student Participation

Wirephoto and Telephoto are trade names which designate the systems allowing the Associated Press and the United Press International to send black-and-white and color pictures by wire. Color separations are made from the original color photograph. A black-and-white print is transmitted for each of the colors. After the black-and-white pictures are made into plate form, the separations carry the proper colors to the paper. The combination reassembles the colors during the printing process.

These systems and radiophotos enable picture syndicates and publications to send and receive pictures in a matter of minutes from across the nation or from remote areas across the sea.

1. How did picture transmission systems such as those mentioned here influence photojournalism?
2. Collect twenty-five pictures (black-and-white and color) from recent daily and Sunday newspapers. Pay particular attention to the syndicate credits at the end of the captions.

(Credit lines on a news picture, just as on a written article, are very important.) Try in this project to gather a few radiophotos, and a few transmitted by satellite. In this study of credit lines, please notice how local newspapers credit hometown photographers.

# Documentary Photography —a Discussion

# 5

Older persons can recall the many pains which marked the growth of photo-journalism during its relatively few years. They remember the Leica camera, which was designed by Oskar Barnack of Germany in 1913 to quickly and economically test exposures in motion-picture work. The Leica, and the horde of miniature cameras which followed, ushered in the age of the candid camera.

Paralleled with photojournalism is the term "documentary photography" exemplified by Farm Security Administration pictures.

## Candid Photography

The skill and dignity exemplified in Germany by Erich Salomon and his type of candid pictures was lost in this country when news photographers in the early 1930s began using the "minnies." It was a popular thing then to capture important people in awkward, embarrassing poses. For example, to catch President Franklin Delano Roosevelt licking his fingers while eating a hot dog or in a more compromising gesture, completely out of context with the story they were covering, was for a few years considered the mark of a good photographer.

While most early candid photography did little to dignify the profession, some serious cameramen like Arthur L. Witman of the *St. Louis Post-Dispatch* used judgment and fair play as a part of their equipment in making pictures with the 35 mm. camera.

In an interview I had with him regarding the 35 mm. camera, Mr. Witman explained, "I had been experimenting with a Leica early in 1934 and have some tear sheets of society pages made in the summer of that year when I toured Michigan and Wisconsin summer resorts, shooting St. Louis society families."

At a time when the 4x5 (with flash on camera) was standard equipment, Witman and a few other newspaper photographers had no difficulty proving the worth of the miniature camera. He showed his editors that a 35 mm. box with 35, 50, and 90 mm. lenses could cover almost any assignment.

Even if the type of equipment is disregarded, news photography generally speaking has always had trouble growing up. There was, for instance, the period during and following the Spanish-American war which historians refer to as "the age of Yellow Journalism." The distinguishing technique of newspaper publishing, at that time, according to Frank Luther Mott was "the lavish use of pictures, many without significance. This practice invited the abuses of picture-stealing and faking pictures."[1]

But even this period did not mark the greatest degradation in photojournalism history. "The bottom really dropped out," Mott reported, "during the 'War of the tabs' in the mid-1920s." It was during this period that Bernarr Macfadden and his editor, Emile Gauvreau, started a new tabloid, the *New York Daily Graphic* (not to be confused with *The Daily Graphic,* which printed the first halftone March 4, 1880). Macfadden's publication used the confession-story technique and the composograph, an illustration made by faked photography. It featured sensational news such as the Hall–Mills murder case, the Ruth Snyder–Judd Gray trials (see page 00) and the Daddy Browning and Peaches story. Describing the messy journalism practiced by some publi-

1. Frank Luther Mott, *American Journalism—A History of Newspapers.*

vis Hine, pioneer documentary photog-
her, once made pictures which Roy
yker used in his economics classes at
umbia University. Fully appreciative of
Hines great sensitivity and capabilities,
yker, without success, sought to hire
a when he first began to document
otographically the American Depression
he 1930s. This picture, made in
08, is one of many Hines pictures
ich pointed out the evils of child labor.
luded in 50 Memorable Pictures exhibit.

cations at this time, Mott wrote that "the older Yellow Journalism seemed pale by the side of the saffron of the new tabs."

Thankfully, this low, gutter journalism was short-lived. Technical and philosophical advances resulted in a change for the better in the early 1930s. Then, abandoning much of their cuteness and irresponsibility, even the tabs showed signs of growing up.

Contributing to the change and to better, more mature photojournalism were (1) the coming of Wirephoto, which gave the cameraman equal billing with the word reporter; (2) the beginning of the picture magazines *Life* (November 23, 1936) and *Look* (January 1937); and (3) a factor not previously discussed, resurgence of the documentary picture.

# Farm Security Administration Photography

Although the documentary style and philosophy of picture taking had been present since the days of Fenton and Brady, the technique was born anew with the arrival of the socially important photographs of Jacob Riis and Lewis Hine and others. But the documentary type of picture, exemplified by Erich Salomon and his peers, came into its own a few years later with Roy Emerson Stryker and the founding of the historic section of the Farm Security Administration (FSA).

Like a huge cake of yeast, the documentary concept and philosophy of the FSA photographers leavened the whole loaf of mass communications. Books, magazines, newspapers, and later television were all influenced by the concept. Considering its importance in the publishing industry, it is well now to find out a bit more about documentary photography. Just what is the difference between a documentary picture and the ordinary snapshot in a billfold or family album?

In his book A. William Bluem, then of the Newhouse Communications Center, thus defined the term:

> . . . Documentary is more than an idea. It is an undeniable form of public communication, functioning within certain ascertainable conditions. Valid documentary must involve more than presentation of the records of life. There must be a second purpose in its conception and the use of a technology which permits a significant impact in its dissemination.[2]

A few years earlier, in 1959 to be exact, Werner Severin pointed out that ideally the time for the rebirth and prolific growth of the documentary picture was in the mid-1930s with the coming of the photographic division of The Farm Security Administration. In the introduction to his master's thesis Severin, now a communications research specialist at the University of Texas, wrote:

> By 1935 the stage was set for documentary photography to record contemporary life on a larger scale than ever before. The technicians had provided the means to reproduce photographs in quantity. The picture newspapers, wire services, and magazines were available to distribute them to millions of readers. Fenton,

One of the greatest pictures to come from the Farm Security Administration photography program in the 1930s is this one by Dorothea Lange. Roy Stryker, director of that project, in his recent book (1973) *In This Proud Land* characterized the portrait of the migrant woman and her children as "the picture of Farm Security." This picture was a favorite in the 50 Memorable Pictures project. (Library of Congress.)

2. A. William Bluem, *Documentary in American Television, Form, Function, Method* (New York: Hastings House Publishers, Inc., 1955, 1968).

Documentary Photography

Brady, Atget, Riis, Hine, the "f:64" group and others [notably Erich Salomon] had shown the way. The dust bowl and the great depression provided the need for this new documentary photography, and the Rural Resettlement Administration (later the Farm Security Administration) filled the need.[3]

After this brief introduction to documentary picture taking, as would-be photojournalists let us consider two important books on the subject: *Portrait of a Decade* by F. Jack Hurley and *In This Proud Land, America 1935–1943 as Seen in the FSA Photography* by Roy Emerson Stryker and Nancy Wood.[4] In these books one learns how Roy Stryker and a small group of FSA photographers took some 270,000 photographs which mirrored the "Portrait of a Decade." Using eloquent, storytelling, challenging photographs, they produced a visual message which improved the life-style of millions of rural Americans.

The FSA pictures were simple, powerful, and believable statements. The photographers who took them were perceptive, sensitive, honest, involved people. Their objective at the outset was to photograph the migrant workers—"that mass of humanity attempting to earn a living from dehydrated, worn-out soil." It was a sad story, but one which needed to be told. The FSA photographers performed their task magnificently. Used extensively in newspapers, magazines, and sociological books, FSA pictures were also shown in libraries, civic auditoriums, and museums. On these occasions their news value was recognized. Many times, too, they were seen as historical documents and in some instances as works of art.

In his master's thesis, Severin described the situation when Stryker, his job at FSA completed, left the government to work for Standard Oil of New Jersey. Of that particular period he wrote: "By the time Stryker left the government, many of the original FSA staff had already found other, more lucrative channels for their talents. The river of realism that was characteristic of Farm Security photography already was branching out into many little streams. As each followed its course, it carried the attitudes toward photography developed under Stryker. Later these streams, swollen with the hundreds they induced to join them on their way, rejoined to make up what is now considered the mainstream of American photojournalism."[5]

If one denies the close alignment between the documentary picture and photojournalism, let him consider the words which follow.

First consider the statement made by A. William Bluem early in his book that:

> . . . In many ways photojournalism closely parallels the documentary movement in still photography. Continuing Bluem pointed out: "The photograph, in conjunction with print, served a distinct social purpose in that it involved a growing public in matters of vital concern . . . In the tradition of William Henry Jackson, the news photographer could record scenes which underscored the need for better social conditions, better laws, and better people."[6]

---

3. Werner J. Severin, "Photographic Documentation by the Farm Security Administration 1935–1942: Cameras with a Purpose" (master's thesis, University of Missouri, 1959).

4. See Bibliography.

5. Severin, "Photographic Documentation."

6. Bluem, *Documentary in American Television.*

Wilson Hicks wrote in the preface to his book:

> One link, perhaps the most important link between photography as art and photography as journalism is, then, the socially significant picture. The question for the young photographer after he enters the profession of journalism is how broadly he can view the social scene . . . as he matures, he still can have an opportunity to act on the reform impulses of his beginning period.[7]

Considerably later, in 1973, at the National Press Photographers convention in Hot Springs, Arkansas, Gifford D. Hampshire, made an interesting statement: "Documentary photography is the genesis of photojournalism and photojournalism is excellent only to the degree that the photographer practices the intellectual discipline of documentary photography."

Hopefully, you have now become a believer in the philosophy that the present-day successful photojournalist is also a documentarian with a camera.

# Project Documerica

Since we have just mentioned Gifford Hampshire, who is director of Project Documerica, let us examine that project. While Documerica corresponds in only a few ways with the photography program of the Farm Security Administration in the 1930s, the two projects do have a few things in common, as Hampshire pointed out in his Hot Springs address: "The founding of Documerica in 1971 was the second time in our history that the federal government has turned to still photographers to document our domestic problems."

Admitting that the experience and achievements of the Farm Security program can never be repeated, Hampshire believes that Documerica is based on concepts of FSA. He is quick to emphasize, however, that there are more differences than similarities—one of which is the fact that three generations of photographers have evolved since the FSA days.

In an announcement explaining the Documerica project, Hampshire and co-workers informed all interested persons that: "The long-term objective of the Documerica project is to document the changing environment in the 1970s–80s. The immediate objective is to establish a visual baseline to show where, as a nation, we are committed to action which should arrest pollution and improve the air, land and water."

The first Documerica assignments were undertaken in April 1972, and by March 1973 assignments had produced thousands of 35 mm. transparencies covering ecological problems. Documerica pictures and transparencies like those of the FSA are available for use by publications and for special exhibits.

Photographers are selected from the ranks of professional photojournalists "who have successfully performed an assignment with major media." The assignments average ten to twenty days, and according to plans rarely does a photographer get more than one assignment a year.

Like FSA, Documerica was set up to serve the public. Transparencies (all in color) are available on a loan basis to magazines, newspapers, and electronic media. Like FSA, too, Documerica frequently is called upon to provide picture

---

7. Wilson Hicks, *Words and Pictures: An Introduction to Photojournalism* (New York: Harper Brothers, Publishers, 1952; Arno Press, 1973).

displays at various libraries and museums throughout the country. For an example of the type of photographs taken by Documerica photographers, see page 209 in the color section of this book.

Transparencies made by Documerica photographers are stored in a computerized retrieval bank in Washington, D.C.

Thus we can see the continuing influence of Roy Stryker and his Farm Security program. Because of him present-day newspapers, magazines, books, and electronic media are better observers and communicators. But that influence does not end here. Documentary pictures are often used in education as research and communicative tools, as the brief discussion by Vme Smith that follows shows.

Another great FSA picture which caused plenty of argument is this one of the dust bowl made by Arthur Rothstein in Cimarron County, Oklahoma, in 1936. "The inference," some displeased Oklahomans have told me, "is that the man and his two children lived in the pig shed behind them almost covered by swirling dust." Included in 50 Memorable Pictures exhibit. (Library of Congress.)

Documentary Photography

# Photography and Sociology

*By Vme Smith*

Vme Smith is Instructor and Research Worker at Northern Virginia Community College.

Photography and sociology work together in contributing to man's understanding of himself and of his society.

"Science begins with observation and must ultimately return to observation for its final validation."[8]

Certainly photography is an excellent observer.

We know photography preserves a moment in time which allows objective examination. We also know that a photograph can cut through cultural and language barriers and can place the emphasis on one particular aspect of human behavior.

Photography can only contribute to man's understanding if the photographer has knowledge, concern, and feeling of responsibility for his subject. To communicate, the photographer must have something to say.

Jacob Riis told the world of the need for slum clearance, and Lewis Hine helped bring about legislation to protect children from long hours at dangerous occupations.

Suzanne Szasz wanted to help parents understand their children better. Eugene Smith, Cornell Capa, and Gordon Parks gave us information about poverty and problems of the elderly. Margaret Mead has brought us the photography of Gregory Bateson, Ken Heyman, and others in her study of different cultures.

We all have a better understanding of the Joseph McCarthy era, the Head Start program, the Chicago convention, migrant workers, racial violence, and antiwar marches through photographs.

The great exhibit of the Family of Man is perhaps one of our most important exports.

As we have mentioned, Margaret Mead specifically used photography in her cultural studies. Other anthropologists, sociologists, and psychologists have done studies using the interpretation of photographs as a measure of ideas and attitudes toward racial issues, politics, authority figures and in market research.

John Collier, Jr., points out "a photograph is a restatement of reality; it presents life around us in . . . new . . . dimensions, and can stimulate the informant to discuss the world about him as if observing it for the first time."[9] Collier also observes that pictures helped in areas where questions seemed too personal, too threatening. The photographs were more precise and helped establish rapport in interviews.

A specific example of the use of photography and sociology is my peer group study of two groups of five-year-old children. One group lived in a "temporary" institution (some children were there for years), and one group lived with their families and were members of a private, parent cooperative kindergarten.

---

8. William J. Goode and Paul K. Hatt, *Methods in Social Research* (New York: McGraw-Hill Book Co., 1952), p. 119.
9. John Collier, Jr., "Photography in Anthropology: A Report on Two Experiments," *American Anthropologist,* October 1957.

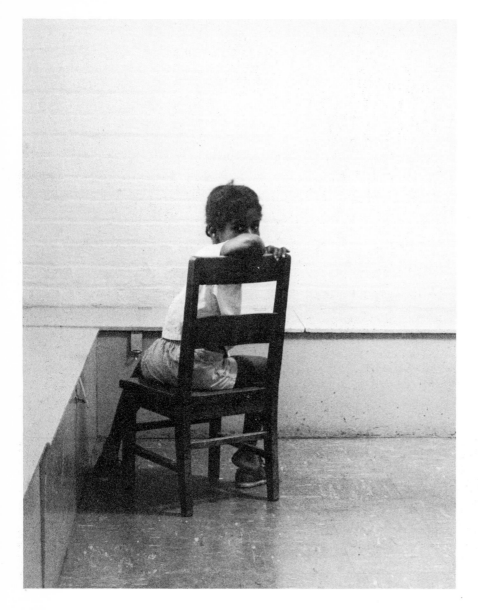

In pointing out how documentary photography can be used as a research tool as well as a means of communication, Vme Smith cited this picture and the one on the next page. The object of this study was to learn how children from normal family situations respond to discipline in comparison to the children from broken homes. Those from average homes were easily corrected with a few words from the teacher. Those from broken homes usually did not respond to words. More often than not they had to be separated from their peers and sent out of the room.

The study was to determine whether or not the children at the institution had stronger peer group relationships to help make up for the lack of family relationships.

The photography was part of the study from the beginning—it was not used at the end of the study to illustrate points already discovered in the research.

The children in the institution were not only without families, they were also without friends. Apparently without the opportunity to learn how to make relationships they were unable to relate to each other, even though they were sleeping thirty to forty in a room.

In addition to showing peer relationships the photographs gave us information about discipline situations and general program content. One group was working with phonetics, while another spent a great deal of time with puzzles suitable for three-year-olds.

In more general terms, photographs of a migrant child being examined by a doctor, a child in small crowded living quarters, and pictures of children in classrooms are important to the research of how migrant families can help improve the educational and health environment of their children.[10]

# More Echoes of Roy Stryker

Long realizing the value of the documentary picture in photocommunication, and recognizing the great contribution Roy Emerson Stryker (right) has made to modern photojournalism, the School of Journalism, University of Missouri, many times has used Stryker's philosophy in the classroom.

In an effort to echo and reecho the Stryker concepts of picture communication, I founded the Missouri Photo Workshop in the summer of 1949. The Master Roy Stryker, John Morris, then Picture Editor of *Ladies Home Journal* and others were on hand at that first Workshop to point it in the right direc-

10. Examples of Mrs. Smith's photographs showing how her camera helped her in the study of educational facilities for migrant children are found on page 44.

For a study of a program for the education of children of migrant workers, Mrs. Smith photographed the pictures on this page. Taken in Geneseo, New York, during the summer of 1973, the pictures indicate how photography was used to "open the eyes" of the children. After learning the fundamentals of both motion-picture and still photography, and after learning about printing the still photography negatives, the children were sent out on their own to photograph that which interested them. The results were indeed surprising. Not only did photography sharpen their seeing, but it also broadened their knowledge of the world about them.

tion. Every year since that time the Workshop has gathered approximately seventy-five "teachers" and "students" (many of them professionals) in some Missouri town. In a week-long soul-searching session, they (students and staff) attempt to see, to think, and to communicate what they have seen with sensitive, understandable pictures. Posing is *verboten,* and the photographs are taken with available light. The serious, in-depth approach to a picture story at a Photo Workshop adds to the spontaneity, the integrity, and the believability of the pictures.

Roy Stryker once proclaimed that one of the important ways for a student photographer to learn was to have a collection of good photographs. He should place them on a table—not hang them on a wall—where he could actually feel them and study them carefully at close range to find out what made them successful as statements—as bits of communication.

In the Missouri Photo Workshop portfolios we adhere to the Stryker philosophy. This set of pictures from recent Photo Workshop exhibits provides you with some fine examples of modern documentary pictures. Study them carefully.

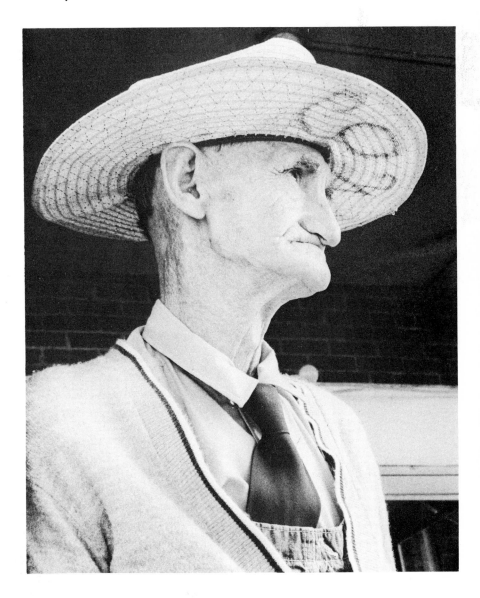

This portrait (*right*) was made by Byron Penick of the *Corpus Christi Caller Times,* at the twenty-fifth Missouri Photo Workshop in the fall of 1973. The workshop was held in Kirksville, Missouri. We are grateful to Mr. Penick and to all other Missouri Photo Workshop Photographers who gave permission to reproduce their pictures in this text.

This picture layout is from a story by
K. Kenneth Paik, picture editor of the *Kansas
City Times*. Exhibited at the 1971 West
Plains Photo Workshop, it portrays the life-
style of a veteran just returned from Vietnam,
and his young wife.

**Cellist.** From the 1972 Washington Photo Workshop. By Lloyd Schallberg, Farmland Industries, Inc., Kansas City, Missouri.

**The Report Card** (*above*). Photo from the 1969 Forsyth Workshop by David Arnold, Topeka, Ks., *Capital-Journal*.

**The Report Card** (*right*). From the 1969 Forsyth Workshop by Medford Taylor, free-lance photographer.

50

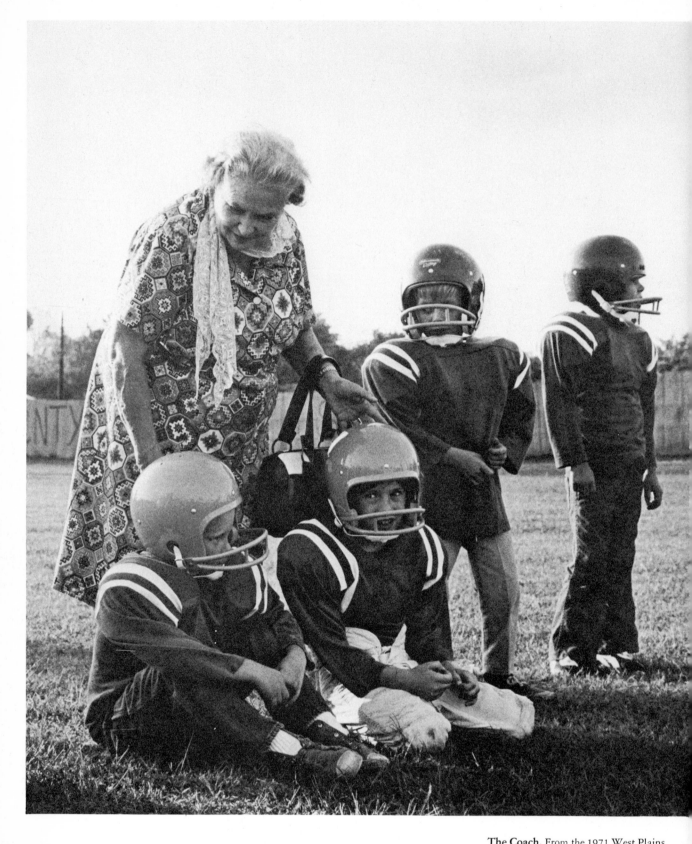

**The Coach.** From the 1971 West Plains Workshop by William Grimes, *Atlanta Journal.*
**School Bus** (next page). By John Flanagan, Wilmington, Del., *News Journal.* Photo is from the 1970 Bolivar Photo Workshop.

52

**Canine on Doghouse** (*above*). From the 1972 Washington, Missouri, Photo Workshop Exhibit, Photo by Lee Romero of the *New York Times*.

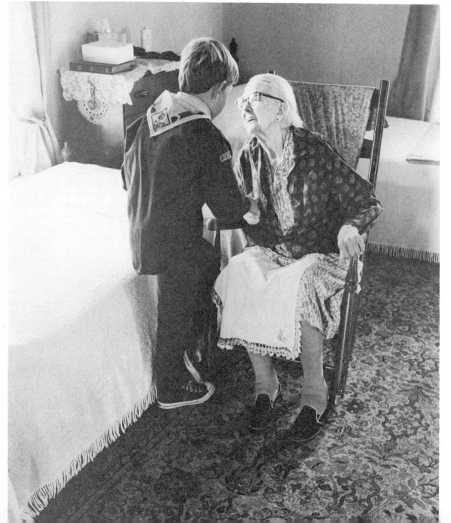

**Elderly Men.** From the 1971 West Plains Photo Workshop. By LeRoy Woodson, Washington, D.C.

**Boy Scout and Senior Citizen** (*left*). From the Bolivar Workshop, 1970. Photo by David Heaton of the *Oklahoma City Oklahoman*.

**The Sawyer.** Pictures by Ann Stevens,
American University, Washington, D.C.
From the 1971 West Plains Photo
Workshop.

**Walks of Life.** By John J. Wozniak, *Kansas City Times*. Picture was taken at the 1972 Washington Photo Workshop.

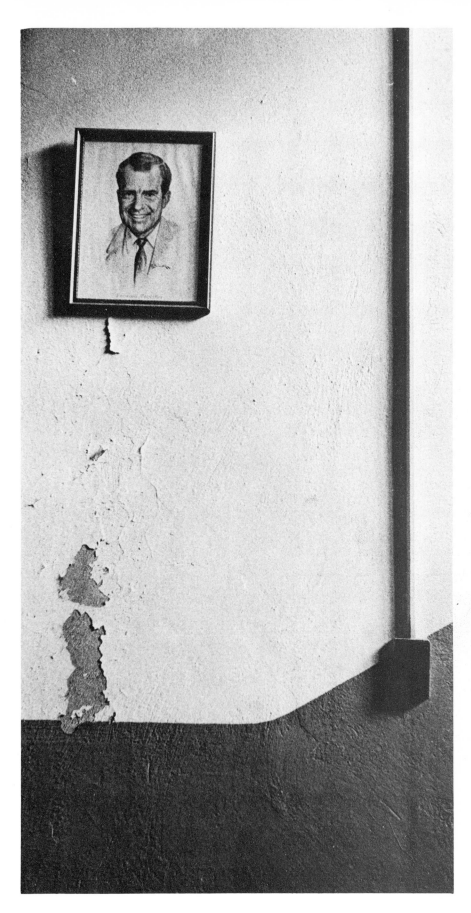

...ace of Nixon. By William L. Stonecipher,
...est Bend, Wis., *Daily News*. From the
...enty-fifth Annual Photo Workshop,
...rksville, 1973.

**The Sheriff Gets a Hair Cut.** From the 1970 Bolivar Photo Workshop. Photograph by Bianca Lavies, National Geographic Society, Washington, D.C.

# Student Participation

Documentary photography, as exemplified by Jacob Riis, Lewis Hine, Erich Salomon, Roy Stryker, Eugene Smith, and many others, is the basis for present-day honest, effective photojournalism.

1. Select three pictures from current newspapers or magazines and tell whether they are snapshots or documentary pictures. Write one paragraph for each picture.
2. The federal government has on two different occasions entered the picture business on a national scale.
   a. What in your opinion was the purpose of the FSA picture program?
   b. What is the purpose of Documerica?
3. William Bluem in his book *Documentary in American Television* made this statement: "In many ways photojournalism closely parallels the documentary movement in still photography." In a paragraph explain what he meant.
4. In this day and age, good photographers—sensitive photographers—often are called upon to provide pictures for textbooks. Look in your public and/or school library for a good example of such a textbook. Bring it to class for discussion.
5. Give an honest critique of the value of the pictures in the Missouri Photo Workshop portfolio in this book. Select three pictures you especially like and tell why. Select three you dislike or like least and tell why.

Note: In addition to the F.S.A. Program and Documerica, which have received emphasis in this book, the United States Government has arranged for special photographic projects dealing with our Bicentennial year. As part of its regular program, the United States Department of Agriculture, inaugurated a year-long project to photograph the Face of Rural America. Pictures thus made were to appear in a Department of Agriculture annual book and in traveling exhibits.

Consideration is now being given to still another such project, to be headed by the well-known photographer Ken Heyman and known as Photo/200. This project was stimulated by a letter from Jes Gorkin of *Parade* Magazine to President Ford and is proposed to be a portrait of America during the Bicentennial year.

**Portrait of a Girl.** By Rick Solberg, Kansas City, Mo., *Star*. From the twenty-fifth Annual Photo Workshop, Kirksville, 1973.

# Thoughts on Photojournalism 6

A good photojournalist is first of all a *journalist*. And a journalist is one who reports for a trade journal, a magazine, or a newspaper, radio, or television. Journalists, some of them at any rate, use their cameras to do the bulk of their reporting. In my mind, a picture editor is also a photojournalist. This fact notwithstanding, the camera reporter, like the typewriter reporter, has a clear concept of news and what makes it. More times than not, a photojournalist has the ability to write with a typewriter, but for reasons of his own, prefers to do most of his communicating with pictures. The fact that he tells the major part of his story with pictures in no way demeans him or sets him apart as a lesser member of the communicative team.

As far as pay is concerned, good news photographers are considered creative individuals and in the same class with reporters and rewrite workers. Where guild contracts are in effect, a photographer does very well—usually in the top-salaried group.

Just how does one become a photojournalist? Photojournalism can, of course, be learned in an on-the-job training program or in a more formal way by attending a trade school, college, or university. The trend is toward the latter, and many of the young people hired as news photographers today have journalism school background. And many journalism schools accept only those college students who have finished their sophomore class. They insist on a good, solid academic backing before a student starts journalism training. It is pretty clear that the time has passed when all a person needed to get a job as a photojournalist was the ability to click a shutter and elbow his way through a crowd.

In fact, if a person knows how to write as well as to take pictures, his chances of securing and holding a job in photojournalism many times are radically increased. This is especially true if one plans to work for a trade journal (house organ), or a small publication as many beginning photojournalists do.

When a small publication believes it cannot afford the luxury of a full-time photo staff, a reporter sometimes is expected to write as well as to take pictures. Certainly, the ability to do both makes him a more valuable person than the one who can only write or only do camera work. It is well to point out, too, that a person who learns to write achieves a discipline which carries over into his photography. He learns how to select the important elements and how to present them.

The modern photojournalist, capable of using either a typewriter or a camera, does most of his reporting with film.

62

Today's successful cameraman is curious about the world in which he lives. He or she must know a great deal about many things. He must have the sensitivity of a poet and the tough skin of a Marine Corps sergeant. Successful photojournalists are knowledgeable, tough, sensitive, perceptive, alive to all that is going on around them.

On his recent visit to Columbia, Missouri Giorgio Lotti of *Epoca Magazine* (Milan, Italy), winner of the 1973 Nikon World Understanding trophy, defined photojournalism as "much more than a documentary fact." He emphasized that the photographer has to put his sensibility and heart into his work. Only in this way can he understand and translate into visual images the reality of things. He must give a message full of humanity and truth.

To many who have watched famous photographers cover a fire, a riot, or a convention photojournalism seems an exciting, glamorous profession. Your definition of photojournalism we hope is far deeper. While it may be "glamorous" and "adventuresome" at times, much of photojournalism is just routine and plain hard work.

Roy Stryker and his crew of photographers in the days of the Farm Security Administration (FSA) referred to their photographs as "statements." And so they were. Hopefully, that is what your pictures will be. It is well to remember, however, that before a worthwhile statement can be made one must have something worthwhile to say. Empty words and empty, thoughtless pictures are a waste of time and money. Every picture cannot be a classic, of course, but every picture can have integrity and can be an honest statement.

Early in their project, FSA photographers learned that to cover a subject professionally one had to do plenty of preparatory work. Once on location, the photographer became an involved, sensitive observer and an honest reporter of the scene before him. An example of the type of research Stryker insisted that his photographers do is described by Carl Mydans in his report of the "cotton" assignment which he did for FSA.[1]

Before leaving to cover an FSA assignment on cotton, Mr. Mydans was called into Stryker's office and asked, "What do you know about this crop?" Stunned by the bluntness of the question, Mydans could not come up with a satisfactory answer, and the trip was postponed. Mydans was taken in hand by Stryker, the old college "prof." Stryker talked all morning, through the lunch period, all afternoon, through dinner, and all that evening about the history of cotton. According to Mydans his "eyeball" lecture covered "the one-crop system and the society that grew up around it." When he got on the train next morning, he had "both a mission and an inspiration," as he later told Severin.

It all added up to an experience which has remained with Mydans through his long and distinguished professional career. One of *Life's* first photographers, he has never forgotten the importance of research.

# Assessments of Present-Day Beginning Photojournalists

I have asked three well-known young professional photojournalists to express their ideas concerning the "shortcomings of present-day beginning photogra-

In his recent study of photojournalism instruction, Steve Lamoreux of Colorado State University found that 55 percent of photojournalism teachers had earned either an M.A. or M.S. degree. Further, in his survey of photojournalism teachers, other staff members, and students he discovered that the majority of those surveyed (70 percent) reject the assertion that photography has little academic background or stature.

1. *See* Werner J. Severin, "Photographic Documentation by the Farm Security Administration 1935–1942: Cameras with a Purpose" (master's thesis, University of Missouri, 1959); and F. Jack Hurley, *Portrait of a Decade* (Baton Rouge: Louisiana State University Press, 1972).

phers." These men were college students themselves a few years ago, and their answers will, it is hoped, help stragglers to find the road to a successful photojournalism career.

## Rich Clarkson, Newspaper Photo Director

First is Rich Clarkson, photo director of the *Topeka Daily Capital-Journal*. Rich has earned the Joseph Costa award and the Joseph A. Sprague Memorial award, the highest honor that the National Press Photographers Association can give. Clarkson's staff photographers have three times earned the News Photographer of the Year title and once a Pulitzer award for photography (1972).

Clarkson has given much time to upgrading photojournalism and to helping young men and women who aspire to become photojournalists. Literally hundreds of college students knock on his door during any given twelve-month period. With portfolio and job application in hand, they have spent hours showing their pictures to Clarkson and telling him of their aspirations.

The following words reveal how he evaluates today's crop of would-be photojournalists.

> This seems to be an era in which everyone is "doing their own thing." This is particularly true among younger people, and while there's a lot to be said for this, photojournalism isn't the 'do-your-own-thing' affair that so many young photographers want.
>
> We're not in the business of pleasing ourselves with our photographs. *The purpose is to communicate something to others.* I look at a couple of hundred portfolios a year and only a handful show any understanding of using the photograph to communicate.
>
> Now, there's nothing wrong with making photographs for one's self-edification nor to decorate your own or someone else's wall.
>
> But that's not photojournalism.
>
> And photojournalism isn't a world of supergraphics either. I see a lot of pictures of graphic shapes and qualities—some even from the sunset-and-silhouette syndrome. But oftentimes, a portfolio full of those pictures is without meat and potatoes. Just frosting.
>
> Many young photographers photograph primarily their own world. This is fine, but while much of today's youth culture is visually loaded and highly photographable and deserving of serious attention, it's not the only thing going on. *Young photographers should be as curious about other people and their worlds as they are of their own contemporaries.*
>
> True, a few young photographers use their works to seriously communicate thoughts, ideas, and feelings. That's the basis of photojournalism.
>
> Another shortcoming much in evidence in a lot of work turned in by young people is a lack of professional discipline—shooting discipline as well as working discipline. This is something that can come with experience, but it is also something that individuals can affect on their own—just by being aware of it and trying to improve one's own working habits. And I'm not talking about little things such as getting to work on time. My reference here is in the way one thinks through his shooting and then how he actually goes about photographing the story. Following that, how he edits and selects and prints.
>
> Professional disciplines are most helpful, and young photographers should be aware of the need to organize one's thinking and efforts.
>
> And finally, there is a general lack of technical expertise in today's 35 mm. generation. Knowing how to expose, develop, and print 35 mm. film properly is fairly general. Many make prints that are exceptionally fine.
>
> But most young photographers have little knowledge of lighting, of other film sizes, and of different cameras and processes. Having enough curiosity to

It is our duty to encourage and assist all members of our profession individually and collectively so that the quality of press photography may constantly be raised to higher standards. (National Press Photographers Association Code of Ethics)

Thoughts on Photojournalism

read, perhaps to experiment, and to at least know where to go for the answers to questions which may arise—this is far more important than many young photographers realize.

This doesn't take a thing away from the serious and more important goals of contemporary photojournalism, and I'm certainly not advocating anything approaching the camera club preoccupation with equipment (which is a problem with some photographers) nor the portrait photographer's preoccupation with formula lighting.

Most young photographers need to be far more technically proficient than they are—and it's not that difficult to learn.

### Jack Kenward, Agricultural Photo Director

The second young man asked to evaluate present-day students is Jack Kenward of Farmland Industries, Inc., Kansas City, Missouri. A longtime news photographer, Kenward has many awards and trophies to attest to his prowess with the camera. Like Rich Clarkson, Kenward has an abiding interest and faith in his profession. Each year in search of a job and/or advice, many young photojournalists come to see Jack Kenward. Following is his evaluation of the present crop.

*What are applicants for jobs lacking in terms of photojournalistic skills?*

The playwright Arthur Miller once said, "A newspaper is people talking to themselves." In that quotation I find identified the basic problem most young photojournalists face, a question of audience. No publication exists without an audience. Few of the aspiring photojournalists we've met in recent years demonstrate any concern for or interest in their existing or potential audiences.

We recently filled an opening for a position on our photo staff. We interviewed thirty or so applicants for that position. Of the thirty, all but a handful demonstrated a more-than-adequate range of technical abilities. Only about three demonstrated any sense of audience. We hired one of those three. The other two also found positions with other publications within a month or two after we made our decision. Many of the remainder are still seeking work several months to more than a year following interviews with us.

Verbal descriptions of photographs are not always precise, but in this group of about thirty portfolios, all but three seemed to be designed to impress other photographers, as though this was the only proper audience for a photojournalist.

If there is any single factor which distinguished for us the differences between the people we wanted and those we weren't interested in, it was this sense of audience—readers, if you please—and a companion sense of commitment to that audience.

I've not been able to precisely define this sense of audience to my satisfaction. I believe it is an important factor in enhancing the communicative quality of photojournalism. I suspect it reflects a degree of commitment to serve that group or groups of people who regularly form the readership of the publication in question. I know the photojournalist with a commitment to serve his audience possesses a markedly different personality from the photojournalist who is concerned simply with the development of his career through the constant parading of his ego in his published photographs and/or writings.

For most young photojournalists, this question of commitment to an audience or to a variety of audiences introduces a new criterion to the evaluation of their work. I believe this commitment and its degree can be seen in the work of individual photojournalists be they job applicant, contest entrant, or candidate for canonization in museums.

In addition to viewing portfolios, we conduct verbal interviews with job applicants which reveal further this lack of commitment to an audience. They have told us they like to travel; they have demonstrated interest in little beyond the narrow confines of their interest in the world of photography; they have

Newspaper headlines should be fully warranted by the contents of the articles they accompany. Photographs and telecasts should give an accurate picture of an event and not highlight a minor incident out of context. (Code of Ethics of Society of Professional Journalists, Sigma Delta Chi)

lacked constantly editors who would grant them "good" assignments; they complain their "best" work is never published. We have learned from these job applicants a complete litany of despair and frustration and alibis, none of which are to us proper excuses for shirking their responsibility to their audience.

Our audiences do not exist to serve us; we exist and work to serve our audiences.

## Gifford Hampshire, Director of Project Documerica

The third person asked to point out the deficiencies in young photojournalists who have crossed his path is Gifford D. Hampshire, Director of Project Documerica. "Giff" received his journalism degree at the School of Journalism, University of Missouri, and for a time was a member of the *National Geographic Magazine* illustrations staff. Following is his answer to my question:

The first deficiency of photographers today is that they are not required to and do not discipline themselves to think logically, as well as emotionally, about *what* and *why* prior to using the camera . . . and too often *how* once they start shooting.

A photographer can be intellectually lazy and still succeed as a "photojournalist." In the institutional framework of a publication, picture researchers, writers, and editors bear editorial responsibility for knowing a subject thoroughly, and articulating a story line to the photographer—sometimes to the point of telling him how to do it.

The beginning photographer whose only thinking is have-camera-will-travel runs a grave risk of complete and permanent rejection. No matter how great his photographic talent or how impressive the portfolio shown, he or she should come to the interview with a prospective employer as an individual, knowing that any good editor or photography director seeking help will examine the applicant's intellectual qualities just as closely as his photographic abilities.

This is particularly true in documentary photography which, in the great tradition, is the product of an individual's mind and heart. Photojournalism is excellent to the degree that the photographer practices the intellectual discipline of documentary photography. I believe the beginning photographer should require of himself, or be required in his schooling, to undertake a documentary assignment. Before deciding on his subject the photographer should ask himself, "What do I want this body of work to say about me as a person as well as a photographer?" . . .

The value of photographing a documentary story lies not only in learning all that is possible about the subject, but also in arriving at an intellectual as well as emotional conviction that the subject is worthwhile. Adequate research allows the photographer to plan his approach and decide how he is going to shoot the assignment.

If all this is done in advance, the photographer's mind and eye should work in harmony as he is shooting. Surprises should be serendipitous instead of tragic . . . In brief, the shooting should be highly rewarding. Finally, after all the film is processed, and the photographer sees all the images, he should be able to make a selection of pictures which meets or exceeds his objective.

There is one final step, in my opinion, which is essential to the completion of the assignment. The pictures or transparencies should be organized and captioned, and the text should be written so that the work can be reviewed by busy editors or photographic directors, and this with or without the photographer. The cameraman should also organize his "seconds" and "rejects" and have them available for review. Most good editors and photographic directors want to see the complete take if they are at all impressed by the photographer's selection.

The second deficiency I see in beginning photographers has a lot to do with the first. Many are taking to photography for the ego trip. Perhaps that's normal, and I know that photographers are part artist (my definition of an artist is one solely interested in self-expression). I think this deficiency will correct itself as the photographer learns intellectual discipline.

The ego comes under the control of the mind and shares a role with the heart, making the photographer more of a likable person.

Lastly, I must say I am shocked to see so much poor color photography by beginning photographers. I realize it is expensive to learn to use color film, but in this day technical mastery of color film is just as important as black and white for anyone calling himself a photographer.

# Advice from Barney Cowherd

To avoid ending this chapter on a pessimistic note let us consider the advice given several years ago to college students by one of their peers. The person speaking was the late Barney Cowherd (see pages 78–81), a very young man who earned the title News Photographer of the Year the first time it was offered. In his unassuming, whimsical, almost Will Rogers style, Cowherd gave this message to a group of college students just a few years younger than he who were assembled to pay tribute to him for winning the coveted title.[2]

Barney was a thinker. He was tired of those flash-on-camera snapshots. He thought, as did I (a young photojournalism teacher at the time), that photojournalism had much more to offer than the news photographers of the day were giving. The message these photojournalism students heard that day was revolutionary. The record of his address is worth playing again and again. Let's listen.

> It appears that there's been some interest in my photographs. This makes me very happy. More than anything else I'm happy because people other than myself like to look at them.
>
> I've decided that these pictures came out of my noodle. The reason they are appealing, if they are, is because I have an ordinary noodle just like most everybody else.
>
> I take pictures of ordinary people doing ordinary things. I've discovered that the ordinary has become fresh because the public is overfed with the unusual, man-bites-dog stuff. We need more stories and pictures of dogs biting man.
>
> A camera is like a typewriter. Typewriters do not write stories and cameras do not take pictures. The human mind writes stories and the human mind takes pictures.
>
> But of course the camera is indispensable. The trouble is that too many of its users don't know that it is unimportant except for its presence.
>
> Expensive cameras and a million gadgets profusely advertised as necessities for good picture making create a false viewpoint for the already struggling student of photography. Some pictures could not have been made without proper equipment, but usually particular cameras and gadgets on them, in them, around them, or underneath them have nothing to do with it.
>
> Quite often the shooting of a flashbulb will kill a shot that would have been good with God-given light, and many a picture has been missed while exposure meter readings were being made.
>
> In addition to what goes on inside your noodle, it's a matter of where you point the camera, the whatever at which you point it, and the particular instant you choose to shoot it. The "where you point it" is easily interpreted from the sad story about the fellow who thought he had taken a beautiful picture and later discovered his failure to include it in his viewfinder.

---

2. Address given by Barney Cowherd at the School of Journalism, University of Missouri, 1948.

Who gives a hoot about the appearance of horse manure magnified a hundred thousand times? This brings us to the "whatever at which you point it." Things of universal, down-to-earth interest kick up quite a storm in comparison to the exotic or erotic.

But the timing probably is of greater importance than the where or what.

It is a certainty that if you fire either much before or much after so-and-so blows his nose, you will not have the ultimate in pictorial value—assuming that everything has pictorial possibilities.

Often it's desirable to catch the action just before the climax. Consider a picture of a partially clothed stripteaser and one of her as a nature girl. The "almost" print keeps you staring because you're curious to know how she'd look if . . . The "all-gone" exposure shows you, but you're left flat, unless you wish to continue the observation for reasons not photographic. By arranging two or more pictures in sequence, we can add considerably to the storytelling possibilities of still pictures and come mighty close to the movies. Of course, we have no audible sound or physical motion, but they can be silently suggested on inanimate paper.

We see a change in time and appearance in the two pictures of the stripteaser. With more pictures, a change of location could be managed, and the imaginative person could even hear the Gayety band by looking at such a photo. A slow shutter speed would render the most active part of the subject's body as a blur, indicating motion.

Among the tribe of people who concern themselves with unimportant stuff, the question of whether photography is art has been overdiscussed. Let us put to death this concern of theirs—by recalling what Alfred Stieglitz once remarked about it. A group of painters said to him, "Of course, photography is not art, but we would like to paint the way you photograph." Stieglitz's reply was, "I don't know anything about art, but for some reason or other I have never wanted to photograph the way you paint."

Some photographers prefer not to call themselves artists; not that they feel that photography is more solid than dabbling, but that names are names and that's all. Possibly that preference is because of the prevailing idea that art has to do with something or other called esthetic—moods, feelings, temper tantrums, and the like.

But it's obvious that these things occur in other people chasing other pursuits. If these idiosyncrasies seem to be present in photographers to any degree, it can be attributed to the extra share of disappointment suffered by them because of their closer relationship with the ungodly manner in which humanity behaves.

The photographer's eyes are diseased with over-sensitivity—they see too much. So many of us engage ourselves in the daily activities of living without being concerned with what our fellowmen are doing, what they look like while they're doing it, or why they do it.

Everybody is different from everybody else. This doesn't sound like too much of a startling observation; however, photographers consciously think in this simple, apparently low level, which is popularly accepted only subconsciously; and, as a direct result, they turn out pictures which are the most honest and realistic records of this life.

We don't spend all of our time trying to figure out what life is all about; perhaps we believe that it can't be figured out, only accepted as it is, such as it is, and presented as it is.

Such as it is, it is not a pretty language. The continuous appearance of the sin-and-strife theme is an indication that we are honest reporters. Our productions are almost in keeping with the modern writers' idea of what's predominantly going on. Unlike the writers, however, we produce a slightly larger percentage of the good-humor variety.

Even though there is an adequate understanding of the technicalities, the mechanics, and the chemistry related to its successful operation, photography continues its insidious habit of getting into man's blood. This is largely because of the miraculous feeling it gives the individual who picks up a picture that he has taken or was in—or even one that was taken while he was looking on.

Whether he realizes it or not, he can hardly believe that such a thing is possible unless the mystics had something to do with it.

# Student Participation

The men quoted in this chapter believe in essence that a word reporter or a cameraman to be successful must have a "sense of audience." In my mind this means that the writer and/or photographer has an obligation to his readers to bring them significant facts about the news or feature event under surveillance. Do you agree?

1. Bring to class for discussion three pictures which are valid reports—pictures which provide information about some local or national happening.
2. Bring to class for discussion three pictures which in your opinion say little or nothing and should not have been printed.
3. Gifford Hampshire, director of the governmental project Documerica, says that "a photographer can be intellectually lazy, and still succeed as a photojournalist." Do you agree? Why? Why not?
4. Read carefully the address given by Barney Cowherd in 1948. Mr. Cowherd was a thinker, an innovater. What are some of the things he said that set him apart from run-of-the-mill photographers?

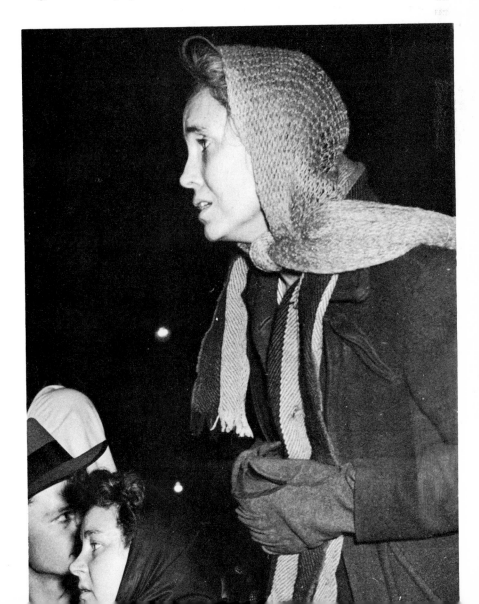

A great picture is a storytelling picture. The picture at *right* by Sam Caldwell of the *St. Louis Post-Dispatch* was taken in 1947 at Centralia, Illinois, where a mine explosion claimed 111 lives. Note the anguish and grief of the woman who, with many others, waits, hopes, and prays that her husband is still alive. Included in 50 Memorable Pictures exhibit.

**Burst of Joy** by Sal Veder of the Associated Press. This picture made a clean sweep of the many competitions in which it was entered in 1973. It earned first place, general news, in the Thirtieth Annual Pictures of the Year competition. Among the other honors were first prize, World Press Photo, Amsterdam, Holland, and the Pulitzer Prize for feature photography. It portrays the return of Lt. Col. Robert Stirm as he arrived at Travis Air Force Base in California after more than five years in a North Vietnam prison. (Wide World Photos.)

**Stormy** (*right*). This picture was made by Bill Eppridge while he was a student at the University of Missouri and has earned many awards and worldwide acclaim. Bill is now a photographer with Time-Life, Inc., and has produced many winning pictures including those for the famous drug story featured in *Life* several years ago and of the assassination of Robert Kennedy.

**Home Town.** This feature photograph from his story of Hartsburg, Missouri, was made by H. Edward Kim, now chief of layout and production, *National Geographic Magazine.* Ed, a South Korean who made a series of excellent pictures on a recent visit to North Korea for *National Geographic,* calls this portrayal of a small Missouri town one of his favorites.

**Flower Power.** To attract and hold attention in today's battle for readers, a picture must be different. This prizewinning picture by Bernie Boston, photo chief of the *Washington Star-News,* certainly qualifies.

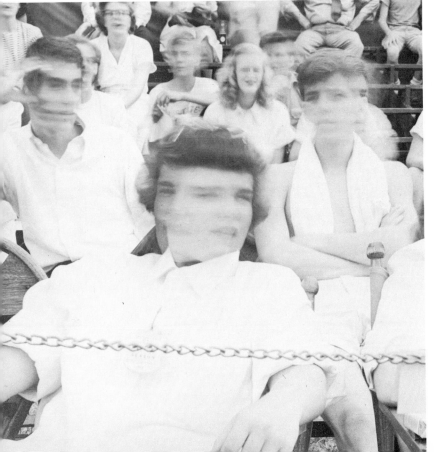

Termed "the most original" of nearly 3,000 pictures entered in nationwide competition, this picture of people watching a tennis match was certainly different. Made by the late Barney Cowherd of the *Louisville Courier-Journal,* it helped earn him the title News Photographer of the Year in 1948.

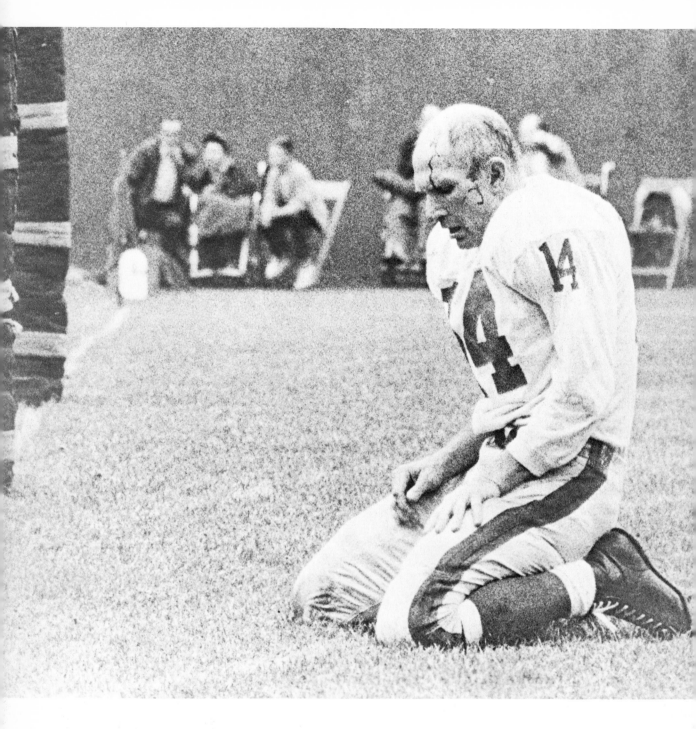

**Y. A. Tittle Topples** by Morris Berman
of the *Pittsburgh Post-Gazette*. This picture
earned first place, sports category, in the 23rd
Pictures of the Year competition. It, like
the picture on the *right*, is a picture that is
different. Emotional and storytelling, it is
the kind of picture sports editors welcome.
(Courtesy of Morris Berman and
*Pittsburgh Post-Gazette*.)

One of the most important parts of a picture
editor's job is to come up with story ideas.
On some publications that responsibility is
shared with the photographers themselves.
The pictures on these two pages by Brian
Lanker are from his Pulitzer Prizewinning
story on natural childbirth. Brian's description of his assignment is given in Chapter 11.

**The Coming of Spring.** Some of the honors this picture has won for Talmadge (Red) Morgan are first-place feature and best-print-of-show, 1973 New York State Associated Press competition. The picture was taken for the Westchester-Rockland Newspapers, New York.

# A Tribute to Barney Cowherd

# 7

## A Perceptive Photographer

Young Barney Cowherd was the first to win the News Photographer of the Year Award in the Pictures of the Year competition, in 1948. Not satisfied with "flash on camera" snapshots, his photographs (made for the *Louisville Courier-Journal*) were different, sensitive, and thought provoking. Barney was considerably ahead of his time.

To learn more about this astounding young man and his philosophies, examine the pictures on the pages that follow and then refer to the address (chapter 6) that he gave to students at the School of Journalism, University of Missouri, in May 1948.

The late Elwood Martin (Barney) Cowherd died in 1972 at the age of 50. He was a sensitive, innovative man, and a pioneer in modern photojournalism.

For thirty years of the half-century allotted him, Barney recorded the Kentucky and Indiana region as though he were a "poet with a camera." He spent the earlier part of his life as a photographer for the Louisville *Courier-Journal* and the *Louisville Times*. Later, he was photographer for Indiana University. Although Barney's "style" changed with the passing of the years, his pictures never ceased to challenge and to please those who looked at them.

As a salute to this man and an acknowledgement of his great contribution to photojournalism, William Strode, Assistant Director of Photography at the *Louisville Courier-Journal,* wrote and produced a book called *Barney Cowherd, Photographer.*[1]

---

1. William H. Strode III, *Barney Cowherd, Photographer* (Louisville: *The Courier-Journal & Times,* 1973).

. . . who in 1948 was the first person to earn the nationwide title of "Newspaper Photographer of the Year."

he frontispiece of the book *Barney*
*whrd, Photographer,* indicative of
rney's sensitivity, was a picture (*left*)
a little girl enraptured by the things she
w in a Christmas display window. This
cture, which appeared in *The Family of*
*an,* was one of Barney's favorites (and
e of the favorites of Bill Strode, who ex-
nined more than 1,600 Cowherd negatives
compiling the book. Strode used this
cture not only as the frontispiece, but also
every division page, much as Edward
eichen used the little flute player in his
amily of Man exhibit. The picture of the
ttle girl served to unify the Cowherd
ictures. Courtesy William Strode, *Barney*
owherd, Photographer (Louisville, Ky.:
he *Courier-Journal* and *Louisville Times,*
973).

**U.S.A. 1948** (*below*). When this Barney
Cowherd photograph appeared in a Museum
of Modern Art display, *Life* reported that it
evoked "more comment than any other picture since the *Mona Lisa.*" That might have
been a slight exaggeration, but there is no
denying that "U.S.A. 1948" commandeered
its share of attention. Barney took the picture
because it "signified the mass confusion
of the time."

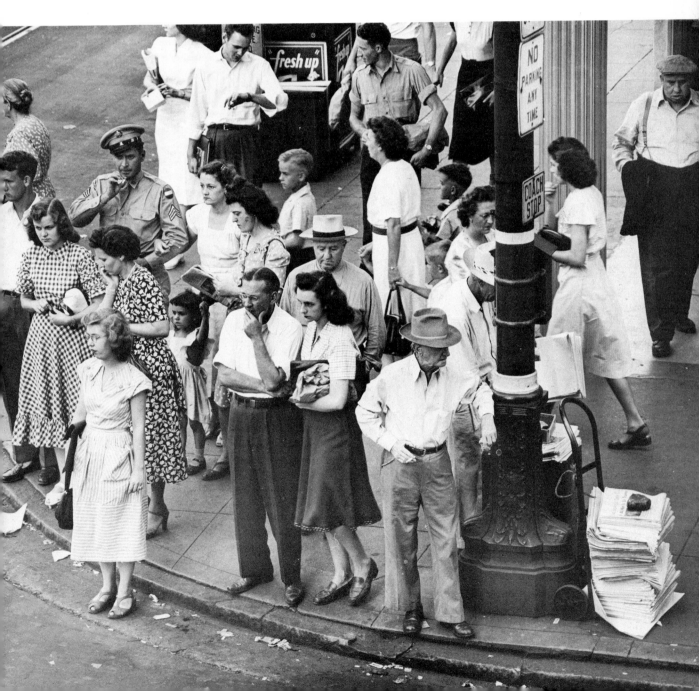

# Picture Editing 8

F ar more pictures were printed this last year than ever before. Paradoxically, only a few publications have bonafide picture specialists on their administrative staffs. Far too many with the title of picture editor are picture editors in name only. They have little or no authority and are not allowed to instigate significant changes. True, not too many of them are trained to assume administrative responsibilities in the photojournalism realm, and unfortunately not too many photographers want to take over directorship of a photojournalism program.

In spite of this foreboding picture, a few publications today do give authority and cooperation to picture editors. A number of these picture editors do an excellent job of getting the most out of the photojournalism dollar. They are recognized as important, well-paid people—and so they are.

In the preface of a book on picture editing you will find these words:

> The key to successful picture editing is the feeling for pictures. This cannot be overemphasized. A person who is going to edit pictures successfully must live pictures, must sense pictures, must interpret every experience in the light of pictures it suggests. Thus far there has been too little of this feeling for pictures. In many a newspaper office picture editing is nothing more than a spare-time job for a newsman. Often the captions are written by anyone who is available, although caption writing is as specialized as is headline writing. Publications (and the whole publishing industry) sadly need people who have a knowledge of picture editing.[1]

## Functions of a Picture Editor

J. Bruce Baumann, a member of the picture staff of *National Geographic Magazine,* gives the following evaluation of picture editors and their status in present-day photojournalism. A fine photographer as well as a fine picture editor, Baumann has had important positions on newspapers in Indiana and Michigan and is well qualified to give an authoritative approach to the subject of picture editing. Here is what he has to say:

---

1. Stanley E. Kalish and Clifton C. Edom, *Picture Editing* (New York: Rinehart & Co., Inc., 1951).

Picture editors should be in charge of all illustrations which appear in print.

In the past, job descriptions have varied for picture editors from place to place, depending on individual management. Today, only a few uneducated managing editors or publishers hold back the authority necessary for a responsible and professional picture-editing job.

The new awareness level of some word editors to accept highly skilled people in the area of pictures is directly responsible for a more sophisticated press. The photographer, who once played the role of illustrator, now takes an active part in the role of journalist. Therefore, as we have had copy editors to polish writer's manuscripts, we have picture editors to make judgments on editorial images.

The role of the picture editor seems deceptively simple. It is, in fact, a job so complex that there have been few textbooks written on the subject. This may further be emphasized by the fact that, although there are thousands and thousands of writers and photographers, there remains only a handful of qualified picture editors. The numbers, however, are growing with each year. A qualified picture editor is much in demand.

What qualifies "qualified"? Two things. He must have a complete administrative and creative hold on the reins. Let's first discuss the administrative aspect.

As established earlier, the picture editor must be in charge of all illustrations which appear in print. It is therefore necessary to regard the picture editor as a member of the news executives. His title is irrelevant as long as he functions with the authority of an assistant managing editor. He must be on a par with the executive news editor, one step below managing editor. At this level of management he is in a positive position to make editorial decisions in the area of graphics.

Why should a single individual be charged with such decisions? Primarily, because committee decisions are inefficient, compromised, and generally non-professional—ineffectual. One person, in charge, can direct a balanced visual product. Second, why would a publisher want to accept anything but a trained, expert, and professional picture editor?

As an administrator a picture editor's responsibilities are these. First, as a *news executive* he should have a list of assignments for each department. He must be aware of all events that concern the publication.

Next, he must sort through the assignments and *determine what is editorially important and visually interesting.* Here he must weed out the mundane and the nonvisual.

The next responsibility is vitally important. *The picture editor must match up the proper photographer* with the *specific assignment.* Similarly, as a sports writer would not be sent to cover a political convention, an unspecialized photographer should not be out covering a specialized story.

The problem of the wrong photographer will remain a problem as long as publications continue to carry a ten-to-one ratio of reporters to photographers. A more practical ratio would be five to one.

A picture editor should provide his photographer with background information. It is his responsibility to provide the knowledge necessary to communcate the story visually.

Second, but not secondary, is the creative aspect of the picture editor's role. It is most certainly an interactive and functional part of his position. It is that ingredient that gives quality to his work.

When the story is completed, the picture editor edits the entire take (either from contact sheets or electronic devices). He must keep in mind the editorial content as well as the visual image. He is, in fact, searching for the accumulative statement—the single frame which communicates with editorial and visual impact.

Having found the photograph which will best exemplify the story, he must first crop the image in a way to project the information that it contains. Many pictures have been lost by a butcherous hand on a grease pencil.

Another of his more vital roles is to carefully select the portion of the image which is to be cropped in (as opposed to being cropped out). I prefer the former terminology to the latter, since what is left in has more importance.

Following this procedure, it is then necessary to determine the proper size that the photograph will appear in print. First, let me say that bigger isn't necessarily better. Sizing a picture larger than it merits only emphasizes its shortcomings. On the other hand, sizing a photograph smaller than it needs to be to communicate its information can reduce or eliminate its editorial importance. Finally, sizing a photograph to fit a predetermined hole is just plain ignorance. Each picture needs individual care and handling. It must be cropped with skill and sized according to merit and need. The chances of properly filling a predetermined hole are as good as filling that same hole in said editor's head.

The placement of photographs on the printed page is as important as any of the previous steps. When a picture is placed on a page, it must work with everything else on that page. It is necessary that headlines, type, and illustrations on a given page complement each other rather than compete.

This may well be the most difficult to achieve. In the rapid pace of production and dissemination of news, it is rare when words and pictures come together at the same time a page editor is planning his product. However, since type wraps, bends, and jumps, it is not an impossible goal.

The creative picture editor knows that ideas are valued commodities. Finding a person who will not close his mind to change is what keeps photojournalism so valid.

The picture editor must be able to sort through the assignment suggestions and decide which stories are best told in pictures and which ones would better be communicated in words.

So many assignments are made because the reporters and editors were struck with telefrightous—the inability to say no over the telephone. The type of assignment that he will accept is based on his imagination of what the potential results might hold. This influential role in the newsroom is the creative activity (which can be a driving force) in producing ideas from writers and editors.

Another important creative function is to guide the photographer's approach. This does not mean, by any stretch of the imagination, that the picture editor should manipulate the photographer. Rather, he should guide him into what should be said photographically, seeing pictures where they are and not contriving them. It is important for the picture editor to keep in mind that he is there to make the photographer think and to remind him that content is the most important substance.

Finally, cropping and layout are the ultimate in picture handling. It is not so strange to expect a picture editor to edit and arrange photographs with as much talent and excellence as is expected of a copy editor and his words.

When laying out sets of photographs, the creative picture editor is the one who knows how to make each picture work with the others. A picture is like a paragraph, beginning and ending with one thought. Each must be arranged and emphasized in the most functional, storytelling manner. Some will be larger because they offer vast amounts of information and visual impact. Others will be smaller because they make a certain point that connects each piece. In the end, the pictures will tell the story.

## Mathematically Speaking

Selecting and preparing pictures for publication are among the many important responsibilities of the picture editor. After deciding a print has the desired content and storytelling qualities, the next step is to prepare it for publication.

The preparation includes cropping the picture, if cropping is called for, and scaling it to the size it will appear in the newspaper. Whether the publication

Among other things, cropping focuses the attention of readers on a given part of the original photo. It allows cutting out of unwanted areas and control of the size of the picture as it finally appears.

is letterpress, offset, or gravure sometimes influences selection and sizing. The fine screen used in photo-offset and the offset system itself permit a more faithful rendition of tonal range than does the coarse screen halftone used in newspaper letterpress. For the latter, the editor would insist on "picture copy" of adequate contrast.

Regardless of the printing method, the editor knows the reproduction should be large enough to be seen and readily understood. Far too many papers—even in these days of cold type and/or photo-offset—"play" their pictures too small.

Granting that most of the time in a newspaper space is at a premium, one still should not use pictures too small. If the twinkle in the eyes reveals character, the reproduction should be large enough for the eyes to be clearly seen. If the bride's gown is essential to the story, then the illustration should be large enough to show it in detail.

Action in a picture means more than a fast-moving person or object. A grimace, a smile—these things, too, often are the story. In such cases, the reproduction should be large enough to let the reader see them.

Crop marks made with a grease pencil on the white border of the picture indicate the portion which the halftone cameraman will reproduce. Cropping should be done to emphasize the essentials and keep the picture from being confusing. Cropping also is a means of controlling the size of the finished illustration. Scaling, or proportioning, allows the picture editor to fit the allotted space on the newspaper or magazine page.

It is easy to figure reproductions and enlargements. The tools used for this job are a line gauge or pica rule, a slide rule, or any other type of calculator. The whole job could be done mathematically, of course, but the "tools," once one knows how to use them, are timesavers.

The reproduction is always in exact proportion to the full size or cropped copy from which it is made. When the width of a picture is increased or decreased, the depth changes proportionately, and when the depth of a picture is increased or decreased, the width proportionately does the same.

When pictures are scaled, the halftone areas increase or decrease in mathematical progression. A one-column picture enlarged to two columns quadruples (not doubles) in area.

One thing to remember in cropping and scaling pictures: Poor pictures often can be improved by cropping. Good pictures sometimes can be made better by cropping. On the other hand, they can be completely ruined and robbed of their storytelling value by careless cropping. If a picture does not need it, *don't crop!*

# Relationship of Graphics and Design to Picture Editing

William Kuykendall believes that graphics and design are closely allied to picture editing, indeed, are a part of the process as he explains in the following:

> Photojournalism must no longer comprise merely the making of fine, story-telling pictures. The time is ripe for renaissance communicators: journalists sensitive not only to relationships within pictures but also to relationships

among pictures; journalists with a feeling for type—its structure, its weight, its mood; journalists with an ear for the written word, both the prose of text and the poetry of headlines and blurbs. There must be journalists who can understand and harness their behind-the-lens creative energies and focus them on the problems of the layout table.

The photographer working only with camera and enlarger is a note taker, an author of paragraphs. The editor to whom he hands his pictures rights or wrongs the story through *his* selection and emphasis of pictures. If the editor goes beyond just arranging pictures with words . . . if he writes and juxtaposes meaningful display lines with the correct pictures . . . if he enhances the story with a complementary type face or a tasteful arrangement of white space, then he rightfully deserves much of the credit for the success of the story. If he fails, only the photographer looks bad . . .

Picture stories are not produced by the sampling method. They require deep involvement yet intellectual detachment. The photojournalist must see the story in depth and perspective just as the writer must . . . Just as the expert interviewer researches his subject and composes a list of incisive questions, the photographer must appear on the scene thoroughly backgrounded and alert for storytelling picture opportunities. He must be aware of subtle nuances of personality in his subject and be prepared to capture them. He must watch for interactions among everyone involved. He must know his equipment and use it automatically. He must think ahead and consider the effect of lens, shutter speed, aperture, light, and camera angle on every scene, every episode. He must choose the appropriate technique, position himself, and anticipate the probable action in time to capture it. And if he guesses wrong, he must be ready to move instantly to a favorable combination without losing the gist of the activity. This applies whether you are photographing politicians at rallies or spinsters at home with their cats. Subtle stories require the greatest discipline . . .

There are few rules in photojournalism. But one guideline that is useful is to consider the progress of your shooting in cinematic terms.

Film producers seeking to establish visual continuity employ some basic devices to orient the viewer and carry him from scene to scene.

First is the establishing shot: This is a long view showing the setting, usually with an important aspect of the subject small, but in the center of attention.

Show the reader where the action is taking place; put it all into context with the establishing shot. Pay attention to small details of composition and have a strong center of interest.

Next is the medium shot: Come close on certain processes or activities; show the major character(s) in relation to the people or objects with which he (they) are interacting.

Then comes the closeup: Move in close to show fine detail or emphasize an aspect of your subject's personality. Always strive for at least one tight, dramatic portrait on your main subject.

Keep in mind the pictures you have shot and watch for opportunities to collect images which differ in content but resemble others in composition, thus enabling you to capitalize on graphic similarities during layout.

You should try to think of your story title while shooting, especially if you are writing it yourself. And think of the lead picture you associate with it. This exercise not only is helpful in securing a strong lead, but also helps you place the overall story in perspective. You should try for a strong ender—one which repeats the overall mood of the story or works as a logical stopper.

The more you "think layout" as you shoot, the more options you will have when it comes time to sit down with pica pole and proportion scale. And the more you work arranging pictures and text, the more sensitive you will become to the editorial realities while shooting. . .

If you have considered the layout while you were shooting and printing, you probably will have arrived at some major design decisions before approaching the layout table.

If coverage is good, you should have an opener, a headline, and an ender in mind. You should know what the story is worth in terms of space and have strong candidates for the body of the layout.

Even if you have decided on your favorites, you should take a fresh, overall view of your pictures.

Lay all of your enlargements on a large table or on the floor and stare at them until you begin to see a progression from picture to picture. Identify your opener and ender. Try to come up with a "meaningful" story title (story labels such as "Picnic Party," "Operation Outreach," or "Local Ladies Help Out Poor" are pretty trite and unworthy of even cheap ink).

As your ideas begin to jell, pick up a small scale layout sheet and sketch in your proposed layout . . .

With the thumbnail layout you can rough in your preliminary designs quickly and evaluate them for balance and harmony. If you are dissatisfied with your first rough, you can put it aside and sketch another. Gradually, as you play with the images in miniature, you should evolve an arrangement of pictures and text which works on the page.

This will be your guide in producing the comprehensive. Do not involve yourself in sizing pictures during the thumbnail stage. Generally, the more you disassociate the mathematical equivalents (points, picas, and inches) from the early creative stages of design, the more you can concentrate on the content of the pictures and their relationships.

It is smart, though, to estimate the amount of copy before starting the thumbnail. This can be a rough estimate based on the commonly used type face set to a 13-pica measure. If, during the course of sketching the thumbnail, you decide on a wider or narrower measure, you still have a basis for estimating the new depth of copy.

Rough in body copy as light horizontal lines on the thumbnail.

Rough in the story title and blurbs in lines approximately their actual "weight" proportioned to the thumbnail. Draw fine, horizontal lines for cutlines and credit lines.

All of these should be included in the thumbnail so that you can estimate the effect of the finished design.

Once a satisfactory effect has been achieved you are ready to do precise headline and body copy fitting, fit cutlines and blurbs, and scale the pictures to the comprehensive.[2]

# Mechanics of Laying Out a Picture Story

Using the experience gained at the twenty-seven-year-old Missouri Photo Workshop, herewith are what I believe are helpful instructions not only for doing story layouts, but also for picture editing.

When he is at work in the field, every photographer is a picture editor. He makes the judgment on whether to take a picture, decides how to compose it, and often has complete editorial control over the picture at the moment of decision. The business of laying out pictures is an extension of editing.

1. Gather all of the materials you will need to work on the layout. This material will consist of 8½-by-11-inch paper, grease pencil, ruler, transparent tape, razor blade or scissors, and magnifying glass or viewer.

---

2. Kuykendall, a free-lance photographer, is a former member of the photojournalism staff at the University of Missouri and has taught both graphics and photojournalism. Quoted here are excerpts from a release he prepared for use at a special agricultural editor's photo school held at Columbia, Missouri.

2. Collect all of your contact sheets. Next, making sure they are identified by roll so that you can find the numbers of the negatives when you need them, circle each frame you think may have a place in the layout.

3. Cut out (make sure the roll number is on the back of each) marked frames from only one contact sheet at a time. Leave sprocket holes and frame numbers. This is the only way you will be able to find the negatives.

4. Do not be afraid to pick too many frames. They can be edited later.

5. Your cutouts are known as "selects."

6. Arrange your selects into subject groups such as portraits, long shots, situations, etc.

7. Decide which pictures are best in each group. So far as possible, choose a horizontal and vertical of each situation.

8. Pick your lead or cover picture. It should be an eye-catcher and a stopper. It should also suggest what the story is about. For instance, if your story is about an individual, it not only should show what the person looks like, but also should suggest the nature of his work or the theme of your story. This picture should be excellent both photographically and editorially.

9. Arrange selects in the order in which you think they will best tell your story. This is where you should do some really hard thinking. Shuffle and reshuffle your contact prints. Look for parallels or contrasts. Remember, the traditional picture story has a beginning, a middle, and an end.

10. Now, begin weeding out the pictures that essentially say the same thing. You must be critical of photographic quality as well as of content. Ask yourself whether your selects say something without the necessity of explaining.

11. Since you are working on a pseudomagazine layout, you must decide whether you want to open your story on a right-hand page or a spread (two pages).

12. Arbitrary rule: Let us not plan for more than six pictures on a spread. A sequence may be considered as a single picture. If you can use less than six, your layout will be better. No layout should be more than six pages, and you probably can do it better with four. Keep in mind that a very effective story can be made on a two-page spread.

13. Find a closer, a picture which says The End to the viewer.

14. Cropping: Not all of your pictures are cropped exactly in the camera. To make a better picture, you may have to crop it in print form. An ugly, space-grabbing tree in the foreground may have to be cropped from the bottom of the frame. A striking horizontal view may be made even more eye-catching by "shallowing" the picture at both top and bottom. A picture of a tall man may make him look even taller when cropped from one or both sides. Perhaps you shot the frame to show a detail. Cropping down on the detail may add emphasis. Watch for the shot that can be cropped, with reason, into an exceptionally deep, narrow vertical. These shapes often permit a spread with real impact. Do your cropping first with a grease pencil and not with a razor blade!

15. Sizing: See the diagram on opposite page for the mechanics of this process.

16. Indicate headlines, copy blocks, and captions on the layout. The copy block is usually composed of straight lines; the captions, by wavy lines.

17. For your miniature layout, use an 8½-by-11-inch sheet of paper, folded through the center, as a two-page spread. With pencil and ruler, draw in

In making an enlargement or reduction, one dimension—either the width or depth—is always known. When using the diagonal system recommended here (see page 89), la a ruler or straightedge across the photograph so that it accurately divides the angles of the lower-left and upper-right corners. If your final illustration is to be 5⅓ inches wide, make a dot at exactly the place where 5½ inches intercepts the diagonal made by the ruler. Dropping a line from this point to the base will give you the dimensions of your enlarged print. This rule of the diagonal will help you to quickly arrive at the size of enlargements or reductions. And you can use it on horizontal shapes as well as on verticals (*dotted lines*).

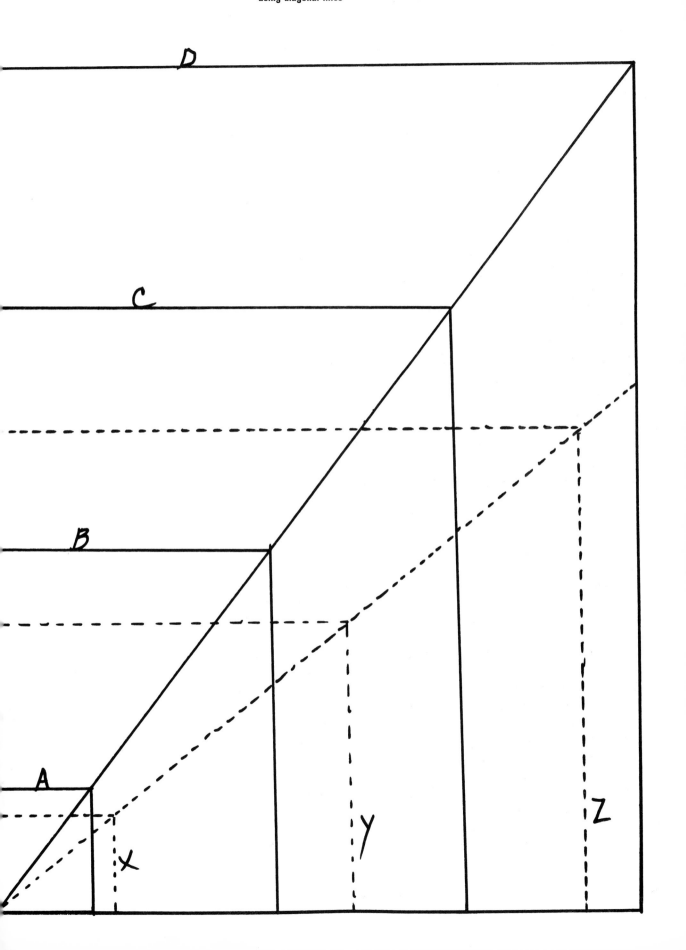

Layout sizing technique
using diagonal lines

In addition to running the activities program at the Boone Retirement Center, Mary Hoffman keeps the patients

# In touch with reality

Mary Hoffman would like to see the stereotype image of nursing homes changed, and through her job as activities director at the Boone Retirement Center, she is doing just that.

The physical conditions at the center are not the best. The building is old, dating back to 1934. The medical facilities and patient conveniences are minimal. They will be improved when the center moves in December to its new building near Boone County Hospital.

But physical conditions are not all-important. They can do little to cure the boredom often found in nursing homes. The patients must have something to occupy their time, and they need someone who cares about keeping them active.

Mary is originally from Wales, where she was trained as an occupational therapist. Her Welsh accent may sound a little out of place in mid-Missouri, but she seems right at home in her work. When she isn't supervising one of her regularly scheduled activities, such as handicrafts or bingo, she can usually be found "making her rounds," helping someone with an individual project, or just chatting with someone in need of a little friendly conversation.

She also coordinates a library book program with the Boone County Library. Twice a month a traveling librarian visits the center, picks up old books and magazines, and with Mary's help, distributes new selections to the residents.

Her job includes a daily session known as "reality orientation." It is a technique used to help those who have lost touch with reality find their way back. It can be used not only for elderly people, but also in the treatment of certain types of mental illness.

During these sessions, Mary asks questions. She might ask what day of the week it is, or whether it's hot or cold in the room. Or she might hold up an apple or a letter of the alphabet and ask the patient to identify it. Simple questions like these can help patients get a grasp on the things they have lost to old age. "The important thing," Mary says, "is to get them to exercise their minds."

At times the sessions are discouraging. Often the patients are not able to respond; sometimes they just don't want to. And Mary's other duties won't permit her to spend as much time as she would like to in the sessions. Ideally,

reality orientation would be a constant activity. But even on a limited basis, the sessions serve an important purpose. Without them, these people would remain idle and drift farther and farther away from reality.

Mary is modest about her role at the center. She has an attitude about her job that makes it more than a job: "It's not enough to just do things for people. You have to want to do them. Then it becomes rewarding for both parties involved." She cares about her people and sees her work as more than making a living. She does it because she wants to.

Although activities programs in small nursing homes are almost unheard of, Mary is proving that it can be done. Such things as handicrafts and bingo give patients something to look forward to each day.

TE
AN
PH
BY
NI
DE

During daily reality sessions, Mary asks patients to identify such

School of Journalism, University of [Mis]souri, has for many years offered a major [in] photojournalism. Along with news [edi]torial, advertising, radio-television, and [oth]er sequences, the Journalism School pro[vid]es a full sequence in photojournalism. [Ph]oto majors learn more than how to click a [shu]tter. Part of their education is devoted [to] word-reporting, advertising, editorial [wri]ting, and all other phases of newspaper [and] magazine work. In addition, the photo [maj]or receives a thorough grounding in the [lib]eral arts. He also receives thorough [tra]ining in photojournalism. He takes photo[gra]phs for the daily newspaper, the *[Col]umbia Missourian,* and learns how to [wri]te feature articles and news stories as well [as] headlines and captions. Going one step [fur]ther, he learns how to scale pictures to the [pro]per size, how to do pasteups, and how to [pro]duce camera-ready pages for newspapers [and] Sunday magazines. The reproductions [of] the newspaper page (left and below) [we]re done under the direction of Prof. [An]gus McDougall, director of the photo[jou]rnalism sequence. (Courtesy of Angus [Mc]Dougall and *Columbia Missourian.*)

[Mo]st newspapers which use picture layouts [som]etimes hold them to something smaller [tha]n full-page size. This horizontal half-page [lay]out (it could have been adapted to per[pen]dicular makeup) is a format frequently [us]ed by the *Columbia Missourian.* (Courtesy [of] Angus McDougall and *Columbia Missourian.*)

the shape and approximate size of each picture. Place each contact-sized print in the lower right-hand corner of the space you have dummied or given to this particular picture. Tack it down with scotch tape and only along the top. Do *not* put tape over the picture itself.

If you do not like the layout as it is, do another and another until you get one you do like. This is the way to find out whether you have told your story clearly and effectively. The procedure given here for magazines is also adaptable to newspaper picture pages. Whether doing magazine or newspaper layouts, make sure that your doodling paper—your miniature layout sheets—will scale to the size of the finished product: the printed page.

# Student Participation

When he selects a picture for publication, the first consideration of a picture editor is to focus on and evaluate the content of the picture. Next, he is concerned with cropping and sizing.

1. Cut a half-dozen pictures from current publications and crop them (with a grease pencil) to increase their effectiveness.
2. Collect a half-dozen pictures from current newspapers or magazines. Using the same yardstick you would use in evaluating a word story (i.e., importance, etc.) explain whether you think the pictures you have chosen are played too large, too small, or the right size.
3. Collect pictures from a magazine picture story or essay and use five or six of the pictures to do a standard (not tabloid) newspaper picture page. Scale the pictures to their final size, draw in headlines, copy blocks, and captions. In selecting your pictures for the newspaper page, make sure you have a beginning, middle, and end.

It was a time for playing, sharing and working, but mainly . . .

# A Time for Friendship

"I'm the only black person here."

"Just pretend that you've got a tan."

Margaret Hayes is a 14-year-old black girl; Sabra Meyer is an 18-year-old white. They shared a river, a canoe and a friendship that will last longer than their one day trip.

Margaret and Sabra met on a Camp Fire Girl float trip down the Currant River. It was a new experience for Margaret, who had never seen a river's rapids. Sabra has been canoeing for several years and was an assistant counselor on the trip.

They stuck together and learned how important teamwork was in floating a river.

Between swimming and playing, Margaret and Sabra shared lunches and spills, and the aching muscles that go with eight hours of paddling.

According to Sabra, "We got to be more than just friends. We really like each other and got along great from the beginning. Margaret is very outgoing and we got to know each other really fast."

Margaret felt that "Sabra is really nice, and funny too. I hope we can get together again. It's kind of hard with her going away to college. I really think of her as a sister."

Racial differences were not ignored; they were something to joke about. "Being black and white made it a little different," said Sabra. "But you really forget it after a while. We could kid each other about it."

When Margaret got tired of paddling, she would sit back and smile at Sabra. "Come on, steer girl. You're the slave now." And they laughed as Sabra answered, "Yes, Ma'am."

Margaret was pleased with Sabra's attitude. "She really got along with my color. It made things really fun."

Their biggest problem in the canoe was steering. Sabra said she "had trouble turning, so Margaret always got into the trees."

But they survived the trip and are eager to go on another one. "Next time," they both agreed, "we have

# Country Roads
By JOHN G. WHITE

Ft. Morgan.
DENVER★

Bethrey McCracken is asked to match her number with same number on chart held by her teacher, Ila Wernsman, at STAR School. Bethrey looks for guidance (left), matches number (above), then is happy (right).

'I happy'

FORT MORGAN, Colo. — "I happy!"

That small shout of exhilaration comes frequently in the Bud McCracken household from their foster child, Bethrey.

Bethrey, a trainable mentally retarded child, was relinquished at birth. At that time, the Social Services Department in Morgan County became her custodian. A few days later, the McCrackens became her foster parents.

As she grew older, it became apparent that Bethrey was retarded. Adoption was improbable.

Ann DuBois, Bethrey's social worker, said that at first "we accepted the custody of Bethrey. She children, she plays, watches cocoon Street, brushes her mother's hair and wrestles with her older brother, Randy, who is 12.

### Sometimes She's Sad

"She has her moments when she is sad," Mrs. McCracken said. "But most of the time she is really happy. It always causes me to smile when she says, 'I happy.'"

In rural areas, there are many children like Bethrey. If they are badly retarded, they go to Ridge Home in Denver. Many schools, like STAR, have been developed, and many families like the McCrackens care for Bethreys. The State Department of Social Services pays for the care of the children and their training.

Bethrey will be in a foster home until she is 18. By then it is hoped funds will be available to develop residential care centers to house the mentally retarded.

Hopefully, Bethrey will be trained to take care of herself and at least, partially, earn a living, Mrs. DuBois said.

"Our society says someone needs to take care of children like Bethrey. That someone in Colorado is the Department of Social Services and people like the McCrackens. It means we must become involved with the children at an early age—to use whatever resources we can to make their lives a little better."

more difficult in this kind of a situation."

The McCrackens made a home for Bethrey and gave her the same love they offered their first foster child 25 years ago.

"We took Bethrey when she was three days old, and it was just a normal adjustment, like with any

Bethrey stands in the sunlight at STAR School (Special Training and Aid for the Retarded) in Fort Morgan and shouts enthusiastically, "I happy!"

Bethrey, 6-year-old trainable mentally retarded child, is occupied with fish in a bowl.

Mrs. Bud McCracken and her foster child look through a story book before dinner.

John G. White, "farm editor" of the *Denver Post*, has at least one picture page each week which is published under the standing head Country Roads. John, who has worked on publications in Kansas, Wisconsin, and Iowa, was a photo major at the University of Missouri. He says that he writes "to tell a story," and that he "photographs to tell a story." White believes that this combination is stronger than either as a separate unit. (Courtesy of John G. White.)

93

This layout (*above*) is a picture story from the 1970 Bolivar Photo Workshop by Bill Luster of the *Louisville Courier-Journal*. Workshoppers select their own stories. Bill was impressed with this wonderful nine-year-old youngster who had lost a leg in a motorcycle accident. He wanted to show that despite her handicap she asked no favors and held her own in the schoolroom and on the playground. It's a beautiful story—one of the most inspiring ever to come from a University of Missouri photo workshop.

climax of Bill Luster's story of the
dicapped youngster is this picture (left).
iows the poise, accomplishment, and
uine happiness which far overshadow the
e girl's misfortune. Exhibited at 1970
ivar Photo Workshop.

**Ethiopian Soldier** by Alfred Eisenstaedt
for *Life* (*above*). This picture was made
during the Italian campaign in Ethiopia. For
those willing to "read" it, it is an outstanding example of a picture that tells a
dramatic story without words. Included in 50
Memorable Pictures exhibit. (Photo by
A. Eisenstaedt, LIFE Magazine, ©
Time/Life, Inc.)

# Principles of Judging Photographs

9

## What Makes a Good Picture?

T astes differ, and no two persons are likely to give the same answer to the question—What is a good picture? Individual judgment, as far as evaluating pictures is concerned, is based on a person's education and background . . . on how closely he or she can associate with the photograph under scrutiny.

This fact came sharply into focus several years ago when I headed a committee to select "The Fifty Best News Pictures of the Last Half-Century."[1] Cosponsors were the National Press Photographers Association and the *Encyclopaedia Britannica*. The same institutions, incidentally, were partners at that time in sponsoring the Pictures of the Year Competition and Exhibition—a nationwide project then in its sixteenth year.

Selecting the Fifty Best Pictures seemed an easy assignment. The committee would be small, it was decided, and all participants would be experts in the communications field.

The committee was finally chosen, and it was a great one: Harold Blumenfeld, executive newspicture editor, United Press International; Joseph Costa, King Features (chairman of the board, National Press Photographers Association); Murray Becker, chief photographer, Associated Press; Arthur Rothstein, Technical Director, *Look;* John Faber, former news photographer, now with Eastman Kodak Co., press division, New York City, and historian for the National Press Photographers Association; Yoichi R. Okamoto, chief, visual media, U. S. Information Agency (and later personal photographer to President Lyndon Johnson); Robert Gilka, illustrations staff (now photographic director) *National Geographic Magazine;* the late Julius Klyman, then editor, St. Louis *Post-Dispatch* Sunday Pictures; the late Dr. Frank Luther Mott, then dean emeritus, School of Journalism, University of Missouri; James Colvin, then public relations director, and Roger Lone, then in the public relations department, *Encyclopaedia Britannica.*

The initial instructions explained that a few years before Mr. Colvin had headed a group to select a number of "classic news pictures." That project was

Dr. Wm. Stephenson, distinguished research professor of the School of Journalism, University of Missouri, explains and vindicates his Q-sort system of research.

---

1. As part of the commemoration of the fiftieth anniversary of the School of Journalism, University of Missouri.

-Day in Normandy by Robert Capa for
*fe*-Magnum. Capa shot more than a
undred pictures on D-Day, but only eight
ere usable because a darkroom worker
erheated the film during the drying
ocess. This error, while it adds something
the dramatic quality, perhaps, is largely
e reason for the fuzziness of the picture.
cluded in 50 Memorable Pictures exhibit.

never completed, but it did provide the nucleus upon which the "fifty best"
picture collection was finally built.

Each member was to have approximately 100 pictures, selected from literally
thousands, with which to work. From the 100 pictures, each judge was to select
25 pictures, listing them in order of preference. Tabulation was to be as follows: First-place pictures were to receive 25 points, second-place pictures 24
points, third-place pictures 23 points, etc. It all seemed so easy—a matter of
simple arithmetic. How wrong I was!

It soon was apparent that we could not agree on the title of the project, let
alone on the pictures. Finally, in the name of harmony, we decided to change
the name from "Fifty Best Pictures" to "Fifty Memorable Pictures of the Last
Half-Century."

But other problems remained, the most important of which was the element
of time. Some committee members were having difficulty making selections.
Would we ever meet the deadline? A careful and honest appraisal of the situation indicated this to be unlikely.

Principles of Judging Photographs

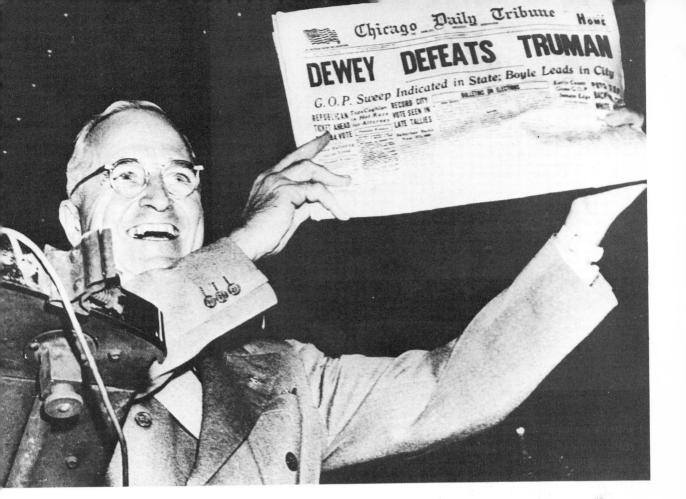

**Last Laugh!** (He Who Laughs Last) by
Al Muto for United Press International
(*above*). The picture was taken in St. Louis
aboard a train enroute to Washington, D.C.
A smiling and obviously pleased Harry
Truman holds a newspaper which proclaimed
Truman the loser, though he had won the
1948 presidential election. Included in 50
Memorable Pictures exhibit. (United Press
International.)

**The Lone Eagle by Frank Merta.** Present
generations find it hard to believe that the
praise given to the late Charles A. Lindberg
because his was the first successful solo flight
across the Atlantic Ocean in 1927 was just
as great as that accorded Neil Armstrong,
the first man to step on the surface of the
moon. Reproduction of this photo (*left*)
had an honored place in thousands of
American homes for many months, if not for
years. Included in 50 Memorable Pictures
exhibit. (United Press International.)

**Well, I'll Be Darned!** by Francis Grady
for European *Stars and Stripes*. In 1951 at
the climax of the Korean War, while Gen.
Dwight Eisenhower was commandant of
NATO forces in Europe, he learned that
Gen. Douglas McArthur had been
relieved of his Korean command by President
Harry S Truman. Eisenhower's reaction
to the news was a quizzical shrug and the
comment, "Well, I'll be darned." Included
in 50 Memorable Pictures exhibit.

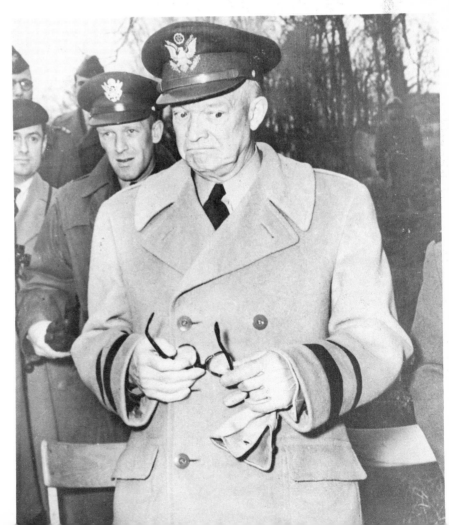

After several months of struggle, I felt that the committee needed expert help from outside the group, and asked William Stephenson, distinguished research professor of the School of Journalism, University of Missouri, to take a hand. He responded with his Q-sort system of judging photographs and saved the day.

The following two paragraphs are excerpts from the news release sent out at the conclusion of the project:

> The Selection Committee and the sponsors make no claim that these are the only great photographs of this period. We concede that other selections could be vigorously defended. We also acknowledge that in several instances where nearly identical photographs were taken by different photographers of the same action it was often almost impossible to select one photographer's work as significantly better than another's.
>
> However, the Selection Committee and the sponsors worked at this project for many months. They accumulated and inspected tens of thousands of prints. The number of man-hours contributed by the Selection Committee was staggering. The sponsors wish to express their appreciation. It seems probable that no photographic selection of a similar scope ever received so much concentrated attention on the part of so many highly qualified specialists.[2]

It is of interest to note that Stephenson is of the opinion today that his research technique has stood the test of time.

Stephenson's report, given on the pages which follow, includes both his present-day assessment of the Q-sort technique of selecting winning photographs and excerpts from the article which he wrote on the system in 1960 for *Journalism Quarterly.*

# Q-Sort System of Judging Photographs

It is nearly sixteen years since the procedure described, in the 1960 *Journalism Quarterly* was used to select fifty memorable news pictures of half a century, (1908–1958) to commemorate the founding of the School of Journalism at the University of Missouri. There is nothing that one can change in either the methodology or discussion of its conclusions. The methodology is secure and viable still. Whether today's photojournalist experts are in the same mold as those of fifteen years ago is of course another matter, and if one had to repeat the selection today, one would be more forward in theoretical respects.

By this, one means that the communication theory is now on hand which puts a distinctive mark on newsworthiness, whether of written, spoken, photojournalist, or filmed news. It is to the effect that news is essentially communicative rather than informational. A funny story is communication; a doctor's prescription is informational. Communication deals with the familiar and the expected —even the unexpected is expected in a funny story—but information is likely to be novel, like a new drug on a prescription.

Now this may seem strangely at odds with photojournalism or with news of any kind. Yet we call news communication, not information (and the *Concise Oxford Dictionary* agrees in this). What we see every day in our newspaper is indeed familiar, rather than entirely novel. It's the same mix of community

---

2. News release, "Fifty Memorable Pictures" project, School of Journalism, University of Missouri, 1958. The findings of this study, together with representative pictures were released in 1958 to newspapers and magazines throughout the country.

Principles of Judging Photographs

deaths, births, and police records; the same familiar comics, editorials; and of course the same sort of hard news and features. The key to the selection of this news is the editor. So the early selection of the 50 photographs was, theoretically, in the best possible hands, but only if they really knew the difference between photojournalism which is highly communicative and that which is merely informative, instructional, or educative.

The interesting point arises, therefore, as to what photographs best fit the communicative framework. They are those that the *public* finds interesting. It is indeed as surrogate for the public that the editor plays a key role. Thus, a photograph of a lovely seascape with sailboats, or of a sylvan country landscape, used to grace the last page of the *London Times* every Saturday morning. It was expected, familiar, and enjoyed every time. Such, according to theory, would be sound *communicative* photojournalism. And the public would give high votes to such photographs every time.

This is not to say that editors merely seek the lowest common denominator, as seems to be the case for prime-time television. Newspaper editors respect their audiences more. Nor is it forgetful of the exceptional and the spectacular. But it is directed toward something that presents a challenge to photojournalism, namely, to show both sides of issues and situations, not for the reason of equal time as in television, but to 'keep the pot boiling,' that is, to keep issues in the forefront of the public mind. Not to change anyone's mind (which is the function of propaganda, advertising, and posters) but merely to keep matters before us. The famous shot of the dead at Hiroshima is a reminder of the horror of nuclear bombing, but it depicts death, not the bitter poignancy of the living as well. Communication asks for both to be seen.

This may merely wet the appetite of theorists, but the methodology employed in this paper of 1960 can be used to probe into questions of the kind just mentioned, so as to bring research to bear on the conventional wisdom and experience of the professional photojournalist, whether as reporter or editor in that role. It was a great pleasure, indeed a highlight in one's past, to work with Professor Edom and the corps of press photographers. One would wish that much more could be done in this field, directed to theoretical questions.[3]

# Fifty Memorable Pictures of the Last Half-Century

Following is a list of the photographs that appeared in the commemorative exhibit of the School of Journalism, University of Missouri, 1958. Page references in parentheses after some of the entries indicate the page in this text on which those photographs appear.

1. "Dead Americans at Buna Beach," George Strock, *Life* (p. 113).
2. "Dazed POW Repatriated," Michael Rougier, *Life* (p. 104).
3. "Christmas in Korea," David Douglas Duncan, *Life* (p. 104).
4. "Ethiopian Soldier," Alfred Eisenstaedt, *Life* (p. 97).
5. "Gestapo Informer," Henri Cartier-Bresson for Magnum (p. 23).
6. "Spanish Soldier Dies," Robert Capa for *Life*-Magnum (p. 23).
7. "D-Day in Normandy," Robert Capa for *Life*-Magnum (p. 99).
8. "Sewell Avery Gets Bum's Rush," Harry Hall, Associated Press (p. 116).
9. "Panic in Chungking Bomb Shelter," F. T. Durdin, Associated Press (p. 112).

---

3. William Stephenson's article "Principles of Selection of News Pictures" is reprinted in the Appendix of this book.

## WAR IS HELL

**Dazed POW Repatriated** by Michael Rougier for *Life* (*above*). Unbelief is written on the face of this GI, whisked from the hopelessness of a prisoner-of-war camp back to his comrades. The incident occurred during the Korean War. Included in 50 Memorable Pictures exhibit. (Photo by M. Rougier, LIFE Magazine, © Time/Life, Inc.)

**Koreans Flee Red Horde** by Max Desfor of the Associated Press (*right*). The pitiful plight of civilian refugees (*right*) has been photographed hundreds of times during the twentieth century, but never has it been shown with more dramatic impact than in this picture. The date was December 4, 1950 and the place, the bridge across the Taedong River. Included in 50 Memorable Pictures exhibit. (Wide World Photos.)

**Christmas in Korea** by David Douglas Duncan for *Life* (*left*). The buildup of Chinese forces resulted in a violent attack upon United Nations troops late in 1950. The retreat from near the Manchurian border gave the free world a bitter foretaste of stalemate. Included in 50 Memorable Pictures exhibit. (Photo by David Duncan, LIFE Magazine, © Time/Life, Inc.)

10. "Boys Against Tanks," photographer unknown; distributed by Associated Press (p. 114).

11. "Weeping Frenchman," George Mejat, Fox Movietone News; distributed by Associated Press (p. 23).

12. "Well, I'll Be Darned!" Francis Grandy, *Stars and Stripes* photograph (p. 101).

13. "Koreans Flee Red Horde," Max Desfor, Associated Press (p. 105).

14. "Yalta Conference," Richard Sarno, United States Army; distributed by Associated Press (p. 109).

15. "Flag Raising On Iwo Jima," (Marines on Mt. Suribachi) Joseph Rosenthal, Associated Press (p. 120).

16. "Russian Revolution," Associated Press (p. 114).

17. "Four Killed at Republic Steel Plant," Carl Linde, Associated Press.

18. "Black Sunday," Lasar Dunner, United Press International.

19. "Death of King Alexander," George Mejat, Fox Movietone; distributed by United Press International.

20. "Hindenberg Explosion," Sam Shere, United Press International (p. 109).

21. "Hungarian Freedom Bridge," Dieter Hespe, United Press International.

22. "Yank Fighter Wheeling Baby," United Press International.

23. "He Who Laughs Last," Al Muto, United Press International (p. 101).

24. "Execution of Communists in Shanghai," Warren Lee, United Press International (p. 117).

25. "Radiant Queen," Charles James Dawson, United Press International (p. 110).

26. "The Lone Eagle," Frank Merta, United Press International (p. 100).

27. "Mussolini and Friends Hanging by Heels," photographer unknown; distributed by United Press International.

28. "Wall Street Bombing," Vincent Palumbo, United Press International.

29. "Firpo Knocked Dempsey Out of the Ring," Henry Olen, *New York Daily News.*

30. "Ruth Snyder in the Electric Chair," Tom Howard, *New York Daily News* (p. 195).

31. "Sinking of the *Vestris,*" Fred Hansen, *New York Daily News* (p. 140).

32. "Bonus Marchers," Joseph Costa, *New York Daily News.*

33. "Wife Beater Gets Whipping," Joseph Costa, *New York Daily News* (p. 198).

34. "Midget on Morgan's Knee," Willie Hoff, *New York Daily News.*

35. "Pea Pickers," Dorothea Lange, Farm Security Administration (p. 37).

36. "Dust Bowl," Arthur Rothstein, Farm Security Administration (p. 40).

37. "Hitler's Jig," United States Office of War Information (p. 110).

38. "Sinking of the *Arizona* [Pearl Harbor]," Official United States Navy photo (p. 117).

39. "Bikini-Baker Day," United States Air Force (p. 108).

40. "Over the Top in World War I," United States Department of Defense (p. 23).

41. "The Babe Bows Out," Nat Fein, *New York Herald-Tribune* (p. 119).

42. "Three Queens in Mourning," Ron Case, Keystone Press Agency, Ltd. (p. 111).

43. "Shooting of Mayor Gaynor," William Warnecke, *New York World-Telegram and Sun* (p. 115).

**ancho Villa on the March.** This picre by an unknown photographer is in ossession of Brown Brothers. Portraying illa and his army of guerillas, it was obably taken in 1916, the year Villa and s raiders attacked Columbus, New Mexico, lling twenty Americans. Included in 50 emorable Pictures exhibit.

Tilliam Stephenson has been distinguished search professor at the School of Journalm, University of Missouri, since 1958. orn May 4, 1902, in Durham, England, Dr. ephenson was educated at the University Durham, the University of London, and xford University. A consultant to Central rade Test Board, R.A.F., a consultant ychologist to the British Army where he nked as Colonel R.A.M.C., and Brigadiereneral, War office. Dr. Stephenson holds embership in many learned British and merican professional organizations. Before ming to the University of Missouri, he d been on the staffs of many British and merican universities. A prolific writer and cturer, Dr. Stephenson has contributed an told number of articles to learned urnals and publications.

44. "Eastland Disaster," Fred Eckhardt, *Chicago Daily News.*
45. "Japan Surrenders," Larry Keighley, *Saturday Evening Post.*
46. "Waiting at the Mine Disaster," Sam Caldwell, *St. Louis Post-Dispatch* (p. 69).
47. "Cotton Mill," Lewis W. Hine, George Eastman House collection (p. 35).
48. "Norman Thomas Hit by Egg," Ralph Morgan, Denver, Colorado.
49. "Crisis in Little Rock," Wilmer Counts, *Arkansas Democrat* (p. 116).
50. "Pancho Villa on the March," Brown Brothers (p. 107).

# Student Participation

In reviewing the list of winning photographs and in carefully examining the photographs from the "50 Memorable Pictures" project included in this text, we must admit that the winners portray hard news events: tragedy, enshrouded usually by an aura of death. Considering that these 50 pictures were taken during a half-century which was predominately a period of war, this is not surprising.

The kinds of pictures called "great," with the exception of undeniable classics such as the Hindenburg Disaster, etc., vary from generation to generation.

With this fact in mind, check through a half-dozen years of magazines, books, and newspapers collected from your home and/or school library and compile a new list of 25 Memorable Pictures of the last few years. Be prepared to defend your choices in class discussion. Among those on your list I predict will be: The assassination of President John Kennedy, man's first step on the moon, views from the Watergate story, and Richard Nixon resigning the presidency.

What changes (if any) can you detect between the taste in present-day pictures and that indicated by the original "50 Memorable Pictures"?

**Hindenberg Explosion** by Sam Shere of United Press International (*above right*). This picture was taken May 6, 1936. The airship was completing its first North Atlantic crossing of the new season when hydrogen used to inflate the balloon burst into flames. The *Hindenberg* was complet[ely] demolished, and thirty-six passengers wer[e] killed. This picture had been considered t[he] greatest news-picture of all time until Joe Rosenthal's picture of the flag raising on Iwo Jima (p. 120). Included in 50 Memorable Pictures exhibit. (United Press International.)

**Yalta Conference** by Richard Sarno (*right*). Taken for the United States Arm[y] the picture was distributed by the Associa[ted] Press. This is one of the few photographs that was selected more for its historical significance than for its drama. In retrospe[ct] the selection committee for the 50 Memor[a]ble Pictures exhibit felt that the emotion aroused by the aftermath of the Yalta Con[f]ference in 1945 lends inescapable drama t[o] the picture. Included in 50 Memorable Pictures exhibit. (Wide World Photos.)

**Bikini—Baker Day.** This photograph helped record the beginning of the atomic age when United States forces conducted "operation crossroads," a test for atomic weapons and their effect on ships and materiel. The picture was taken in 1946 o[n] Bikini Atoll in the Marshall Islands. Included in 50 Memorable Pictures exhibit. (U. S. Air Force photo.)

**Hitler's Jig** (*above*). This picture is from a frame of motion-picture film shot by an unknown photographer. It was made available in this country through British sources during World War II. The Fuehrer is shown gleefully dancing after the surrender of France in the same railway car in which German officials had surrendered in 1918. The jig took place in the Forest of Compiègne in 1940. Included in 50 Memorable Pictures exhibit. (United States Office of War Information.)

**Three Queens in Mourning** by Ron Case, Keystone Press Agency, Ltd. (*right*). The picture shows Queen Elizabeth II after the death of her father, George VI. With the queen, forming this tragic group of mourners, are her mother and grandmother. Included in 50 Memorable Pictures exhibit.

**Radiant Queen** by Charles James Dawson (*left*). This picture is accepted almost universally as one of the finest portraits ever made of royalty. It portrays Queen Elizabeth II passing in a royal carriage shortly after her coronation. Included in 50 Memorable Pictures exhibit. (United Press International.)

**nic in Chunking Bomb Shelter** by
**T.** Durdin (*left*). The horrors of war are
ᵐly portrayed in this picture of a
ᵃnese air raid. Seven hundred persons
ᵈ in the stampede to the shelter. The
ᵗᵘre was distributed by the Associated
ˢˢ. Included in 50 Memorable Pictures
ᵃibit. (Wide World Photos.)

**Dead Americans at Buna Beach** by,
George Strock for *Life* (*above*). This is one
of the first pictures of American military
dead released during World War II. Many
more Americans died before the coming of
victory. Included in 50 Memorable Pictures
exhibit. (Photo by G. Strock, LIFE
Magazine © Time/Life, Inc.)

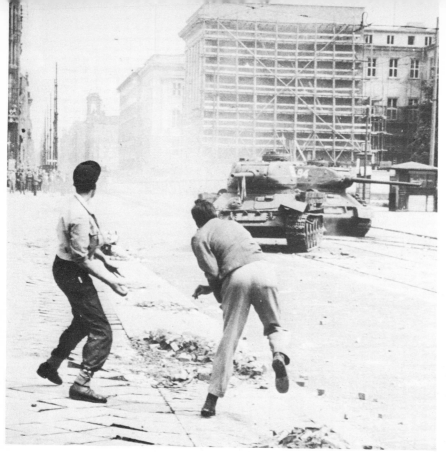

**Boys Against Tanks** (*left*). Here is a picture by an unknown photographer w like the the one *below*, was distributed Associated Press. The incident occurred 1953 during the rebellion against Russ occupation forces in Berlin. Included i Memorable Pictures exhibit. (Wide W Photos.)

**Shooting of Mayor Gaynor** by Willi Warnecke, *New York World-Telegram Sun* (*right*). William T. Gaynor, Maye New York, was shot but not killed on August 9, 1910, by a discharged city employe aboard the deck of a liner on which he was to sail for Europe. Other photographers had taken their pictures departed. Warnecke's late arrival perm him to get this famous "scoop." Include in 50 Memorable Pictures exhibit.

**Russian Revolution** (*below*). One of most powerful pictures in the history of photojournalism, this tragic scene was recorded in May, 1917, by an unknown tographer. The setting is a street scene Petrograd (now Leningrad) when revo tionists began firing machine guns. The picture was distributed by the Associate Press. Included in 50 Memorable Pictu exhibit. (Wide World Photos.)

**Sewell Avery Gets Bum's Rush** by Harry Hall, Associated Press (*left*). All prizewinning photographs are not hard to get. Some, like this one could have been taken by a 12-year-old child with a box camera. It was selected for the 50 Memorable Pictures exhibit because of its social significance. Several photographers took similar pictures of this event in 1944, when Avery was forcibly removed from his Montgomery Ward and Company office in Chicago as the United States government forced compliance with wartime labor regulations. Included in 50 Memorable Pictures exhibit. (Wide World Photos.)

**Pearl Harbor** (*right*). Crumpled and listing, the battleship *Arizona* pours clouds of smoke into the air after the surprise Japanese attack on Pearl Harbor, Hawaii, December 7, 1941. A bomb reportedly passed down the smokestack, exploding the boiler and forward magazine. Damage at Pearl Harbor was so extensive that it was carefully concealed by the federal government. (Official U. S. Navy photograph.)

**Crisis in Little Rock** by Wilmer Counts for the *Arkansas Democrat* (*below*). One of the violent incidents in the 1958 struggle over the integration of Little Rock Central High School. Included in 50 Memorable Pictures exhibit. (Courtesy *Arkansas Democrat*.)

**Communists in Shanghai** by Warren Lee (*below right*). Before abandoning Shanghai to Chinese armies in 1949, Nationalist police executed communist prisoners in the streets. Included in 50 Memorable Pictures exhibit. (United Press International.)

**The Babe Bows Out** by Nat Fein for the *New York World-Telegram.* This portrayal of Babe Ruth's final appearance in New York's Yankee Stadium in 1948 is one of the most famous of all sports pictures. Cited as a classic example of good photographic thinking, instructors often point out that Mr. Fein did not "follow the pack" in selecting the spot from where he would take the picture. By isolating himself from the others, he was able to come up with this great picture. Shooting from Ruth's rear, he made the lonely, easily recognized figure the center of interest. Adding to the storytelling quality of the picture is the vast crowd shown paying the final tribute to the bambino. Fein also recorded the Babe's teammates and a few photographers at work. Included in 50 Memorable Pictures exhibit.

**Flag Raising at Iwo Jima** (Marines
on Mt. Suribachi) by Joe Rosenthal of
the Associated Press. For many years after
it was made (February 23, 1945) this
picture undoubtedly was the most reproduced
picture in history. Like a gigantic breath of
fresh air it swept the nation, raising morale
and symbolizing the march to victory.
Included in 50 Memorable Pictures exhibit.
(Wide World Photos.)

# 10 Research in Photojournalism

*Keith P. Sanders*

Although considerable research has been done, there is much which needs to be done before visual communication receives full recognition. Dr. Keith P. Sanders, professor of communication research at the School of Journalism, University of Missouri, tells us what has been learned about pictures and about the area which needs further study.

People like pictures. Pictures make people laugh, cry, sympathize. Pictures communicate. Yet, despite common sense and what hard facts we have—both of which tell us that photographs are very important—very little research has been conducted into photojournalism.

Malcolm S. MacLean, Jr., who probably has contributed more to the understanding of photojournalism than any other researcher, once wrote: "It is curious how little research has been done on pictorial communication. A good picture, we believe, can tell a lot—fast—and with a big wallop that the readers won't forget. Yet we have practically no research on how we can best make or select those 'good' pictures to do such jobs for us. Despite the thousands of readership and other studies, editors and photographers still have to pretty much fly by the seat of their pants in their decisions on pictorial communication."[1]

People like pictures of themselves and pictures of other people, other places, other things. Pictures are so popular, in fact, that numerous studies have shown that photographs in newspapers and magazines consistently draw more readers than the words in print which the photographs accompany. The Continuing Study of Newspaper Reading, for example, demonstrated that the popularity of news photographs was several times that of written material.[2] The study reported that the average news story in newspapers was read by only 13 percent of the men and only 11 percent of the women. In the same newspapers, however, three times as many men and four times as many women read the average one-column picture as read the average news story (and readership increased considerably with an increase in the size of the picture).

A picture may not actually be worth a thousand words, but its appeal either as a separate entity or as a complement to a verbal story goes beyond the strength of the words. Arnold summarized the impact well: "With their distillation of a moment's essence, pictures command attention in a way that words cannot. A memorable picture tells the story. If the picture is good enough, no

Keith P. Sanders is professor of communication research, School of Journalism, University of Missouri.

1. Malcolm S. MacLean, Jr., and Anne Li-An Kao, "Picture Selection: An Editorial Game, *Journalism Quarterly* (40): 230–232.

2. Advertising Research Foundation. *The Continuing Study of Newspaper Reading* (New York: started in 1939).

further explanation is necessary. As adjuncts to words, pictures also exercise their strength. As a segment of an integrated story, pictures expand the ability of the words to explain, just as the words expand the graphic interpretation of the pictures. Here, words and pictures balance and add to each other, making the final whole greater than the sum of its parts."[3] It is not a question of photographs *competing* with words. It is a question of what combination of words and photographs will most effectively communicate an idea to a reader.

Research has served photojournalism well, although much more needs to be done. In the 1930s the *Des Moines Sunday Register* studied reader interest in pictures using recently developed techniques by a newcomer to the research field—George Gallup. It was found that readers were more interested in looking at pictures than they were in reading columns of unbroken print. After trying various combinations of pictures and words, the newspaper's circulation increased by 50 percent.[4] In addition to showing the potential for increasing readership, the study presented evidence that pictures spoke a universal language, a language that seemed to appeal to all people. Gardner Cowles saw the possibilities of publishing a magazine that would concentrate on the use of a "picture language"—a language that could reach and inform millions of people regardless of age, sex, income, education—and founded *Look.*[5]

The remainder of this chapter is devoted to a review of photojournalism research. The review is not intended to be inclusive; rather it concentrates on research that seems to have particular relevance. If the reader is interested in pushing deeper into the literature, he is invited to consult the bibliography included at the end of the chapter. There have been thousands of readership studies, but very few of them are reviewed here for the reason that one readership study is pretty much like all previous such studies—only the names and places have been changed. Although every newspaper should regularly conduct readership studies, such studies produce little that can be generalized to picture readers elsewhere. This review, therefore, has opted for research findings that have particular theoretical value. The final section of the chapter is devoted to a discussion, albeit brief, of where photojournalism research might go from here.

Keith P. Sanders is professor of communication research at the School of Journalism, University of Missouri. He also has taught at Bowling Green State University and at the University of Iowa.

Dr. Sanders, a former newspaper sports editor and television sports newscaster, has had both professional and research interests in photojournalism.

In 1973 he received the Joyce A. Swan Distinguished Faculty Award, which is presented annually to a member of the Missouri School of Journalism faculty in recognition of outstanding achievement.

He is a member of the International Communications Association, Sigma Delta Chi, Kappa Tau Alpha, Omicron Delta Kappa, and the Association for Education in Journalism (twice serving as research chairman for the Mass Communication and Society Division.) Dr. Sanders is the author of several articles published in scholarly journals such as *Journalism Quarterly* and *Journal of Broadcasting.*

# Content: The Crucial Variable

What is it about a photograph that attracts people to it? In a word, it's content. Of the various "variables" one can use to judge a photograph—such as composition, focus, balance, rhythm, unity, lighting, contrast, etc.—the content variable stands far out from all the rest. Subject matter orientations have consistently been found to be the main determinants of interest in a photograph.[6,7,8]

---

3. George Arnold, "Theoretical Views of the Photography Editor as Gatekeeper" (master's thesis, University of Missouri, 1974).

4. Gardner Cowles, "Visual Excitement in Modern Publishing," in *Art Directing* (New York: Hastings House, Publishers, 1957).

5. Ibid.

6. Randall P. Harrison, "Pictorial Communication," *Search,* vol. 6. National Project in Agricultural Communication, East Lansing, Michigan, 1962.

7. Cliff Ganschow, "Contribution of Certain Compositional Factors to Photographs' Effectiveness." Mimeographed. Department of Technical Journalism, Iowa State University.

8. William R. Hazard, "Responses to News Pictures: A Study of Perceptual Unity," *Journalism Quarterly* (37): 515–524.

One of the earliest systematic attempts to determine what kinds of photographs are most read concluded that pictures of babies and children had particularly high overall interest value. Pictures of travel, scenery, people, animals, nature, and science were found to have middle-range appeal. Pictures of sports, society, fashion, and finance were found to have low overall interest. Conducted in the 1930s by the Advertising Research Foundation, the study attempted to summarize dozens of newspaper readership studies.[9] The conclusions need to be tempered by the fact that the previous studies are difficult to compare because of the use of many different category and definition systems.

Swanson studied the readership of 3,353 photographs and found that the most read categories were Fire and Disaster, War, Weather, Consumer Information, Human Interest, Major Crime, Country Correspondence, Accidents and Mishaps, Science and Invention, Defense, Local Government, and Agriculture. The lower read categories, in ascending order, were: Home and Family, Fine Arts, Sports, Popular Art, Entertainment and Features, Social Relations, and Relation and Morals.[10] Swanson found that men and women have quite different photographic preferences in certain areas. There were major differences in readership of Home and Family photographs, for example, which were read by only 14.2 percent of the men but by 55.4 percent of the women. Comparatively, women much preferred the categories of Social Relations, Popular Art, and Fine Art, while the men preferred Sports. However, Swanson noted that women in general seem to be far more picture-minded than men. Although there were only two categories that received less than 45 percent readership by the women (with a low of 24 percent), there were 10 such categories for the men (with a low of 14.2 percent). Other researchers have found differences in content preferences between men and women. Harrison found that men tend to prefer photographs of events and women tend to prefer pictures of people. Both sexes look at pictures of women more than at pictures of men.[11] Woodburn found that men rated high photographs of Human Interest, National Defense, Crime, Servicemen's News, and Sports. They rated low photographs of Food, Fashions, Women's and Society, and Weddings and Engagements. Women rated high photographs of Weddings and Engagements, Children and Babies, Women's and Society, Crime, and Human Interest, but rated quite low Sports.[12]

Instead of concentrating on actual readership of published photographs, MacLean and Hazard conducted an experiment to determine women's interest in different types of photographs.[13] They asked 152 women to rate a set of 51 news magazine photographs. Factor analysis of the photograph ratings produced six factors, or groupings, of photographs that had been scored in similar ways. The six basic content groups, or factors, were:

1. Idolatry: This group included pictures of successful, glamorous, and wealthy women, especially if portrayed in a "happy family" situation.

9. Advertising Research Foundation, *The Continuing Study.*

10. Charles Swanson, "What They Read in 130 Daily Newspapers," *Journalism Quarterly* (32): 411–421.

11. Randall Harrison, "Pictorial Communication."

12. Bert W. Woodburn, "Reader Interest in Newspaper Pictures," *Journalism Quarterly* (24): 197–201.

13. Malcolm S. MacLean, Jr., and William R. Hazard, "Women's Interest in Pictures: The Badger Village Study," *Journalism Quarterly* (30): 139–162.

2. Social Problems: This group included pictures of people causing "trouble," such as strikes and riots, pictures about people "on the wrong side of the tracks," and pictures of people who did not "fit in" with popular ideals.

3. Picturesque: This group included salon pictures, moody pictures, dynamic pictures, pictures portraying loneliness and escape from other people, and pictures of people doing things with their hands.

4. War: This group included pictures of war, fear of involvement in war, horror at the gruesome results of war, pictures depicting the glory of American armed power, and pictures exhibiting sympathy for the victims of war.

5. Blood and Violence: This group included pictures of people injured or killed through crime or accident.

6. Spectator Sports: This group included action pictures of sports that normally command large audiences.

Most readership studies concentrate on overall readership and, consequently, ignore the commonsense notion that people are different. A quite different approach to photograph readership, then, is to group people together on the basis of their similar preferences. Ideally suited to such an undertaking is Q-methodology, as described by Stephenson[14, 15, 16] and MacLean.[17] MacLean and Kao used Q-methodology to develop *types,* or groupings, of people who had similar preferences for photographs.[18] They asked people to literally sort through a set of 60 photographs and to indicate how much they liked or disliked each. Each person's "Q-sort" was then correlated with every other person's sort and then factor analyzed. Four major factors or types resulted. Each factor was composed of people who had sorted the photographs in very similar ways. The factor thus represented a "hypothetical person," a "type" of reader—a composite of the people who sorted the photographs in similar ways. The determination of the four types represented but one phase of the MacLean–Kao study. Some of the other phases will be reported later in this chapter. The current phase will be reported here in length not only because of its innovative and imaginative contribution to research methodology, but also because of the rather considerable insight it provides into what kinds of photographs people like and why.

Type A liked pictures about young marriage, fame, performance, glamour, and art and readily identified with the subjects or things portrayed in such photographs. Throughout, there was a strong sense of self-identification. Type A rated high pictures of a family scene, flowers, a party, an outdoor scene, a mother and son, animal loving, and the like. Type A liked those photographs because he considered them to be "real," "beautiful," or to have

14. William Stephenson, "Principles of Selection of News Pictures," *Journalism Quarterly* (37): 61–68. (See Appendix)

15. William Stephenson, *The Play Theory of Mass Communication* (Chicago: University of Chicago Press, 1967).

16. William Stephenson, *The Study of Behavior: Q-Technique and Its Methodology* (Chicago: University of Chicago Press, 1953).

17. Malcolm S. MacLean, Jr., "Communication Strategy, Editing Games and Q," in Steven R. Brown and Donald J. Brenner, eds., *Science, Psychology and Communication* (New York: Teachers College Press, 1972).

18. Malcolm S. MacLean, Jr., and Anne Li-An Kao, *Editorial Predictions of Magazine Picture Appeals* (Iowa City, Iowa: School of Journalism, University of Iowa, 1965).

general interest, for escape or enjoyment, because of good expression and good composition. "Beauty" is a word the people who composed this type used frequently to explain their liking for the pictures. Type A liked children, family togetherness, peacefulness, the carefree life, sports, and sex. Type A admired talent and athletic ability. In all these, he could either actually or ideally identify with what was depicted in the pictures. Type A disliked death, war, destruction, crime, and victims of poverty or a bad system. These caused the Type A person to feel uncomfortable, disgusted, and disagreeable; he tried to avoid such things. MacLean and Kao noted three obvious tendencies about the Type A person: The Type A women all agreed on their Like-Dislike pictures; Type A people, especially women, tend to like what they can ideally or actually identify with; higher educated Type A men tend to like more humane and feminine subject matter as the Type A woman does.

Type B had the strongest feelings for pictures about death, soldiers, performance, young marriage, social problems, sports, and offbeat material. Type B was indifferent about art, fame, politics, pattern, science, and show. Among the highly accepted pictures for Type B were the strikingly sad and horrible, and the pleasant, happy family, and performance scenes. Type B people commented that they hated war and violence. Some of the photographs reminded them of their own sad experiences. These pictures showed suffering, agony, pain, and sorrow. Hatred of war, sad memories, unbearable scenes of suffering, and pictures of pleasant life were the main elements that elicited strong feelings, although not necessarily a *liking* for the picture, in Type B. Type B rejected all three pictures of big, gala parties, and most of the close-ups. Type B also rejected photographs of people "doing nothing."

Although somewhat similar to Type A, Type C was clearly more interested in a physical and masculine type of content. The people composing Type C were predominantly men and were very athletically inclined. Type C liked the pictures of sports, particularly those of a physical and spectacular nature. He also liked pictures of sex, design, and glamour. He identified and felt strongly toward such matters. Type C's identification is readily understandable when one considers his sports participation. Type C was an active participant; he played at least one kind of sport and very likely belonged to some kind of league or had recently entered some kind of tournament. He sensed the power, beauty, and meaning of action to be found in photographs showing physical sports. Type C rejected photographs portraying fame, pattern, death, soldiers, and politics.

Type D was made up of young people, college students for the most part. Type D rejected identification with scenes depicting death and misery, soldiers, and social problems. He identified with those depicting sports, politics, performance, and offbeat material. Type D was concerned with global tension, his own future, and with current events. He praised glorious actions and muscular expressions and advocated hard work in everything. He liked and cared about what he had experienced. Type D didn't care for art, and some of the pictures of girls and children seemed ridiculous to him.

From a theoretical standpoint one of the major findings of the MacLean–Kao study was the relationship between subjects' Like-Dislike and Intensity-of-Feeling Dimensions. They found a consistent U-shaped curve between the two. This means simply that the pictures that aroused the strongest feelings in people were the ones people either strongly liked or disliked. A photograph that does not arouse strong feelings is not likely to be *either* much liked or disliked. This finding substantiates the earlier observation by Kalish and Edom that a picture's *impact* is a major determinant in how well liked or disliked the picture will be.[19]

The literature on photographic content preferences is neither extensive nor consistent. It can be seen that certain types of content—animals, people, scenery, and highly topical news items—are well liked and highly read. Pictures of war, destruction, death arouse great intensity and are highly read, but apparently are not well liked by most people. Women seem to be generally more picture "conscious"—at least, they consistently read more pictures than men do. There are quite clear-cut preferences between men and women. One reason for the sometimes conflicting results, of course, comes from the fact that so many different categories have been used. MacLean and Kao point out, for example, that two photographs that normally would be placed in the same category can get quite different ratings. For example, Type C liked sports photographs containing a great deal of highly physical action, but disliked most other sports photographs. Then, too, one must keep in mind the constant changing of our society. During World War II, for example, photographs that showed the glory of the American war effort likely would have received high ratings. A study involving similar photographs conducted during or after the Viet Nam War, however, very likely would receive quite different ratings, at least from a significant portion of the reading public. It is for such reasons that a photography editor must periodically "reacquaint" himself with his readers and their likes and dislikes.

# Perception: The Hidden Dimension

Photographs are rich in connotative meaning. The meaning people perceive in a photograph is of considerable interest. As Osgood and Tannenbaum put it, "the effect of a photograph is closely related to the attitude or meaning a person has toward the photograph. It is therefore important in studying the effects of photographs to look at what the photographs mean, and why they mean what they do, to the readers."[20] Meaning and attitude are interrelated; that is, one's attitude influences the meaning he will perceive in a photograph and the meaning he derives will influence the continual process of attitude formation.

What a photograph "means" to a person is the result of a complex interaction between the photograph and the person's prior experiences and perceptions (his apperceptive mass). The *intention* of the photographer is relatively unimportant; people will perceive what they want to see. There probably is no more humbling experience for a professional communicator than to expend great amounts of time and effort to produce a message only to have the audience fail to see what you were trying to accomplish. Studies have shown that photographs are effective in creating attitudes, changing attitudes, and generally persuading people—although not necessarily in the direction intended. One is

19. Stanley E. Kalish, and Clifton C. Edom, *Picture Editing* (New York: Rinehart & Co., Inc., 1951).

20. Charles E. Osgood and Percy H. Tannenbaum, "The Principle of Congruity and Prediction of Attitude Change," *Psychological Review* (62): 42–55.

reminded of the classic Mr. Biggott studies.[21] The purpose of this experiment was to see if strong prejudice could be reduced or eliminated by getting the subject to see how absurd prejudice was. The procedure was to show people a cartoon series featuring Mr. Biggott, a prudish figure with exaggerated anti-minority attitudes. It was thought that if people saw how foolish Mr. Biggott's attitudes were, they would change their own attitudes. Instead, the propaganda served to reinforce the existing prejudice!

Although there have been several studies that tested photographic effects, very few of them have been concerned with news photography. Mehling concluded that a newsphotograph with a cutline was more effective in producing attitudinal change than a newsstory lead with a headline.[22] Kishiyama studied the effect photographs have on how a suspected criminal was perceived. He presented people with a set of pictures portraying the "suspect" with varying facial expressions. He found no difference between the various photographs.[23]

People look for, and find, meaning in photographs with which they can identify. Hazard found that readers respond positively to pictures related to their own daily concerns.[24] Spaulding observed that people like pictures that relate to their daily life and to daily events that are personally significant.[25] Schramm and White found that photograph readership increases with education and higher economic status.[26] This is consistent with the identification concept since it has been repeatedly shown that one effect of education, and higher economic status to a somewhat lesser degree, is to expand a person's experiential world. Or to put it another way, educated people are likely to have more subjects with which they can identify. Harrison observed that readers are more likely to accept messages that offer opportunity to identify in sex, age, race, and major social characteristics.[27]

The MacLean–Kao study delved deeply into the matter of identification, particularly with news photographs.[28] In reviewing the MacLean–Hazard study (see note 13), they noted two chief essentials of content: visible forces and intangible forces. The visible forces (close-ups, action, contrast) served to *attract* readers. The intangible forces (interest, drive, and feeling for the picture—such as adventure, ambition, combat, love, romance, anger, hate, etc.) served to *arouse a response* in the reader. MacLean and Kao broke the two elements into four dimensions: Like-Dislike, Intensity-of-Feeling, Ideal Self-Identification, and Actual Self-Identification. They found that Self-Identification, especially Ideal Self-Identification, had a lot to do with liking of pictures. The pictures the readers liked or disliked most were the ones that aroused the strongest feelings.

21. E. Cooper and M. Jahoda, "The Evasion of Propaganda," *Journal of Psychology* (23): 15–25.

22. Reuben Mehling, "Attitude Changing Effect of News and Photo Combination," *Journalism Quarterly* (36): 189–198.

23. David N. Kishiyama, "News, Photographs and Attitude Change" (master's thesis, University of California at Los Angeles, 1973).

24. William R. Hazard, "Responses to News Pictures."

25. Seth Spaulding, "Research on Pictorial Illustration," *Audio-Visual Communication Review* (3): 35–45.

26. Wilbur Schramm and David M. White, "Age, Education, Economic Status: Factors in Newspaper Reading," *Journalism Quarterly* (26): 149–159.

27. Randall Harrison, "Pictorial Communication."

28. Malcolm S. MacLean, Jr., and Anne Li-An Kao, *Editorial Predictions.*

# Stylistic Elements: What Works?

Although content has been shown to be the primary focus of the reader's attention, other elements are at work as well.

Research has shown that picture size is an important variable in determining readership. Woodburn reported that the *Continuing Study of Newspaper Reading* (see note 2) found that readership increased in direct relationship to an increase in the size of the photograph.[29] For men, readership increased from 37 percent for a one-column photograph to 49 percent for two columns, 62 percent for three columns, and 64 percent for four columns. For women, readership increased from 45 percent for a one-column picture to 61 percent for two columns, 67 percent for three columns, and 73 percent for four columns. Spaulding reported similar findings[30] and Neubert found that cropping decreased comprehension and impact.[31] Particularly high readership has been found for picture pages.[32, 33] In the first 100 studies reported in *The Continuing Study of Newspaper Reading,* full picture pages received a phenomenal 89 percent readership, while other pages averaged about 60 percent. Sanders and Chang found that a picture page was the most read page of the paper.

Greenlee tested to see if color photographs were preferred to black-and-white photographs. He found that a well-liked photograph is a well-liked photograph regardless of whether it is black and white or in color.[34] Spaulding, on the other hand, concluded that color increases readership. The apparent discrepancy may be explained this way: for "good" photographs color makes little difference, but for "poor" photographs color may attract more readers than will black and white.

Culbertson studied photographic iconicity—the resemblance between a pictorial symbol and its referent. He hypothesized that the more precisely the photograph represented its subject—in terms of shape, detail, and magnitude—the greater would be its effect. Although he found no significant differences in degrees of iconicity, he did note some evidence to suggest that iconicity of magnitude may aid comprehension.[35]

Hazard found that shape and concentricity of the organization of the photograph ranked behind subject matter as determinants of interest.[36] Leu concentrated on three aspects of composition: balance, rhythm, and unity. He found a tendency, although not significant, toward "systematic differences in the way compositional elements are used in the judgment of photographs."[37] He also noted that compositional elements become more important to people in judging

---

29. Bert W. Woodburn, "Reader Interest."

30. Seth Spaulding, "Research on Pictorial Illustration."

31. Michael T. Neubert, "The Effects of Selection and Emphasis Upon Reader Responses to News Pictures" (master's thesis, University of Wisconsin, 1966).

32. Seth Spaulding, "Research on Pictorial Illustration."

33. Keith P. Sanders and Won Ho Chang, "What They Read in the *Columbia Missourian.*" Mimeographed. School of Journalism, University of Missouri, 1974.

34. Robert D. Greenlee, "The Influence of Subject Matter Areas on Preference for Color vs. Black and White Photographs" (master's thesis, Iowa State University, 1968).

35. Hugh Culbertson, "Basic Research in Visual Communication: Iconicity." Paper presented to the Photojournalism Division, AEJ Convention, Lawrence, Kansas, 1968.

36. William R. Hazard, "Responses to News Pictures."

37. Jon Robert Leu, "The Effects of Photographic Compositional Elements on the Selection of News Pictures by Various Groups of Individuals" (master's thesis, Iowa State University, 1972).

photographs as their background in art and photography increases. Spaulding made these recommendations about pictorial composition: young children prefer simple drawings, while older children and adults prefer complex illustrations; illustrations should be constructed in keeping with the clockwise motion of eye fixations; the number of items in illustrations should be limited to assure notice of what is most important; the most significant objects and actions should be emphasized by placing them in the center and upper left of illustrations; illustrations require the motion of eyes in horizontal paths rather than in vertical ones.

Lighting angle has been found to be a significant compositional element. Tannenbaum and Fosdick tested four lighting conditions: 45-degree lateral angle, below, flat, and with the light at the camera. The most favorable effect was that caused by the 45-degree angle condition.[38] Contrary to the views of many experts, lighting from below did not lower ratings.

In a later study, Tannenbaum and Fosdick studied how a group of professional news photographers used compositional elements to encode a message in a photograph.[39] They concluded that "certain stylistic elements are used in consistent ways to modify the meaning which a message topic will have for the reader." The photographers used similar techniques in the use of light contrast, number of lights, background tone, and print density. There also was significant agreement on camera angle and image size.

Photographs with captions or overlines have been found to increase both readership and understanding.[40, 41, 42, 43, 44] In two separate studies, Kerrick found that captions can change or modify the meaning of a picture, especially when the picture itself is complicated and/or ambiguous. A caption can make a picture "sad" or "happy," "good" or "bad." Captions that are incongruent with the content of the picture will be ignored and interpretation will be based primarily on the picture alone. Kerrick noted that, although the influence of a caption can usually be anticipated by the writer, captions sometimes produce meanings opposite to those intended. The combined effect of a picture and a caption is stronger than that of the picture alone or the caption alone. Kerrick observed that the caption tends to lend more evaluative meaning, but the picture tends to lend more potency or strength. This latter finding was reinforced by Mehling, who found that photographs with words were more effective in changing evaluative judgments than were words or pictures alone.[45] Harrison noted that readers prefer full and informative captions to increase comprehension.[46] Misunderstanding is particularly likely to arise when the message is complex, where there is ambiguity, and where the object or event is unfamiliar.

---

38. Percy H. Tannenbaum and James A. Fosdick, "The Effect of Lighting Angle on Judgment on Photographed Subjects," *Audio-Visual Communication Review* (8): 253–262.
39. James A. Fosdick and Percy H. Tannenbaum, "The Encoder's Intent and Use of Stylistic Elements in Photographs," *Journalism Quarterly* (41): 175–182.
40. Jean S. Kerrick, "Influence of Captions on Picture Interpretation," *Journalism Quarterly* (32): 177–184.
41. Jean S. Kerrick, "News Pictures, Captions and the Point of Resolution," *Journalism Quarterly* (36): 183–188.
42. Seth Spaulding, "Research on Pictorial Illustration."
43. Randall Harrison, "Pictorial Communication."
44. Reuben Mehling, "Attitude Changing Effect."
45. Reuben Mehling, "Attitude Changing Effect."
46. Randall Harrison, "Pictorial Communication."

# The Photo Gatekeeper: Where It All Begins

Pictures are "nonverbal messages, encoded by a communicator in much the same manner as are the verbal messages of the poet, the novelist, the newspaper reporter, or the radio news commentator."[47] The choice of a suitable picture to accompany a story can be a crucial decision in the communication process. The person who daily makes this decision—the photography editor—will often have the ability to influence, if not determine, the reactions of his audience to the events described in the story he is illustrating. Since photographs have the potential to create far greater impact than mere words, in a very real sense the photography editor's selections of which photographs to use are more important than the selections a word editor must make. The intentional or subconscious reasons for which he selects pictures for publications can, and likely will, mold the attitudes of his audience.

Despite the many studies that show the power of photographs to increase readership, to enhance effective communication, and to shape the attitudes of readers, the photography editor has frequently been treated as an ill-favored stepchild in the newsroom. Blake, writing as recently as 1965, observed that "many editors think of photographers as 'shutter-trippers'—lacking an appreciation of news value and a knowledge of journalism fundamentals. They have not accepted the photographer as a member of the editorial family. This type of editor complains that photographers don't understand editor's picture needs and seldom produce pictures with sufficient news content."[48] Earlier Walters reported that in most newsrooms photographs were handled as nuisance jobs by city editors, news editors, or managing editors. "These busy men do not make the same study of cropping or reproduction or the news value of the picture that they make of the written word."[49] The second-class status of photographs was demonstrated in 1952 by Siebert. He found that whenever space was restricted, photographs and other graphic materials were usually the first things cut. On the other hand, when extra space became available, graphic materials were not as quick to expand as were the other, verbal, types of content.[50]

Kalish and Edom and Walters pointedly rejected the idea that photojournalists were lacking in journalistic ability. Walters said, "There should be little distinction in newspaper offices or in courtrooms or any other place between the men who report a story through the photographic lens and those who use the typewriter."[51] And Kalish and Edom said, "It should never be a question of 'pictures versus words' when a decision is reached about the content of the paper; rather it should be 'pictures *and* words.'"[52]

The ideal journalist, Leahigh reasoned, would be one who combined the

---

47. Fosdick and Tannenbaum, "The Encoder's Intent and Use."

48. Donald P. Blake, "The Editor vs. the Photographer," *Quill,* December 1965, pp. 18–20.

49. Basil L. Walters, "Picture vs. Type Display in Reporting the News," *Journalism Quarterly* (24): 193–196.

50. Fredrick S. Siebert, "Trends in the Use of Pictures by Three Newspapers," *Journalism Quarterly* (29): 212–213.

51. Basil L. Walters, "Picture vs. Type Display."

52. Stanley E. Kalish and Clifton C. Edom, *Picture Editing.*

talents of the newswriter/reporter with the talents of a photojournalist. On the typical American newspaper, of course, a person is either a photographer or a reporter. Leahigh, however, studied a newspaper (the *Daily Pantagraph* of Bloomington-Normal, Illinois) that combined the functions. The paper used a system in which each reporter was equipped with a camera and was expected to take his own pictures. Leahigh asked, "If a newswriter could master a thorough understanding of pictorial reporting and if he could appreciate reader interest problems involving pictorial matter and display, would he not, theoretically, be able to operate as effectively and as efficiently as a traditional news photographer?"[53] Leahigh compared the *Daily Pantagraph* photographs with those from three comparable newspapers. He found that its photographs were rated slightly higher than two of the traditional system newspapers but considerably lower than those of the *Telegraph Herald* of Dubuque, Iowa. The *Telegraph Herald* has been generally recognized as one of the most photography-conscious newspapers in the Midwest.

Principles of photograph selections have been the focus of several studies. One of the most significant, and earliest, was conducted by Stephenson (see note 14) and is reported elsewhere in this book (Chapter 9 and the Appendix). Ganschow found a high level of agreement among professional photographers concerning what is effective composition, as did Tannenbaum and Fosdick.[54, 55, 56] Wagner found that one group of people with experience in picture selection consistently gave low ratings to obviously posed photographs.[57] Other low-rated photographs were described as trite, staged, or generally lacking in clear expression of any kind of human experience. The editors placed emphasis on spontaneity of the photographs, and ranked high photographs that portrayed either action or social problems of poverty and hunger. The expression of human emotion was a common theme among the highly rated pictures.

The photography editor has a dual function: to determine if a picture should be printed and to decide how it should be played. In selecting a picture, the editor's ability to sense a good picture is important. Equally important is the fact that readers will interpret the picture in the light of their personal feelings and experiences. Successful picture selection consequently combines a feeling for pictures with an understanding of the audience.[58]

The most thorough and systematic study of picture editing to date is that done by MacLean and Kao.[59] In the final phase of their five-phase project, they attempted to determine what kinds of information about the audience would be most useful to picture editors. They selected three kinds of photography editors: "Senior Editors"—professional editors, picture editors, and photographers of publications; "Junior Editors"—students majoring in journalism who knew photography and who had had experience in some sort of picture editing; "Naive Editors"—junior and senior education majors in college who had not had any experience in photography or in picture editing.

---

53. Alan Kent Leahigh, "Reporters with Cameras: A Comparison of Newspaper Photography Systems" (master's thesis, University of Missouri, 1971).

54. Cliff Ganschow, "Contribution of Certain Compositional Factors."

55. James A. Fosdick and Percy H. Tannenbaum, "The Encoder's Intent and Use."

56. Percy H. Tannenbaum and James A. Fosdick, "The Effect of Lighting Angle."

57. Barbara Wagner, "Picture Value of Potential Editors," Mimeographed. School of Journalism, University of Missouri, 1973.

58. Gardner Cowles, "Visual Excitement."

59. Malcolm S. MacLean, Jr., and Anne Li-An Kao, *Editorial Predictions*.

**Table 1**
Correlations Between Editors' Predictive
Sorts and Readers' Actual Sorts

| Picture Editors | Demographic Information | Overall | Male | Female |
|---|---|---|---|---|
| *Senior editors* | 1. Minimal information | .27 | .48 | .07 |
| | 2. Detailed information | .26 | .37 | .16 |
| | 3. Predictee's Q-sort | .44 | .43 | .45 |
| | 4. Q-sort & detailed information | .55 | .49 | .61 |
| | overall: | .39 | .44 | .32 |
| *Junior editors* | 1. Minimal information | .24 | .25 | .23 |
| | 2. Detailed information | .38 | .41 | .35 |
| | 3. Predictee's Q-sort | .56 | .42 | .70 |
| | 4. Q-sort & detailed information | .47 | .36 | .58 |
| | overall: | .43 | .36 | .47 |
| *Naive editors* | 1. Minimal information | .31 | .37 | .24 |
| | 2. Detailed information | .23 | .05 | .40 |
| | 3. Predictee's Q-sort | .53 | .43 | .64 |
| | 4. Q-sort & detailed information | .52 | .50 | .53 |
| | overall: | .42 | .34 | .45 |

"Typical" readers were asked to sort through two sets containing 60 photographs each. The three types of editors were then given differing amounts of information and asked to sort the same photographs as they thought the readers had sorted them. In short, they were taking part in a complicated editing game that involved the prediction of what readers liked and disliked. There were four types of information provided:

1. Minimal Demographic Information: Age, Sex, and Level of Education.
2. Detailed Demographic Information: Age, Sex, Education, Occupation, Position in the Household, Income, Family Members, House Ownership, Type of Dwelling Unit, Newspaper and Magazine subscriptions, Car Ownership, Religion, Politics, Hobbies, Favorite Sports, and Movie Going.
3. Subject Q-sorts: The editors were shown how the subjects actually sorted one of the sets of photographs. The editors were then asked to sort the second set of photographs as they thought the subject would have sorted them.
4. Subject Q-sorts and Detailed Demographic Information: The editors were given the information described in no. 2 and no. 3 above.

MacLean and Kao hypothesized that the more information the editors were provided, the more accurate they would be in predicting the likes and dislikes of the readers, and to a certain extent that's what they found. The editors' predictive Q-sorts were correlated with the actual sorts of the subjects.[60] The

---

60. The Pearson Product Moment Correlation Coefficient, as used in this study, can be considered a measure of agreement. If two people liked exactly the same pictures and disliked exactly the same pictures, their correlation would be +1.00. If they completely disagreed—the pictures one liked the other disliked and vice versa—their correlation would be −1.00. If they agreed on some but disagreed on others, their correlation would fall somewhere around 0.00. The correlation, thus, ranges from −1.00 to +1.00.

Research in Photojournalism

correlations ranged from a low of —.069 to a high of .799. Statistically, a correlation of less than .260 could be obtained by chance alone—merely by assigning photographs to ranks at random, for example. A correlation greater than .260, however, could only very rarely occur by chance, and the higher the correlation, the greater the accuracy in prediction.

As predicted, accuracy of prediction increased according to the amount and kind of information provided to the editors, but the pattern was less than perfect. The Senior Editors did barely better than chance when given Minimal Demographic Information (.270) and Detailed Demographic Information (.260). Accuracy improved considerably for the Senior Editors who had been given the Predictee's Actual Q-sort (.439), and it increased still more when given the Q-sort and Detailed Demographic Information (.554). It is interesting to note that accuracy actually decreased when the Junior and Naive Editors were given the maximum information.

It is clear that providing editors with examples of the types of photographs that people actually like gives the editor the best information he needs to accurately predict reader response. Minimal Demographic Information is not terribly valuable. Surprisingly, highly Detailed Demographic Information did not help much. This suggests that the editors were unable "to figure people out" and to make the deductive leap from one set of data (demographic information) to another set of data (liking of pictures). The concern here must be with the editor's *understanding* of his audience. The editors' inability to grasp what people are like suggests that they do not understand people nearly as well as they should.

Overall, the three types of editors were equally successful (statistically speaking) in predicting reader preference. The fact, however, that the Senior Editors were not more accurate than the others is strong evidence for the need for additional study of audiences by photography editors and would-be photography editors. The Senior Editors, given their experience, would have been expected to have done better than they did, which suggests once again that they may be out of touch with readers. The Senior Editors were surprised at the

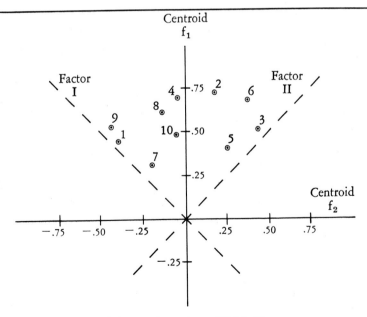

Fig. 1 (From data of Table 1)

picture preferences of the readers in this study. Quite clearly they had developed stereotypes about reader preferences, and this study showed that those stereotypes were not very accurate.

Nowhere was this more evident than in the Senior Editors' predictions of women's photographic preferences. Until the Senior Editors were shown the women's actual Q-sorts, they were quite inaccurate in their predictions, correlating only .069 with Minimal Information and .157 with Detailed Demographic Information. On the other hand, they were easily the most accurate at the first two levels of information in predicting men's readership. To their credit, the Senior Editors made the most of the additional data, even to the point that one editor, armed with Detailed Demographic Information and the Q-sort, predicted a woman's preferences at .705. It is interesting to note that the Naive Editors did the best job of predicting women's readership when given only Minimal and Detailed Demographics. This probably can be explained by the fact that these "editors" were, after all, readers and not editors and that they were therefore "close" to understanding fellow readers. Once again, this supports the observation that Senior Editors are out of touch with their readers.

MacLean and Kao concluded that information about the typologies of audience members in terms of their reaction patterns helped editors predict better than the traditional kind of survey research demographic information.

# Where Do We Go From Here?

The research literature on photography as an art form is extensive and rich, but the research literature on photography as a journalistic form is not very extensive. Aside from a few studies, most photojournalism research has constituted a part of some larger research project. Most readership studies look at photographs almost as an afterthought. A recent National Survey of the Content and Readership of the American Newspaper didn't include photographs at all![61]

Despite the pioneering efforts by Stephenson and MacLean, we still know relatively little about how photography editors choose pictures. One approach that might prove valuable would be to study intensively a few photography editors as they perform their selection process, along methodological lines developed by White, Gieber, and Snider in their studies of wire editors.

There is evidence to suggest that photography editors still use a "fly by the seat of their pants" approach to selecting pictures. The relatively poor performances of professional editors in the MacLean–Kao study indicate a continuing need for photography editors to assess the interests of their readers. Local readership studies, therefore, are particularly beneficial. Such studies, however, should concentrate on actual picture preferences instead of on mere demographic data unless the editors are prepared to make more of such data than they have in studies thus far conducted.

The problem with the typical readership study is that it groups people together on the basis of some demographic variable—or a combination of

---

61. Newspaper Advertising Bureau, Inc. "A National Survey of the Content and Readership of the American Newspaper" (New York: 1972).

demographic variables. The simple fact remains, however, that all too frequently demographic variables are poor indicators of picture interest. One thirty-year-old college-educated woman with a high income may very well read quite different photographs than another thirty-year-old college woman with a high income. The concern in finding reader preferences, thus, should be with grouping people together on the basis of their preferences, not on the basis of their demographics.

Successful communicators know that the most important consideration in communication is to "Know Thy Audience." People are unique. Fortunately, people have similar patterns of preference that make it possible for us to deal with both their uniqueness and their similarity. What is needed is a system for identifying major patterns of preferences. If that can be done, we can vastly simplify, and at the same time vastly improve, the editing process. MacLean stated the advantage: "Instead of trying to deal with some amorphous man-in-the-street, or at the other extreme, with five million different individuals, we can develop strategies for aiming communication differentially to perhaps five or six different types of persons, types which pretty well cover the five million individuals."[62]

MacLean and Kao devoted much of their concluding statements to a discussion of how such types can be developed. They suggested a combination of Q-methodology with Talbott's Q-block approach.[63] Briefly, the system consists of showing a relatively small sample of people, say twenty-five to thirty, a selection of photographs and asking them to rank them on a Most-Liked to Least-Liked basis. The Q-sorts would then be factor analyzed, probably producing about three or four factors, or types of people. After weighing the rankings according to the factor loadings, the photographs would be ranked (by standard scores) for each type. The photographs that were ranked particularly high or low would in essence "define" the type. Using only those photographs, a much larger sample would be contacted. Those people would be asked simply which photographs they liked. People would be assigned to types on the basis of how many times they picked photographs that a particular type had earlier selected. The advantage of such a system is two-fold: first, it enables one to identify what percentage of the readers "belong to" what picture preference type, and, second, the assigning of people to types is fast, efficient, and easy to do. In the likely event that the photography editor does not have access to either someone familiar with factor analysis or a computer program to actually do the analysis, the same result can be achieved more simply, although perhaps with less precision. The procedure would be something like this: Have a small number of people go through a relatively large set of photographs (say, 60) and rank them on a 7-, 9-, or 11-point scale or Most Like to Least Like. Correlation coefficients, which are quite easy to compute, would be calculated between each pair of people. Still simpler would be to note the number of times two people agreed on the rating of photographs. In short, any system that would group people together on the basis of their similarities in picture preferences will suffice. Finally, take those photographs that were ranked particularly high or particularly low and conduct a survey.

62. Malcolm S. MacLean, Jr., "Some Multivariate Designs for Communications Research," *Journalism Quarterly* (42): 614–622.

63. A. D. Talbott, "The Q-block Method of Indexing Q Typologies." Paper presented to the Theory and Methodology Division, AEJ Convention, Lincoln, Nebraska, 1963.

We have a long way to go to develop a better understanding of why people like photographs. For example, it seems particularly strange that so little attention has been given to the importance of stylistic elements in news photographs. Once again we find a considerable amount of such research in the photography-as-an-art-form research literature, but little in the photojournalism literature.

A follow-up study on the massive MacLean–Kao study seems much in order. The study is rich with theoretical implications very much in need of testing. Why is it, for example, that the Naive Editors performed so well, compared to the Senior Editors? One also wonders how well the editors would have been able to predict if they had been given *no* information. After all, it is exactly that situation—no information about the audience—that the typical photography editor has to confront all too frequently.

## Bibliography

Advertising Research Foundation. *The Continuing Study of Newspaper Reading.* New York: started in 1939.

Arnheim, Rudolf. *Art and Visual Perception.* Los Angeles: University of California Press, 1966.

Arnold, George. "Theoretical Views of the Photography Editor as Gatekeeper." Master's thesis, University of Missouri, 1974.

Arpan, Floyd G. ed. "Photo-Journalism." *Journalism Quarterly* 24:193–249.

Baker, E. L., and Popham, W. J. "Value of Pictorial Embellishments in a Slide-Tape Instructional Program." *Audio-Visual Communication Review* 13:397–404.

Baker, Stephen. *Visual Persuasion.* New York: McGraw-Hill Book Co., 1961.

Ball, John, and Byrnes, Frances C. eds. *"Research, Principles, and Practices in Visual Communication."* East Lansing, Michigan, National Project in Agricultural Communications, 1960. (Washington, D.C.: Department of Audio-visual Instruction, NEA, 1964.)

Bartley, S. H., and Adair, H. J. "Comparisons of Phenomenal Distance in Photos of Various Sizes." *Journal of Psychology* 47: 699–704.

Berlo, D. K., Lemert, J. B., and Mertz, R. J. "Evaluations of the Message Source: A Basis for Predicting Communication Effects." Research Monograph, Department of Communication, Michigan State University, East Lansing, Michigan, 1966.

Blake, Donald P. "The Editor vs. The Photographer." *Quill,* December 1965, pp. 18–20.

Bourisseau, W., Davis, O., and Yamamoto, K. "Sense-Impression Responses to Differing Pictorial and Verbal Stimuli." *Audio-Visual Communication Review* 13:249–258.

Brown, Roger. *Words and Things.* Glencoe, Ill.: The Free Press, 1959.

Bush, George S. "Survey Shows New Needs for Photo-Journalism." *Journalism Quarterly* 38:216–217.

Bush, George S. "Technique vs. Meaning in Photo-Journalism." *Journalism Quarterly* 37:97–101.

Butts, G. K. "An Experiential Study of the Effectiveness of Declarative, Interrogative, and Imperative Captions on Still Pictures." Ph.D. dissertation, University of Indiana, 1956.

Carlson, V. D. "The Resolution of Photographic and Labelling Factors in Affective Impressions." Ph.D. dissertation, Vanderbilt University, 1963.

Cook, J. J. "Indices of the Meaning of Photographs in Relation to Concomitant Physiological Activity." *The Psychiatric Institute Bulletin* 2:4.

Cooper, E., and Jahoda, M. "The Evasion of Propaganda." *Journal of Psychology* 23:15–25.

Cooperman, Gary. "A Historical Study of *Look* Magazine and Its Concept of Photojournalism." Master's thesis, University of Missouri, 1966.

Cowles, Gardner. "Visual Excitement in Modern Publishing," In *Art Directing*. New York: Hasting House, Publishers, 1957.

Culbertson, Hugh. "Basic Research in Visual Communication: Iconicity." Paper presented to the Photojournalism Division, AEJ Convention, Lawrence, Kansas, 1968.

Culbertson, Hugh. "Words vs. Pictures: A Comparison as to Perceived Impact and Connotative Meaning." Paper presented to the Graphics Division, AEJ Convention, Carbondale, Illinois, 1972.

Culbertson, Hugh, and Powers, Richard. "A Study of Graphic Comprehension Difficulties." *Audio-Visual Communication Review* 7:97–110.

Davies, Edward J. "The Effects of Photographic Compositional Elements on the Selection of News Photographs and Abstractions of Photographs by Artists, Photographers, and Non-Professionals." Master's thesis, Iowa State University, 1969.

Dickinson, John A. "A Q-Sort Analysis of Men and Women's Reading Interest in Pictures." Master's thesis, Louisiana State University, 1972.

Edom, Clifton C. "Photo-Propaganda: The History of Its Development." *Journalism Quarterly* 24:221–226.

Fosdick, James A. "Stylistic Correlates of Prescribed Intent in a Photographic Encoding Task." Ph.D. dissertation, University of Wisconsin, 1962.

Fosdick, James A., and Tannenbaum, Percy H. "The Encoder's Intent and Use of Stylistic Elements in Photographs." *Journalism Quarterly* 41:175–182.

Ganschow, Cliff. "Contribution of Certain Compositional Factors to Photographs' Effectiveness." Mimeographed. Department of Technical Journalism, Iowa State University.

Gervin, Robert E. "Photography as a Social Documentation." *Journalism Quarterly* 24:207–220.

Gibson, L. "A Theory of Pictorial Communication." *Audio-Visual Communication Review* 2:3–23.

Graham, M. D. "The Effectiveness of Photographs as a Projective Device in an International Attitudes Survey." *Journal of Social Psychology* 40:93–120.

Greenlee, Robert D. "The Influence of Subject Matter Areas on Preference for Color vs. Black and White Photographs." Master's thesis, Iowa State University, 1968.

Gropper, M. "Why Is a Picture Worth a Thousand Words?" *Audio-Visual Communication Review* 11:75–95.

Hall, Edward T. *The Silent Language*. New York: Doubleday & Co., Inc., 1959.

Harrison, Randall P. "Pictic Analysis: Toward a Vocabulary and Syntax for the Pictorial Code, with Research on Facial Communication." Ph. D. dissertation, Michigan State University, 1965.

Harrison, Randall. "Pictorial Communication." *Search*, vol. 6. National Project in Agricultural Communication. East Lansing, Michigan, 1962.

Hazard, William R. "Responses to News Pictures: A Study in Perceptual Unity." *Journalism Quarterly* 37:515–524.

Hicks, Wilson. *Words and Pictures*. New York: Harper and Brothers, 1952.

Hochberg, J. "The Psychophysics of Pictorial Perception." *Audio-Visual Communication Review* 10:22–54.

Kahan, Robert S. "Magazine Photography Begins: An Editorial Negative." *Journalism Quarterly* 42:53–59.

Kalish, Stanley E., and Edom, Clifton C. *Picture Editing*. New York: Rinehart & Co., Inc., 1951.

Kelly, Wayne. "Effectiveness of News Photographs in Attitude Formation." Master's thesis, University of California, 1963.

Kepes, Gyorgy. *Language of Vision*. Chicago: Paul Theobald & Co., 1959.

Kerrick, Jean S. "Influence of Captions on Picture Interpretation." *Journalism Quarterly* 32:177–184.

Kerrick, Jean S. "News Pictures, Captions and the Point of Resolution." *Journalism Quarterly* 36:183–188.

Kessen, W. "The Role of Experience in Judging Children's Photographs." *Journal of Abnormal and Social Psychology* 54:375–379.

Kishiyama, David N. "News, Photographs and Attitude Change." Master's thesis, University of California at Los Angeles, 1973.

Korn, Jerry, *et al. Photojournalism*. New York: Time-Life Books, 1971.

Leahigh, Alan Kent. "Reporters With Cameras: A Comparison of Newspaper Photography Systems." Master's thesis, University of Missouri, 1971.

Leu, Jon Robert. "The Effects of Photographic Compositional Elements on the Selection of News Pictures by Various Groups of Individuals." Master's thesis, Iowa State University, 1972.

Leuba, C., and Lucas, C. "The Effects of Attitudes on Description of Pictures." *Journal of Experimental Psychology* 3:517–523.

Lippmann, Walter. *Public Opinion*. New York: Macmillan Co., 1922.

Logie, M. "Photojournalism." *Gazette* 3:109–128.

MacLean, Malcolm S., Jr. "Communication Strategy, Editing Games and Q." In Brown, Steven R., and Brenner, Donald J., eds. *Science, Psychology and Communication*. New York: Teachers College Press, 1972.

MacLean, Malcolm S., Jr. "Some Multivariate Designs for Communications Research." *Journalism Quarterly* 42:614–622.

MacLean, Malcolm S., Jr., and Hazard, William R. "Women's Interest in Pictures: The Badger Village Study." *Journalism Quarterly* 30:139–162.

MacLean, Malcolm S., Jr., and Kao, Anne Li-An. *Editorial Predictions of Magazine Picture Appeals*. Iowa City, Iowa: School of Journalism, University of Iowa, 1965.

MacLean, Malcolm S., Jr., and Kao, Anne Li-An. "Picture Selection: An Editorial Game." *Journalism Quarterly* 40:230–232.

Mare, Eric de. *Photography*. 4th ed. Baltimore: Penguin Books, Inc., 1968.

Marphetia, Toranj A. "Image Creating Potential of Photo Journalism." Master's thesis, Marquette University, 1973.

Mehling, Reuben. "Attitude Changing Effect of News and Photo Combination." *Journalism Quarterly* 36:189–198.

Mich, Daniel D. "The Rise of Photo-Journalism in the United States." *Journalism Quarterly* 24:202–206.

Nafziger, Ralph O., MacLean, Malcolm S., Jr., and Engstrom, Warren. "Useful Tools for Interpreting Newspaper Readership Data." *Journalism Quarterly* 28:441–456.

Neubert, Michael T. "The Effects of Selection and Emphasis Upon Reader Responses to News Pictures." Master's thesis, University of Wisconsin, 1966.

Newspaper Advertising Bureau, Inc. "A National Survey of the Content and Readership of the American Newspaper." New York, 1972.

Osgood, Charles E., and Tannenbaum, Percy H. "The Principle of Congruity and Prediction of Attitude Change." *Psychological Review* 62:42–55.

Otto, W. "The Differential Effects of Verbal and Pictorial Stimuli Upon Responses Evoked." *Journal of Verbal Learning and Verbal Behavior* 1:192–196.

Rhode, Robert B., and McCall, Floyd H. *Press Photography*. New York: Macmillan Co., 1961.

Sanders, Keith P. "A Q Study of Editors' Attitudes Toward Journalism Research." *Journalism Quarterly* 49:519–531.

Sanders, Keith P., and Chang, Won Ho. "What They Read in the *Columbia Missourian*." Mimeographed. School of Journalism, University of Missouri, 1974.

Sanders, Keith P., and Pritchett, Michael. "How Appearance Influences Television Newscaster Appeal." *Journal of Broadcasting* 15:293–301.

Schramm, Wilbur. "The Nature of News." *Journalism Quarterly* 26:259–269.

Schramm, Wilbur, and White, David M. "Age, Education, Economic Status: Factors in Newspaper Reading." *Journalism Quarterly* 26:149–159.

Scodel, A., and Austrin, H. "The Perception of Jewish Photographs by Non-Jews and Jews." Journal of *Abnormal and Social Psychology* 54:278–280.

Severin, Werner J. "Cameras With a Purpose." *Journalism Quarterly* 41:191–200.

Severin, Werner J. "The Effectiveness of Relevant Pictures in Multiple-Channel Communications." *Audio-Visual Communication Review* 15:386–401.

Severin, Werner J. "Pictures as Relevant Cues in Multi-Channel Communication." *Journalism Quarterly* 44:17–22.

Sidey, Hugh, and Fox, Rodney. *1000 Ideas for Better News Pictures.* Ames, Iowa: Iowa State University Press, 1956.

Siebert, Fredrick S. "Trends in the Use of Pictures by Three Newspapers." *Journalism Quarterly* 29:212–213.

Spaulding, Seth. "Research on Pictorial Illustration." *Audio-Visual Communication Review* 3:35–45.

Spencer, Otha C. "Twenty Years of *Life*: A Study of Time, Inc.'s Picture Magazine and Its Contribution to Photojournalism." Ph.D. dissertation, University of Missouri, 1958.

Stephenson, William. *The Play Theory of Mass Communication.* Chicago: University of Chicago Press, 1967.

Stephenson, William. "Principles of Selection of News Pictures." *Journalism Quarterly* 37:61–68.

Stephenson, William. *The Study of Behavior: Q Technique and Its Methodology.* Chicago: University of Chicago Press, 1953.

Swanson, Charles. "What They Read in 130 Daily Newspapers." *Journalism Quarterly* 32:411–421.

Swink, Eleanor Sue. "Effects of Priming, Incubation and Creative Aptitude on Journalistic Performance." Master's thesis, University of Missouri, 1966.

Talbott, A. D. "The Q-block Method of Indexing Q Typologies." Paper presented to the Theory and Methodology Division, AEJ Convention, Lincoln, Nebraska, 1963.

Tannenbaum, Percy H., and Fosdick, James A. "The Effect of Lighting Angle on Judgment on Photographed Subjects." *Audio-Visual Communication Review* 8:253–262.

Wagner, Barbara. "Picture Value of Potential Editors." Mimeographed. Paper, School of Journalism, University of Missouri, 1973.

Walters, Basil L. "Picture vs. Type Display in Reporting the News." *Journalism Quarterly* 24:193–196.

Wendt, P. R. "The Language of Pictures." *Etc.* 13:281–288.

Wilcox, Walter. "The Staged News Photograph and Professional Ethics." *Journalism Quarterly* 38:497–504.

Willem, Jack M. "Reader Interest in News Pictures." In Morgan, Willard D., and Lester, Henry M., eds. *Graphic Graflex Photography.* New York: Morgan & Lester, 1946.

Wolseley, Roland E. "Photo-Journalism: An Annotated Bibliography." *Journalism Quarterly* 24:243–249.

Woodburn, Bert W. "Reader Interest in Newspaper Pictures." *Journalism Quarterly* 24:197–201.

Wrolstad, Merald E. "Adult Preferences in Typography: Exploring the Function of Design." *Journalism Quarterly* 37:211–223.

# Student Participation

Research has shown that the best communicators are those who know and understand their audiences. A corollary is that all too frequently we make mistaken assumptions about our readers. The following exercise will help you better understand your readers and your photographs. Approach the exercise with an open mind and be prepared for some surprises.

First, collect a set of six photographs. You can clip them from magazines or newspapers, or you can use photographs you have taken yourself. Get at least two photographs that you think are very good and at least two photographs that you think are very bad. Try to vary the content somewhat (don't make them all portraits, all pictures of children, or all of animals, for example). For ease in handling, mount the pictures on cardboard.

Select a couple of people you know well (friends, roommates, spouse). The advantage of starting with someone you know is that you can practice your interviewing"technique" on them. Armed with your photographs, interview each person individually. Start by asking them to choose the photograph they liked the most and the one they liked the least. Ask them what it is about the photographs that they liked or disliked. What do they "see" in the photos? What makes them interested in a particular picture? Do they normally pay much attention to photographs in newspapers and magazines? Did they like the same photographs you liked? For the same reasons? The object of this questioning is to get them talking about photographs in general. Your selection of photographs should help considerably.

Friends and associates, of course, are apt to be very much like you, with the same interests and experiences—indeed, that is probably why they are friends. So, after you have talked to a couple of friends, deliberately seek out a couple of people who are quite different from you (in terms of factors such as age, sex, education, social status, and the like). Go through the same procedure with them.

You likely will find that some of your assumptions about people were incorrect, but you also will be pleased to find that many of your assumptions were right on target. At any rate, you should now have a much better basis for communicating effectively through photographs.

**Sinking of the Vestris.** Many great news pictures, and this is a good example, have been taken by amateur photographers. This dramatic photograph made by Fred Hansen, an assistant pantry man on the *Vestris*, was taken with a camera purchased just before the start of the tragic voyage. The sloping deck of the British steamer and the fear on the faces of passengers are storytelling, indeed. The *Vestris* sank with a loss of 112 lives. Hansen sold his roll of undeveloped film to the *New York Daily News* for nearly $1,000. Included in 50 Memorable Pictures exhibit.

# Winning A Pulitzer Prize

ian Lanker, formerly with the
opeka, Ks., *Capital Journal,*
lls us how he photographed the
ory on natural childbirth and
ained worldwide acclaim.

rian Lanker has earned just about every
ossible honor in newspaper photography. A
aff photographer of the *Topeka Capital-
ournal* when these pictures were taken,
anker has earned three National Press
hotographers Association regional Photog-
pher of the Year awards, one in Region 8
n 1968) and two in Region 7 (1969–
970). Topping this fine record, Lanker was
e youngest photographer to that time
1970) to earn the title Newspaper
hotographer of the Year. Going one step
urther, Lanker won the Pulitzer Prize for
eature photography for a story on natural
hildbirth in 1972 (p. 141).

Note: On this page we begin translation of a tape recording dictated especially for this book by Brian Lanker, prizewinning photographer on the *Daily Capital-Journal,* Topeka, Kansas. Editing has been kept to a minimum to insure that you get a true picture of Lanker's thoughts and feelings as he went about producing the story which won for him a 1972 Pulitzer award in photography. (See pictures on pages 143–45, and Moment of Life—An Experience Shared on a page which follows. The translation:

June 10, 1974

Right now it is 2:30 in the morning, and about 4 o'clock, less than two hours from now, I leave for a several-day trip to western Kansas to do a custom harvester story. But this seems the best time to get things done as the days are so hectic with tornadoes, etc.

In regard to the childbirth story: It started out by my seeing an article in our paper on the Lamaze classes. One of our photographers did the story showing how the husbands and wives, as a part of a class of instruction, go through different exercises to prepare themselves for the birth of a child.

For me, and for the community, the natural childbirth approach was new. It was new especially to see the relationship of the husband and wife during a natural childbirth, as opposed to the norm, where so many times the husband is shoved to the far end of the hospital where he reads a magazine or chews his fingernails. It was news to me—and to a lot of people—to find out that the husband is a vital part of the natural childbirth story.

Up to this time, the big problem with a birth story, in my mind, was that they had really missed what it was all about. They missed showing the birth, missed showing the two of them—mother and father—together.

So I set out to find a couple who would not mind a photographer in the delivery room with them. I didn't think it would be easy, but little did I know how hard it would be. Well, six months' worth of these classes (each class lasts only a month) meant that six groups went by before Jerry and Lynda Coburn came along and said "Yes, we really believe in the Lamaze method of childbirth, and we think it would be good if in some way we could let other people experience what natural childbirth is all about." With their permission to photograph the birth of their baby, things started to happen.

The story really never was scheduled for the paper. I didn't go to a great deal of trouble to tell them what I was doing. I was playing it low key because I had no idea of what kind of photographs might come from this story. The only thing I did in regard to the staff in the newsroom was to constantly leave a number where I could be contacted should a call come from the Coburns. I stayed home at nights, refraining from all other activities so I would be available. I did, however, go to the Coburn home many times—became acquainted with them, had tea, and joked with them. They gave me a book on *Childbirth Without Pain.* I read it at home. That basically is where the preparation for shooting the story and my relationship with the Coburns began. It wasn't a close relationship at the start, but it was destined to become very close. When it came time for the child to be born, I was the first to receive a call. Lynda advised she was calling her husband and the doctor and asked if I was ready.

Of course I was ready, but the same day the child was to be born—and almost at the same time as it worked out—I was scheduled to give a talk at the local Rotary Club. The executive editor at the newspaper had made the arrangements, and I couldn't say no to the several hundred Rotarians—mostly out-of-towners in Topeka to attend the legislature then in session.

I had this speaking engagement hanging over my head as I went to the hospital that morning. The real excitement and anxious moments, however, came from thoughts of the impending birth. I guess I sort of prayed things would work out. And they did. Recalling the situation I can tell you that I didn't have an inkling of an idea about the excitement in store for Jerry, Lynda—and myself, as well.

I was so elated and so involved with the whole idea of birth and this birth in particular that by the time the baby was born, I really felt like it was mine. I guess this goes against the journalistic principle which insists that you have to be an uninterested, objective observer. I was quite a bit a part of this birth—so much so, in fact, that I don't remember actually seeing the images and then clicking the shutter, as I usually do on assignment. Things were happening too fast, and the camera just became an extension of my eye. I focused fortunately —and wound the film—but until it was over, I was unaware of what really was going on.

Lynda gave birth to Jacki Lynn just moments before noon. I finished photographing, and quickly removed the cap, gown, and protective covering for my shoes, all of which were worn in the delivery room. Frantically I rushed to the hotel where the Rotary Club was meeting. Although I arrived too late for the luncheon, I was in time to make the scheduled talk and slide presentation. During the talk I explained where I'd been and what had just happened. Several days later when many of those in the room finally saw our newspaper and the picture page, I suppose, they understood a little better the excitement I was talking about. . . .

Usually, after an assignment I return to the office where an hour or so later I process the film. I didn't do that this time. Admittedly I had qualms about how well I had covered the situation. I didn't feel that whatever I had done could come close to capturing the feeling, the aura, and the importance of the husband and wife experiencing this very beautiful moment together. I put the film away and developed it several days later. The winning of the many photographic honors is now a matter of record.

**From Contact Sheet to Printed Page.** With a self-assigned story, "The Moment of Life," Brian Lanker earned the 1972 Pulitzer Prize for feature photography. During the time he was in the delivery room with the parents (Jerry and Lynda Coburn) Lanker was so involved that he was not sure he had actually taken the important pictures. Professionalism won out, however, and Lanker had many fine exposures on his contact sheets, one of which is pictured *above.*

How the story was used in the *Topeka Capital Journal* is shown on page 144.

Life comes with a tug.

A mother's face tightens white against her cheekbones, her face rushes red as she makes the final effort to deliver the child.

In the psychoprophylaxis method of delivery, such as the Lamaze childbirth method once reserved for the hardy few, the man stands next to his wife, letting her squeeze his hand, reminding her to push down. It is an alternative to the usual anesthetized, and isolated delivery room procedure.

Topeka hospitals report a growing number of Northeast Kansas parents are using the new method. In it the mothers are trained in the latter two months of pregnancy to develop conditioned responses through muscle relaxation and breathing exercises to intercept the pain stimuli and thus reduce pain. They learn what to expect at each phase of delivery and how to apply the breathing and relaxation techniques effectively.

Stormont-Vail and St. Francis hospitals report the method is growing in popularity with from two to six mothers, including some hospital personnel, each week choosing it.

"I was excited beyond belief. I kind of forgot what to do. It was a true high. I needed him to tell me what to do," she said.

"I couldn't do much being there but she needed me," he said.

"It was the most important thing to me, having him there."

Both believed the reserved waiting room where he could sit in a plastic molded chair surrounded by Redbook magazines and smouldering ashtrays was not the place to be at the moment of childbirth.

It's his baby too.

Dressed in hospital garments, Jerry sat with his wife throughout the delivery.

# The Moment of Life
# An Experience Shared

While Lynda Coburn was in labor at St. Francis Hospital, her husband Jerry was right there with her, ready to give both moral and physical support whenever needed.

During the final contractions Lynda strained every muscle in her body and then radiated joy upon arrival of their daughter.

Jacki Lynn Coburn was born to Mr. and Mrs. Jerry Joe Coburn in St. Francis hospital at 11:45 a.m. on Thursday the 27th day of January, 1972.

"One minute your stomach is so then in a second you have this ho heavy, wet, body on top of you, a it's overwhelming."

Topeka Sunday Capital-Journal
for and about THE FAMILY

It was all over. Jerry walked from the now empty delivery room where moments earlier he had helped to deliver his daughter. "I didn't think it would move me that much, but I was very surprised and

The childbirth pictures were entered in the National Press Photographers Association clip contest, the Pictures of the Year Competition, the Missouri-Kansas Associated Press contest, and of course for the Pulitzer Prize . . . . The photographs and the story of natural childbirth must have an almost universal appeal. Never did they lose a competition nor were they ever given second place. They were picked first in every competition in which they were entered.

It is not that being first—or even second—is important. What is important is that these pictures really got close to people. They really communicated something, and that is what we are trying to do.

In concluding his story Lanker dictated these words which should be of interest to persons in photojournalism:

After finding a couple for my story, there was a little research to be done. I read the book *Childbirth Without Pain*. I also got permission to photograph the event from the hospital and from the doctor. It was an easy matter to meter the light and figure the exposures before the happy event occurred. I knew what the conditions and the light were going to be. I knew what lenses and what camera settings I would use. There weren't any surprises—photographic surprises—I was in for.

# One Last Thought

In 1972, the year Brian Lanker earned a Pulitzer Prize, another Pulitzer Prize in photography was given for a photograph from Vietnam. This one, by Nick Ut of the Associated Press, portrayed the horrors of war, showing a group of screaming, frightened children just subjected to an accidental Napalm strike. So: we have a Pulitzer Prize won on one hand by a horror picture of a distant war and on the other hand by portrayal of a very beautiful moment, the birth of a baby in middle America. That's what photojournalism is all about.

**Terror of War** by Huynh Cong (Nick) Ut
of the Associated Press. This picture won
first place, spot news, in the thirtieth annual
Pictures of the Year competition. He also
won the Pulitzer Prize for spot news the
same year that Brian Lanker of Topeka
earned the Pulitzer Prize for feature
photography. (Wide World Photos.)

# 12 Photo-Offset Newspapers

The strike by compositors on the *Chicago Daily Tribune* in 1947 gave us the first crude glimpse of the cold type and photo-offset newspapers which were to follow.

**B**ecause of the increasing demand for more and better pictures in magazines and newspapers, each year since invention of the halftone screen the search for better methods of reproduction has continued.

Cold type, now so widely used by newspapers throughout the country, probably came into national focus in December 1947 concurrently with the compositors' strike at the *Chicago Daily Tribune. The Tribune* explained to its readers:

> For the last two weeks *The Tribune* has been published without the aid of printers. From a somewhat uncertain start, and utilizing makeshift methods, employes who remained at work since the strike of the typographical union have progressed steadily toward their goal: Production of a newspaper that affords the same news coverage, advertising and public service as the prestrike editions.
>
> Great strides already have been made, with present issues carrying more than double the news of earlier ones, legibility is much improved, and the speed of production increased. . . .
>
> . . . The new type reproduction process required that virtually every bit of news matter and part of the advertising had to pass through the newspaper's photo-engraving department, adding greatly to its regular work . . .
>
> . . . In the linotype process, copy, either news or advertising, is sent to the composing room after it is written by reporters or copywriters. The linotype operator reproduces the words and letters in metal casts automatically by operating the keyboard of the machine which somewhat resembles that of a typewriter . . .
>
> In the photo-engraving process, the copy prepared in the editorial and advertising departments must be type-written twice before it goes to the composing room. The first time it is written on typewriters in column form with a notation at the end of each line telling how many spaces have been taken in the line.
>
> This copy goes to Varitype operators who adjust their machines according to the notations made by the pre-typers so that each line in the column of the finally typed product is "justified," i.e., comes out even on the right hand margin. Thus these pre-typists and Varitypists serve the purpose of a composing room in the new process.
>
> The finished copy from the Varitypers, together with the original written material supplied by writers and reporters, is passed along to a table where editorial employes have been pressed into service to check the typists' copy against the original.

SOCIETY DESK

TYPEWRITERS

FEATURES DESK

FINANCIAL DESK

PICTURE DESK

VARI-TYPERS

A view of the newsroom on the fourth floor of The Tribune which for the last two weeks has been published without the aid of printers who are on strike. Legends indicate the var produce editions

# lish Every Day Without the Aid of Printers

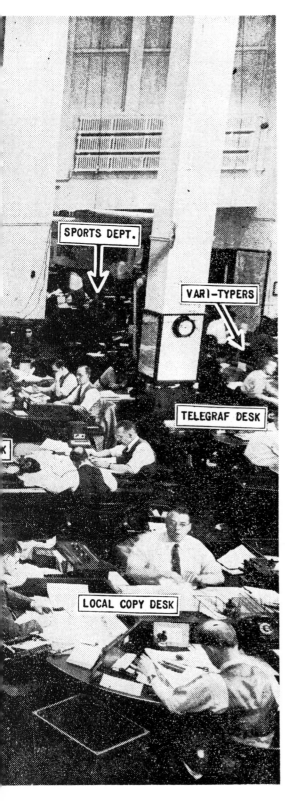

SPORTS DEPT.

VARI-TYPERS

TELEGRAF DESK

LOCAL COPY DESK

-engraving process has made it possible to
tories.  (Tribune Photo)

One of the desks at which heads are set by taping
cardboard letters together.  (Tribune Photo)

In the meantime, headlines for each story are written by copyreaders and sent separately to the art room where columns of Varityped material have been assembled. There the headlines are set by pasting strips of individual letters together with Scotch tape. When the typed stories are brought in from the proof readers they are matched with the proper headlines and pasted on sheets of cardboard which have been marked to show where news matter and advertising matter are to be placed on each page.

These pasted pages are sent to the engraving room where they are reproduced as zinc etchings by the photo-engraving process. The etchings are then put together page by page. Pictures and advertising displays are fitted into the news matter like pieces of a jigsaw puzzle until each page is complete . . .

. . . Once all the pieces of the page are in place, the stereotype process of pressing a mat, drying it and casting a type metal shell for the press cylinders is carried out in the usual manner . . .[1]

Thus, the practicality of cold type was proved. Today, the use of computerized typesetting or a far more sophisticated system of cold type is on the increase to the benefit of everyone.

# The Cold Type Offset Process

Photo-offset and cold-type composition have contributed even more to visual communication. Let us see how the *St. Louis Post-Dispatch,* a large and venerable Mid-West daily and Sunday publication recently went from letterpress to cold type offset production. The discussion that follows appeared in a special section of that newspaper at the time the changeover was made.[2]

### THE ST. LOUIS POST-DISPATCH SPENDS $10,000,000 FOR IMPROVEMENTS

Radically new methods of printing and distribution are now being used by the *Post-Dispatch,* which is spending more than $10,000,000 in a program to improve legibility of the newspaper and provide much quicker delivery to readers.

New presses, computers, and other automated machinery have been put into operation, making the *Post-Dispatch* the first large metropolitan newspaper in the United States to be printed by the offset process instead of letterpress. In another major change, the newspaper is discontinuing use of hot metal in a switch to what is called "cold type."

The combination of cold type and offset printing is designed for more exact duplication of type and superior reproduction of pictures. Construction of an auxiliary printing plant in St. Louis county makes possible speedier delivery of papers to subscribers in outlying areas where population growth is greatest.

For almost 100 years newspapers have been using type that was set mechanically, by pressing keys on the clanking machine called a Linotype, a typesetter produced lines of type cast from molten lead, or hot metal. As he typed, he had to judge as best he could whether a line was running short and should be

---

1. *Chicago Daily Tribune,* December 8, 1947.

2. Special Section, *St. Louis-Post Dispatch,* June 24, 1973. Written by Harry Wilensky of the *Post-Dispatch* staff. Photographs by Robert C. Holt, Jr., technical director of photography for the *Post-Dispatch,* unless otherwise noted.

spaced out, or running long and should be compressed by allotting less space between words. Now this guessing is eliminated. A computer into which a dictionary has been incorporated takes care of spacing out the lines of type and hyphenating when necessary.

Abandoning the cumbersome Linotype, the printer now perforates tape by using a typewriter-like keyboard. The tape goes into the computer, then through a high-speed photocomposition machine. A lens in the photocompositor picks up images of type characters and transfers them to a paper film. After being run through a developing processor and dried, the picture of the type called cold type is pasted into the proper location on a page. Composition of advertisements is handled in the same way.

The *Post-Dispatch,* which also prints the *Globe-Democrat,* has installed five offset presses, each geared to print up to 55,000 papers an hour. A sixth press has been ordered.

The October 18, 1974 Research Institute Bulletin, published by the American Newspaper Publishers Association, featured a talk on Printing Plate Systems by Frank J. Stanczak. Among other things, Mr. Stanczak revealed that of the more than 1100 "newspapers with a circulation of 50,000, 68% are produced by photo-offset; 21% stereotype letterpress and 11% from direct zinc, magnesium, or a photo polymer plate." Although the percentage varies in newspapers having a circulation of 10,000 and the larger ones, a breakdown gives a clue as to how printing processes are changing in the newspaper publishing world. Photo-offset has had a big effect on photojournalism—especially in the many suburban newspapers around large cities. Photo-offset production is more economical. More than that, it allows more versatility and greater fidelity in the reproduction of photographs.

The letterpresses printed from the raised surfaces of metal plates. The raised surfaces, after being inked, carried the impressions onto the paper, while the depressed surfaces did not print. The new offset presses print from flat, rather than raised, surfaces and use thin, lightweight aluminum plates instead of heavy castings.

The offset process is based on the natural repulsion between grease and water; moisture prevents greasy ink from sticking to the plate except where there is matter to be printed.

After the cold type and photographs have been pasted into place, each page of the newspaper is photographed to make a negative.[3]

Light passes through the negative and exposes the image onto the treated sheet of aluminum, and after the plate is placed on the press, a thin film of water is constantly directed on it. The part of the plate with the image rejects water and accepts ink; the nonimage area (constantly bathed in water) rejects ink.

The inked-plate image is not directly impressed on the paper. It is transferred from the plate to a rubber blanket wrapped around a metal cylinder. The transfer is called "offset" and gives this form of printing its name: the inked image is offset to the rubber blanket, and the newspaper is printed from the blanket.

---

3. Some newspapers prescreen the photographs to make a print, which is pasted in its proper place on the page layout. Then, using the process camera, they shoot the entire page as line copy before making the metal plate. Others shoot the line negative, and strip in the halftone negatives before printing the offset plate on metal.

Offset printing, by virtue of much finer detail, provides better reproduction than letterpress.[4] Type (as well as illustrations) is more clearly defined, making for improved legibility.

The *Post-Dispatch* and offset printing

The glass disk (*top,* opposite page) is one of the integral parts of the cold type printing process the *St. Louis Post-Dispatch* has combined with offset press work in its new printing plant in St. Louis county. The two systems, and others in the new plant, represent some of the most advanced technology in the newspaper printing industry—a space age away from such hallowed figures in the printing world as Gutenberg and Caxton . . . .

Briefly described, the process begins with glass disk, on which are printed a number of alphabets, sets of numerals, and punctuation symbols in various type faces. Five such disks are installed in photocompositor machines, which photograph sequences of characters to make up lines of type.

Pasteups of full individual newspaper pages are then made and photographed. The photograph is called a "PMT print" (photomechanical transfer) and looks like the one at *lower left* (opposite page) emerging from a print dryer.

Using a telephoto transmission system similar to that used to transmit wirephotos, the picture of the page is sent to the *Post-Dispatch* printing plant.

It is received as a negative, such as the one being examined on the light table (opposite page, *lower right*). This negative, in turn, is used in the production of metal printing plates for the presses.

*Post Dispatch* narration by Harry Wilensky and photographs (except as noted) by Robert C. Holt, Jr., both members of the *Post-Dispatch* staff.

# Photo-Offset and Computerization Are Here to Stay

In an article titled "Newspaper Industry Moving Into Computer Age" Roy Malone of the *Post-Dispatch* staff gave some interesting information:

> While some big city newspapers have folded or merged because of economic problems, the newspaper industry generally appears healthy. Since World War II the number of dailies has increased from 1,749 to 1,774 and the circulation rose from 43,384,188 in 1946 to 63,147,280 in 1973. In the last two years (1971–73), total circulation has gained by more than 1,000,000 according to figures in the *Editor and Publisher Yearbook* . . . And the Occupational Outlook Handbook of the Labor Department for 1972–74 said growth can be expected in the newspaper industry with a 5 to 6 percent yearly increase in revenues amounting to about 12 billion dollars by 1980. . .
>
> More than 100 newspapers in 1973 installed some type of new electronic copy processing system, using visual display terminals in place of typewriters or optical character readers.
>
> Visual display terminals [it was explained] consist of machines "with a television screen above a typewriter keyboard, linked to a computer, on which stories or advertisements can be written. Editors can call the copy onto their

---

4. Offset printing is a "kiss" impression and not a "squeeze" as is letterpress. Because of this, even though offset paper is little different than regular newsprint, it permits a much finer screen to be used.

The glass disk on which are printed a number of alphabets (*above left*) is one of the integral parts of the cold type printing process that the *St. Louis Post-Dispatch* has combined with offset press work in its $10,000,000 modernization program. A PMT (photomechanical transfer) print emerges from a dryer (*lower left*). *Next*, a telephone transmission system similar to that used to send pictures by wire is used to send the PMT print to the printing plant miles away. In the printing plant the transmission is received as a page-size negative (*lower right*) which is used to make the offset plate which goes on the press.

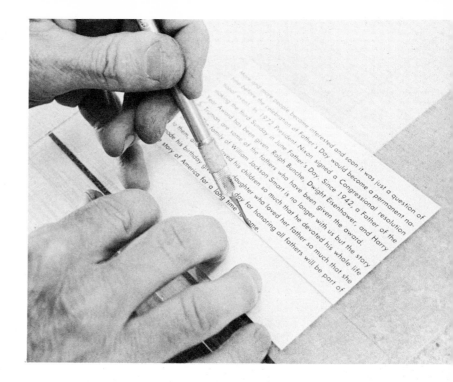

Type is set by computers in the photo-offset–produced *Post-Dispatch*. A tape (*below*) is perforated and processed through a computer to obtain line hyphenation and justification. The computer provides a new tape which operates a phototypesetting machine at the rate of 150 lines per minute. This unit photographs the characters and transfers them to a sensitized paper which is used in the pasteup of advertising and news pages. (See illustrations at *right*.)

Workers at the *Post-Dispatch* (*above*) in the letterpress composing room use considerably more space than is required with the computerized cold type system. The hot type process in which the typesetting machines squirted hot lead into a mold to make the required "lines of type" also were used to make matrices (*left*) with which to cast lead shells in the stereotyping department. (Photo by Jack January.)

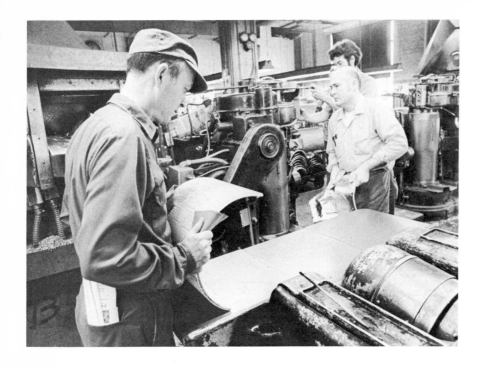

The picture (*left*), taken in June 1973 at the *Post-Dispatch* downtown plant, shows the casting of a lead shell or plate in the stereotyping department. This casting is placed directly on the letterpress printing unit. This operation is not used in the offset printing method. Instead, a plate processor produces an aluminum plate that is mounted on the offset press.

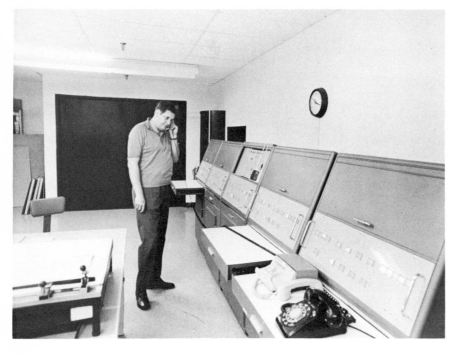

The *Post-Dispatch* uses five transmitters and five receivers connected by Southwestern Bell Telephone cables. A Velox print is placed on a transmission cylinder. It is electronically scanned and transmitted to the northwest plant where it is received as a film negative. After processing and drying, the negative is used for making an offset plate. Each transmitter can send a page in 2.55 minutes.

screens for changes or proofreading and then route it electronically to photo-composition devices for typesetting. (Picture storage and recall, too, is being used today.) At the *Post-Dispatch,* page layout is by pasteup, but eventually full pages, or the entire newspaper, may be set electronically."[5]

From the foregoing, we can see that newspapers, like photojournalism itself, are certainly not dead. Techniques will continue to change, of course, and the photojournalist of the future must be much more knowledgeable than was his successor a half-century ago.

5. *St. Louis Post-Dispatch,* April 28, 1974.

Photo-Offset Newspapers

# Student Participation

As mentioned in a previous chapter, two of the three printing methods are letterpress (raised surface or relief), and photo-offset (planography). The third method of printing is gravure (intaglio).

1. Which of the three printing methods was used by the *Chicago Tribune* in the late 1940s when type compositors were on strike, and typewritten copy was photoengraved before being locked in a form, matted, and stereotyped?
2. How does this type of composition differ from metal slugs produced on a Linotype or Intertype linecasting machine?
3. What are some of the advantages of photo-offset printing as now practiced by the *St. Louis Post-Dispatch?*
4. Generally speaking, why does offset printing in a newspaper result in finer detail and better halftone printing than does letterpress?
5. Once again, as for Chapter 3, select three examples each of newspaper letterpress printing, of offset printing, and of photogravure printing—all nine examples in color.

# Photojournalism Today

# 13

By William H. Strode III

A newspaper's function is to serve the public. This service takes many forms: keeping people informed about local, national, and international happenings, making the news clear and relevant, and at the same time providing human interest and entertainment.

The photographer plays an important role in fulfilling these functions. Lewis Hine, who photographed in the early 1900s, said, "Photography could light up darkness and expose ignorance."

Photographs used skillfully in a newspaper can accomplish these ideals. So newspaper photographers must be responsible journalists who follow the advice of Carl Mydans, "Take your pictures with your mind, heart, and a camera."

This is the approach to which we aspire at the *Courier-Journal,* The *Louisville Times,* and the *Courier-Journal & Times Magazine.*

To achieve these goals, we seek to put as much responsibility as possible on the individual photographer. He is thought of as a journalist. He is encouraged to produce his own ideas. And he is responsible for the content of his photographs. With these concepts in mind, we built our present photographic operation.

There seems to be a new feeling, a new horizon as to what today's newspapers are trying to achieve. As Norman Isaacs, former executive editor of the *Courier-Journal* and the *Louisville Times,* once said, "Many descriptions have been given of what we are seeking to achieve in depth reporting, and in interpretive journalism, in bringing about the evolution to a form of a daily news magazine".[1]

Whatever the description, what we say we are striving for is a journalism different from what we have today. We are striving for a way to take the news of this complex society of ours and present it in a far more intelligible form. We want our readers—and viewers—to have something other than the bits and pieces of today's journalism. We want them to see the world in a broader context with a background and interpretation that will enable the citizen to understand the real meaning of the events that evolve around us.

The photographer as a communicator must use his pictures to enable the reader to understand his fellow man and discover the world around him. The

Wm. H. Strode III, assistant director of photography, explain the philosophy behind the photographic operation of a great, modern newspaper, the Louisvil *Courier-Journal* and the *Louisville Times.*

Wm. H. Strode III

photographer must probe the individual mind and probe the larger society. He must present people to people. His pictures must have content and meaning, and they must convey this meaning to the reader and viewer.

In our constant effort to achieve meaningful pictures, we try to give each photographer time to cover his assignment adequately, regardless of whether that time is one hour or three months. We try to find photographic assignments that are meaningful to the community, and we expect the photographer to photograph with understanding and feeling.

There is a commitment to good photography from management and from editors. And there is a continuing education program professionally and academically for photographers. Daily picture page and magazine photographic essay ideas are discussed by editor and photographer. Our stories often look not only at the event, but also behind the event to report its cause or deeper meaning.

Obviously, not every photograph in the newspaper is a profound statement. There is a definite place for pictures that simply and quietly mirror the world around us and the way we live in it, pictures that bring a smile or a moment of relief to a reader in an otherwise hurried day. The little things as well as the big make up life.

# Structure of Photographic Department

Our photographic department has a combined staff of thirty-four people who work for both the *Courier-Journal* and the *Louisville Times*. The department is organized into many areas of responsibilities.

*News*

Thirteen general-assignment photographers produce the news and feature pictures and picture stories for both the morning and evening papers.

*Sunday*

In addition to the general-assignment photographers, three photographers work exclusively for the combined *Courier-Journal & Times* Sunday paper and the *Sunday Magazine*.

*Special Assignment*

Even though each photographer is capable of covering any type of assignment, we have several areas where the majority of work is done by specialists. Most of our aerial photographs are taken by one person, who also pilots our plane. The single-engine plane is flown almost daily for taking aerial photography, for making film pickups, or for transporting reporters and photographers around our two-state (Kentucky and Indiana) coverage area. Color food photography is another area of specialization. *Scene,* a Saturday tabloid leisure magazine, has one photographer who does the majority of its work.

---

1. Norman Isaacs, Speech in Louisville before the National Press Photographers Convention, 1968.

*Advertising Photographs*

Two photographers work exclusively for the newspapers' advertising department.

*Photographer Beats*

Many of the general-assignments photographers are interested in specific areas of news coverage. One photographer is interested in police and penal institutions, another in wildlife and farming, another in the fire department. We have been experimenting in allowing these photographers time to pursue their areas of interest.

*Laboratory Technicians*

Even though our photographers do much of their own laboratory work, we have five specially trained technicians.

*Picture Editors*

The *Courier-Journal* and the *Louisville Times* each has a picture editor and an assistant picture editor. Even though they are part of the combined photography department, each set of editors works only for his or her particular paper.

*Administrators*

Administrators include the directors of photography, a photographic department manager, and a secretary.

# Picture Editors

The picture desks are the focal points for all visuals produced by each paper. Assignments for both pictures and artwork are the responsibility of those on the picture desk, who also advise how they are to be used.

Picture editors work with the city desks, reporters, and photographers to produce the daily picture assignments. Each department's requests for picture assignments are filtered through the picture desk, where they are approved or killed. Part of the picture editor's job is to see that there are enough pictures each day to meet the demands of publication and also to make certain we do not cover more assignments than we can use. When assignments are held to a reasonable number, the photographer knows the paper has the room and the intention to publish his picture if the event turns out to be as worthy as anticipated. This puts a responsibility on the photographer to produce. It also helps give him the time he needs to make good pictures by eliminating marginal assignments that could keep him running instead of thinking and photographing.

The picture desks are also responsible for the selection of pictures. This is sometimes done by conferring with the photographer, but more often than not the editor makes his selections from contact sheets. These selections are then presented to page editors. At this point, too, the picture editors discuss cropping and sizing with the page editors and at the same time do a bit of lobbying for what they believe is the most effective use.

Besides the pictures and photographic illustrations that go with stories, the newspapers publish many freestanding pictures. Assignments for these pictures come from the picture editors. It is up to them to ferret out the news events that have visual human interest potential independent of story coverage. These possibilities are gleaned from future stories, suburban or community newspapers, area magazines, working relationships built up with news sources in agencies and organizations, photographers, reporters, and telephone tips. The picture editor, in effect, is a visual city editor.

Even though the picture editors are part of the photographic department organizationally, they are on a level with city, womens', and sports editors.

The *Louisville Times* produces a "picture page" each day, the minimum size being 9½ by 14¾ inches. This picture layout, which is always on a single subject, sometimes is related to a front page story. More often than not, however, it is a feature layout telling its own story. Sometimes a series may run for three or four days on a single topic. Both features and news stories are used for the picture page.

The picture desk gives the photographer the opportunity to conceive, photograph, and lay out the picture page if he wishes to do so. Even though the photographer is given the opportunity to present a completed package, more often than not the picture editor and the photographer work together on the picture selection and layout.

The picture editors also work with all the department editors and the art department on other picture layouts in the other sections of the paper.

There are times when a drawing or sketch will illustrate a story better than a photograph. The picture editors work directly with the art department in planning such illustrations.

Dull and posed pictures, those depicting check passing, ground breaking, handshaking, and large groups of people are almost never assigned or used in the *Courier-Journal* or the *Louisville Times*. Instead, we use our time and effort to make pictures that are of more concern to the entire community, pictures with content that tell the important story of a news-related event or the reason for the event. For example, we would seek to publish a story and pictures of overcrowded conditions at the community hospital—the reason for a new hospital ground breaking—rather than a picture of the ground breaking itself.

Freestanding feature pictures often result from the enterprise system. Under this system, a photographer is allowed time to photograph an idea he has or to roam the city or countryside looking for pictures.

Our photographic coverage sometimes takes staff photographers across the country and sometimes around the world, but our primary job, we feel, is to give good local coverage to Louisville and good regional coverage to Kentucky and Indiana.

Because we believe our first responsibility is to our community, we photograph city council meeting activities (or related problems), local high school

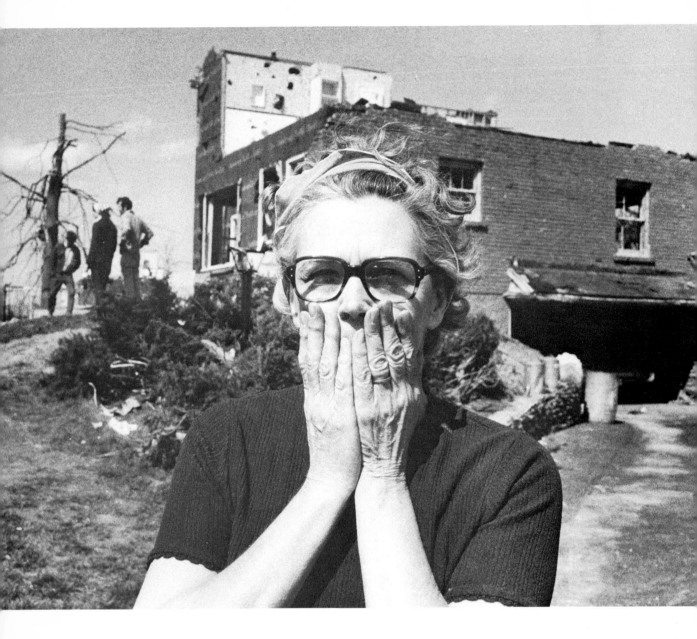

Pictures must have content and meaning.
A successful picture is one that makes a
statement or tells a story. This one tells us
that more than a tornado had come through
town. It shows the reaction and emotion
of a tornado victim.

and college sports events, and other local events more than we do national or
international events.

We use many criteria in selecting a staff photographer. The most important
are: his ability to "see" photographically, his feeling and understanding of
people, his potential, and his educational background.

We expect our photographers to have the ability to handle any photographic
situation including available-light candid photography, 8-by-10-inch studio
photography, fashion and food pictures, and lighting of complete buildings
or arenas.

A picture that is different—one that tells a
story—is the objective of every photojourna
ist. The page-one picture used in the
*Louisville Times* Tuesday evening, July 14,
1970, met these requirements. This picture
by staffer Bryan Moss portrays the reactions
of local people when President Nixon came
to town.

Photojournalism Today

TOIL 'N' BROIL

# THE LOUISVILLE TIMES

RED FLASH

VOL. CLXXIII—No. 64 ★★★★★    LOUISVILLE, TUESDAY EVENING, JULY 14, 1970    48 PAGES    TEN CENTS

# Enthusiastic Welcome by Kentuckians Draws Happy Response From President

## Top Aides Also Arrive For Meeting

By DICK KIESCHTEN
Louisville Times Staff Writer

President Richard Milhous Nixon, on exuberant strode into the heart of America, shook hands with citizens on Louisville street corners early this afternoon.

The President, whose plane touched down at Standiford Field slot moments before noon, left by automobile twice to mingle with the crowds in his motorcade wended its way toward the new Federal Building.

Mr. Nixon, who was here to confer with the governors of 13 Appalachian states, and representatives of two others, arrived at enthusiastic welcome from

**More pictures on the President's visit to Louisville are on Page B1.**

thousands of sun-drenched citizens with placards massed at the airport and lined the route of his downtown passage.

Police estimated the crowd at Standiford Field variously at 5,000 and 7,500.

Police Chief C. J. Hyde said about 7,500 persons were at the airport. He said he drove the route of the President ahead of the President's car and estimated the number of persons along the route at 50,000 or so.

Mr. Nixon arrived at the Federal Building at 1 p.m.

Hands high and face beaming, President Nixon is surrounded by a welcoming crowd at the Federal Building. Presidential counselor Daniel P. Moynihan is at left.

## Louisvillians Get a Look At a President

The youngster—he couldn't have been more than 10 years old—was pushed forward by the press of the crowd.

He looked up at a face a few feet in front of him, one of many in the pushing throng. He recognized the face immediately.

"Boy, it's the President," he exclaimed.

This was the scene at Fourth and Broadway where President Richard M. Nixon paused in his motorcade trip from Standiford Field to the new Federal Building shortly after noon today.

Mr. Nixon was greeted by enthusiastic crowds as his car swept along Broadway from the North-South Expressway to Fourth, but the most excited response came as he ordered his car stopped and stepped out into the crowd at Fourth.

**Bodyguards Look Worried**

The President, flanked by worried-looking Secret Service agents and Louisville police officers, was immediate to swamped by hundreds who had awaited his arrival under a very hot noonday sun.

Mr. Nixon beamed as he briskly shook the proffered hands. After several minutes of mingling—and occasionally struggling with the crowd, he returned

to his car and again turned to the people.

The President spotted a black youngster boosted onto someone's shoulders and beckoned for him to be brought closer. Leaning precariously from his open-roofed car, Mr. Nixon grasped the child's hand.

More hands were offered. A few were briskly gripped and shaken.

Gov. Louie B. Nunn, traveling in the same car as the President looked uncomfortably hot and at one point lapsed into a grimace which quickly turned into a smile.

The governor joined in the handshaking, and then the brief stop was over.

At the corner of Fourth and Walnut, the cheering and clapping continued, and then a hush came down as the President left his car to shake hands and thank his welcomers.

After working through the crowd for awhile he returned to his car, climbed on its roof and offered a now familiar gesture, spread hands above his head. Then he hopped down onto the crowd.

The visiting over, the President climbed back in his limousine, not to get out again until he reached the Federal Building.

At about Founders Square, Mr. Nixon dropped his smile for a moment, checked

his watch, and the procession sped on, police reporters and Secret Service men all breaking into a run.

He whipped past a small contingent of young people carrying anti-war signs, such as "Get Off the War" and "Thanks for Cambodia" at the corner of Walnut and Sixth.

At the Federal Building the 113th Army Band from Ft. Knox struck up "Ruffles and Flourishes" and "Anchors Aweigh" just before the President's arrival a few minutes before 1 p.m.

The President and Gov. Nunn stood together with their hands and shoulders through the open sunroof of the presidential limousine. Perspiring Secret Service men trotted on foot in front of and beside the presidential car and police on motorcycles forced the crowd back on each side.

The President shook hands with a large number of spectators and waved several times at the federal employees who used the windows of the building above him.

The 13 visiting Appalachia-area governors emerged from the Federal Building before the President's arrival. Most of them stood in a group, chatting on the

See LOUISVILLIANS
Back page, col. 1, this section

## Governors Are Lent A Presidential Ear

easier as the crowds pressed toward the President, but there were no untoward incidents.

At the Federal Building, approximately 2,000 people crowded into the Federal Square park southwest of the building, awaiting Mr. Nixon. The President, after shaking hands with the Appalachian governors, pushed his way through the dense to the microphone and introduced himself.

He said, "I want to tell you how very grateful I am for this wonderful reception.

The President spoke haltingly at first, still breathing heavily from his exertion in pushing through the crowd. He said, "The President meeting with the governors is not unusual. It's not unusual for the Cabinet to meet with the governors. What is unusual in Washington coming to Kentucky, the government coming to Kentucky."

In his brief remarks at the airport, Mr. Nixon commented on the theme that the "real America" and, by implication, the real currents of public opinion, is to be found in such areas centers as Louisville.

The President was accompanied by several of his top advisers including presidential counselors Bryce N. Harlow, John Ehrlichman, and Daniel Patrick Moynihan; George Shultz, director of the newly created Office of Budget Management; Donald Rumsfeld, director of the U.S. Office of Economic Opportunity; Secretary of Agriculture Clifford M. Harding, and Secretary of Labor James Hodgson.

Mr. Nixon, tanned and wearing a blue suit, was greeted at Standiford Field by Kentucky Gov. Louie B. Nixon, Jefferson

See ENTHUSIASTIC
Back page, col. 1, this section

---

JUDGE SAYS IT'S OK

## The Latest in Courtesy: Offer a Lady a Barstool

FRANKFORT, Ky. (AP) — Franklin Circuit Judge Henry Meigs has ruled that women cannot be prohibited from tending bar to bring served mixed drinks at...

The judge said the state civil-rights ordinances or superseding statutes that were luck activities in women.

The anti-discrimination statute, he said, takes the state and necessary implicating that law against women in this field to be insured.

The ruling was handed down yesterday.

The state Alcoholic Beverage Control Board, had suspended for five days the alcoholic beverage licenses issued to Diane Sherston Burke doing business as Diot's Blues Room.

Prosecution argued that Mrs. Burke is operating a tavern bartender, and all the women to be served at the bar.

A Kentucky ABC regulation permits a woman to act as a bartender only if she holds the license for the establishment.

yes in violation of both state and federal law.

The ABC board did not indicate immediately if it would in turn appeal Meigs' ruling to the Court of Appeals, Kentucky's highest court.

The statutes involved say that women may serve only as waitresses, ushers or cashiers in premises where liquor or beer is sold and may be served only at tables where food is served—though food need not be served at the same time as liquor.

Meigs said the ABC board order against Mrs. Burke was "unreasonable and contrary to law" because the civil-rights statute repudiates what he called the discriminatory portion of the other statutes.

A similar suit was filed in March 1969 in U.S. District Court in Lexington by a Covington cafe owner and his barmaid, John Reed and Betty Morris, on the basis of federal anti-discrimination laws.

Today, we can understand that.

Inside the license for the establishment.

## In Today's Times

**Louisville Needs Pride**

A dose of "fierce emotional commitment" would result in a new stadium to serve as a symbol of the city's pride, businessman William Stone declares in "Sound Off," The Times' forum for comment, Page A11.

**Just Like Old Times**

Ex-Yankee Jim Bouton describes

his return to a pennant race in the last of a 10-part series on B5.

### Where to Look

| | | |
|---|---|---|
| Business | B10 | Movies, Stage A16 |
| Calendar | | News of Record A15 |
| Of Events | A14 | Obituaries A12 |
| Editorials | A10 | Sports B4 |
| Lemme Doit | B1 | TV, Radio B2 |
| | | Women's News A18 |

## President Doesn't Sway Weather

Leaping lizards! Mr. Weatherman:

Sure, we want our Very Important Visitor to feel at home. And we know Washington, D.C., is noted for its uncomfortable summer weather.

Today, we can understand. But, tomorrow, too?

Tomorrow is expected to be mostly

sunny and humid again, with a high in the mid-90s after a low tonight in the low-70s (the added ingredient tomorrow will be a 30 per cent chance of rain).

Thursday is supposed to be slightly cooler, but with a chance of thundershowers.

Louisville's cup of hospitality runneth over.

## Governors Are Lent A Presidential Ear

By JIM RENNEISEN and FRANK CLIFFORD
Louisville Times Staff Writers

The governors of Appalachia had a blue ribbon audience for their lobbying efforts here today.

Seated around a rectangular conference table in Room 629 in the new Federal Building were President Richard M. Nixon and several of his top aides.

Eleven Appalachian governors were looking on behalf of the regional concept of dealing with the nation's domestic problems.

Reporters were not allowed inside the conference. However, according to a presidential aide, Mr. Nixon told the governors:

Sometimes when we think of Washington, those of us at the highest levels feel as though we are in an isolation booth, like in the old quiz shows where the man inside cannot hear what's going on outside. We're trying to break out of the iso-

lation booth . . . . We have come here today to get your views.

At the start of the meeting, it was learned that the governors outlined the basic administrative guidelines that they are necessary to adapt the approach of the Appalachian Regional Commission (ARC) on a nationwide basis.

In essence, the guidelines would continue state and federal resources for the sake of solving regional problems and for setting regional improvements.

The governors said: During the last five years we have witnessed the implementation of a highly successful and innovative program conducted by the ARC. We believe that the major key to the success of that program has been the partnership and the decision-making role that has been given to the Appalachian states.

The governors represented 13 states from Pennsylvania to Mississippi.

Kentucky Gov. Louie B. Nixon was a

See GOVERNORS
Back page, col. 3, this section

O beautiful for spacious skies, for amber waves of grain,
For purple mountain majesties, above the fruited plain.

# AMERICA, AMERICA

God shed His grace on thee,

And crown thy good,
With brotherhood,
From sea to shining sea.

This picture page (*above*) in the *Courier-Journal & Times Magazine* is an example of teamwork by both photographer and picture editor. Bill Luster had been shooting this July 4 feature for several weeks while covering other assignments.

Killer Tornado

# Twisted Brandenburg ...

## Pastor has seen it before—in war

By HOWARD ROSENBERG
Louisville Times Staff Writer

BRANDENBURG, Ky — An Army chaplain from Ft. Knox looked inside Central Elementary school and decided he had seen it all before.

In Vietnam.

And the Rev. Thomas Stokes, pastor of Wolf Creek Baptist Church in nearby Battletown, stood outside the building and said:

"Some of them don't even look like they got faces. One woman got a stick right through her face."

This is tornado-ravaged Brandenburg, Ky. It's the seat of Meade County, just down the Ohio River from Louisville.

Earlier in the day, the school had been a building of laughing and playing children.

Last night it was a building of death, a temporary morgue, caught in the piercing flash of blue emergency lights and the bark of police radios. Men in jackets with shirttails out stared into the lights with glazed eyes.

Inside were the disfigured remains of those who died in the tornado—36 had been counted by 6 a.m. The town's population is about 1,700.

Many more were missing and the death toll was expected to rise with the coming of daylight.

It was a grotesque, unforgettable sight, bodies resembling torn rag dolls lying in the school's dimly lit corridor.

They were on the floor. There weren't enough cots to go around.

A middle-aged man walked up to the building. "Anybody know who is in there?"

"Looking for someone?"

"My wife and three kids."

Practically everyone was still looking for someone.

The dead were removed from the morgue during the night and taken to area mortuaries for embalming. They were to be returned in the morning for viewing and identification.

Mr. Stokes was there to comfort relatives of victims. A few identifications were made by close relatives. Most bore up well.

But one man asked Mr. Stokes, "If God is a good god, and He loves us, why did it happen?"

"That was a good question," Mr. Stokes said.

"I answered that God didn't do it. It happened."

Evidence of the happening was everywhere. "You pick bodies up, and they break all to pieces," said a state trooper.

Meade County Judge James Greer was in his Courthouse office, talking to a man who wanted a beer license, when the twister touched down in Brandenburg at approximately 4:10 p.m. "I could hear a whistle in the background," he said. "And it kept getting stronger and stronger."

Postmaster Thomas Tichenor was coming. "We wanted to get to a wall. It was kinda twisting back and forth. We didn't know which way to go."

Tichenor made it under a table just before the Post Office window blew in. "It screamed like it was a jet," he recalled.

But Post Office clerk Owen Dugan's

See BRANDENBURG
Back page, col. 2, this section

# THE LOUISVILLE TIMES

VOL. CLXXX—No. 130    88 PAGES    THURSDAY EVENING, APRIL 4, 1974    TEN CENTS    HOME EDITION

Copyright © 1974, The Louisville Times

Big new homes became piles of sticks and bricks yesterday after a tornado struck the sixth-class city of Northfield. This view looks southward from Newmarket Drive. In the background is the Watterson Express.
Staff Photo by Billy

# Killer tornado rips 10-mile gash in count

By MARTIN E. BIEMER
Louisville Times Staff Writer

Nature's forces collided over a broad part of the nation yesterday, and it may take Louisvillians many weeks to recover.

A tornado, part of a storm system that stretched from Alabama to Ontario, cut a 10-mile-long swath through densely settled residential and commercial areas in Louisville.

The death toll was almost miraculously low. Officials said four people died as a direct result of the storm in Jefferson County.

For the nation, it was the worst tornado disaster since Palm Sunday, April 11, 1965, when 271 people were killed.

For Kentucky, it was the worst tornado disaster since March 27, 1890, when at least 76 people lost their lives in Louisville alone. Seventy-seven persons reportedly died across Kentucky.

In addition 63 persons were reported dead from twisters in Indiana.

The tornado that struck Louisville yesterday apparently was the same one that struck Brandenburg, Ky, about 25 miles southwest of Louisville along the Ohio River.

The death toll at Brandenburg was 30. John Burke, meteorologist-in-charge at

## Storm section

Coverage of yesterday's storm is concentrated in a special section, which begins on Page B1.

the National Weather Service station at Standiford Field, said the twister was tracked on weather-service radar.

He said it apparently lifted into the air after leaving Brandenburg, passed over West Point and Kosmosdale, and may have clipped the top of the hill in Iroquois Park.

"It touched down in the parking lot right here at the airport," he said. "A piece of roof from the west wing of the terminal blew off."

Then, Burke said, it continued to swirl "along the ground or very close to it" in a northeasterly path across the city until it appeared to lift into the clouds somewhere northeast of Brownsboro Road and Lime Kiln Lane.

Burke said the swirling winds in the funnel probably reached "200 to 300 miles per hour" as it smashed across the city.

The extensive damage began at the Kentucky State Fairgrounds and continued through Audubon Park, Calvary Cemetery, along Eastern Parkway to

Cherokee Park, through the over or past the Interstate 64 Grinstead Drive, past the Water Co.'s filtration plant, through the suburbs of Rolling Indian Hills, Northfield, and tween them.

More damage was reported of Northfield, near the entra Harbour Manor subdivision ne Lane and Brownsboro Road.

Kentucky National Guards all available police officers

See KILLER TORN
Back page, col. 1

# Water expected to be restored today; boil before drinking, company warns

By RICHARD KRANTZ
Louisville Times Staff Writer

Water was expected to be restored to most Louisville homes and businesses by early afternoon today. But all drinking water should be boiled until further notice, spokesmen for the Louis...

About six main roads in eastern Louisville and Jefferson County were partially blocked during the morning, but officials said they hoped to have them open by noon today.

These streets included sections of Bardstown Road, Eastern Parkway,

Frankfort Avenue, Grinstead Drive, Brownsboro Road and Top Hill Road.

As dawn broke over Louisville, the crippled city seemed to face several days of struggle before its daily life returned to a semblance of normalcy.

Water shortage was the most critical problem that threatened the city immedi...

# Cooler weather is returning with clouds

Cooler weather is returning to Louisville with a low tonight in the upper 30s and a high tomorrow of around 50.

Tomorrow will be mostly cloudy, with a 30 per cent chance of showers.

Gusty winds to 20 miles an hour ...

# Aides say Nixon may ne a loan to make tax paym

By FRANK CORMIER
Associated Press

White House officials say President Nixon, facing a federal tax bill for about half his reported net worth, probably will be forced to borrow money to make the payments.

Mr. Nixon announced through aides last night that he would pay about $465,000 in back income taxes and interest after being told privately ...

Nixon proposed to meet a tax est bill of about $465,000; us use some resources and pay for the rest.

The White House announce the IRS report contained no fraud on the part of the Pre...

The IRS contended that claimed deductions for a controversial gift of dential papers to the Nat... The papers were valued at ...

It was a time for comforting and consolation among family members.

# Northfield: a community in the wake of tragedy

One of the areas hardest hit by yesterday's tornado was the suburban development of Northfield, at the junction of Interstates 71 and 264. People left homeless and in shock by the storm dug out and began leaving the area to take refuge elsewhere.

STAFF PHOTOS BY LARRY SPITZER, EXCEPT AS INDICATED

Leigh Ann Jaggers, 7, cried as her mother led her from their home in Northfield.

Several residents of Northfield made the trek away from the area, passing by a scene of destruction in the background.

# COWHERD

*a photographer's last look at Indiana*

Some many months ago The Courier-Journal & Times Magazine com-
missioned Barney Cowherd, a nationally known photographer, to
create a photo-essay to be entitled "In Search of Indiana." Cowherd,
a Louisvillian who had become a Hoosier by choice, accepted the
assignment with a sense of personal curiosity. He had experienced
Indiana as a matter of course for years; what would he find if for the
first time he focused deliberately on scenes so familiar to him? Barney
Cowherd never fully accomplished his mission. Last month, after a
long struggle with cancer, he died. What he did complete was a
series of photographs that will ever remain a tribute to his skill. And
something else; as he says below, Barney Cowherd found himself.

*At Mount Vernon*

### By BARNEY COWHERD

Most people think everything that happens in a state
happens in a city. That's not entirely true.
In search of Indiana I went to the land. Anyone could
go around his home block and find man if he
would only stop and look. What I found around
the block of rural Indiana was a place
where you can still enjoy the land—and yourself.

*Near Bloomington*

*A church at Columbus*

*A tree near Nashville*

### COWHERD

Man leaves his mark on the land, and man leaves his
mark on man. The two cannot be separated, for man now is
part of the land. Each must contribute to the other. We must live
in harmony with the land. This harmony is evident
in the delicate beauty of Indiana for all who stop and view.

*A farm near Franklin*

**Photo Essay.** This photo essay on Indiana
is typical of those run by the *Louisville
Courier-Journal & Times Magazine.* The
essay was a tribute to the memory of Barney
Cowherd and appeared with appropriate
black border in the issue of September 10,
1972, after Barney's death.

Paoli

Monroe County

Near Bramer

Pekin/Posey(?)

## COWHERD

Have you ever listened to
the clippity-clop
of a squeaky Amish buggy,
the wash blowing
in the breeze, or the
laughter of the young?

Have you ever listened to
the trees growing?
Sometimes just sit and
listen. You will find
another Indiana, and maybe
another you. I did.

Greenville

---

Hindostan Falls near Loogootee

MeLissA I Love you
9/27/70

Near New Albany

## COWHERD

Small, unrelated things brought the biggest
question of my search: Whatever happened to love?
I saw a man wanting to sell his love seat
and asked why. He said he didn't need it any more.
The bad news of the war, crime in
the streets, tensions and fears, they were all right
here in Hoosierland. But in the young people
I saw love — and answers to many
questions. Behind the masks of long hair, drugs,
free love, nudity and the rest, there
were only people. I do not know if I found
Indiana in my search. But I found that among
the people and places I photographed, I belonged.
In my search I found a home
and myself. Too bad it was too late.

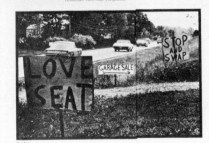

Borden

169

# Ethics

Over the years newspapers have built a credibility gap of their own. The remark that "you can't believe what you read in the newspapers" applies to photographs as well as to words. Unfortunate as it is, there are many reasons for this kind of thinking. The credibility gap of the visual image has been widened by television's early exploitation of photography.

If the desecration of the visual image continues, even the long established fact that photography is rooted in reality will not save it. Photographers must protect the faith in the photograph. To do this, they must be responsible, and responsibility among other things means serving with good taste. It also means operating with regard for the public and photographing only the truth.

If a photographer pictures—and we publish—an untrue situation, even if only one person is involved, two people will know it. The person photographed and the photographer. That is two too many.

The responsibility demanded of journalists today is far beyond anything we may have ever dreamed possible, and we can never forget it.

To this end we do not set up situations on the pretense that they are actually happening. We do not contrive pictures. (We do use photographic illustrations, but they are clearly identified as such.) We do not mutilate photographic prints by cutting, extensive retouching, or pasting in objects. These are all lies, and our paper does not publish lies.

If an honest, human mistake is made in our paper, we correct the error as soon as it is discovered in columns called "Beg Your Pardon" and "We Were Wrong."

In another area which has to do with ethics, our news people do not accept free tickets, free transportation, free samples, free memberships, or anything free from our news sources. Members of the news staff also do not work for pay (moonlighting) for any company or any other profit or nonprofit organization in our circulation area.

This policy is absolutely necessary, because our papers claim always to be neutral and fair in their handling of news, if we are to be *believed by others* to be neutral, fair, and untainted by outside influence.[2]

# Sunday Magazine

Locally edited Sunday magazines have a unique opportunity to add another dimension to newspapers by providing a magazine approach to news.

Magazine journalism is quite different from newspaper journalism in its approach, style, and content. Newspaper magazines on a regional level help fill the void created by the demise in recent years of several major national magazines.

Locally produced stories, written or photographic, about and for local people have a distinct advantage that national magazines cannot provide.

Unfortunately, far too many Sunday magazines have been forever gentle, unprovocative, and sweetly amiable. There is certainly a place for beautiful fashion, for peaceful scenes, and for light, lovely essays. In addition to these light features, however, Sunday magazines must also have a solid, vigorous voice and an impact of their own.

At the *Courier-Journal & Times,* we try to create such a magazine in a regional situation by using the best techniques of photography, writing, and editing found in the national magazines. This means giving writers and photographers the opportunity and time to produce in-depth stories and essays. It also means giving advanced thought and planning to stories and to carefully use space to take full advantage of the opportunity for good reproduction of photographs and illustrations.

Here, even more so than on the daily papers, photographers are called upon to be professional journalists. They are continually asked for story ideas and layout suggestions. There are no written assignments for the magazine photographers to follow. The concept used is a team approach with photographers, writers, and editors collaborating on story ideas. Some stories are photographic essays with the writer producing text to fit a photographic layout. At other times, the photographer is illustrating a written story. The approach that best communicates the story is the one used.

Daily news photographers are encouraged to submit ideas to the *Sunday Magazine.* If they are accepted, the photographer is given the opportunity and time to photograph that particular story.

Many editorial decisions are made at a weekday meeting where editors, photographers, writers and art director discuss upcoming stories and look over the photographs that have been taken. On occasions such as this, a critique of the previous week's magazine is also held.

Food Pictures

Each week the magazine has a food feature, written by our food editor and photographed by one of several photographers. It is the photographer's responsibility to decide how and where the food picture will be taken. He has known for several months what type of food he will photograph on a particular day, and he must have all the necessary props available and have decided if he wants to photograph on location with a 35–mm. or 2¼ camera, or a 4×5 or 6×10 camera in our color studio, adjoining the food editors' kitchen.

The decision as to which camera to use is made by the photographer on the basis of what equipment will do the best job. Most news assignments are photographed with 35 mm. cameras, but staff photographers will use the camera which best lends itself to the job.

Even with advance preparation it often takes one or two days to complete one food picture. The photographer is responsible for his picture's content, but the food editor, photographer, and art director work together during the shooting session.

Both transparencies and color negatives are used for the food pictures.

Fashion

The majority of fashion layouts produced for our papers are published in the *Sunday Magazine.* The use of color, the magazine format, and space make the magazine the logical choice. The same type of advanced planning that is necessary for food photographs is also necessary with fashions.

Much careful thought about presentation, style, approach, and lighting is necessary before a shooting session takes place. Models must be chosen, loca-

# plum good

By LILLIAN MARSHALL, Food Editor

IN TEMPERATE parts of the world, the plum has endeared itself to humans for thousands of years. Of 100 recognized plum species, some 35 are indigenous to North America, the rest mostly to Japan and Europe. Consider that the 100 species break down into a couple of thousand distinguishable varieties and you might expect to step on several plums in the course of a short stroll. Yet, for some reason, we have left it to the Europeans to glorify this elegant fruit. One of the most delectable desserts imaginable is plum goulie (dumplings) that Mrs. William Turner Jr. of Corinth, Ky., learned to make from her late grandmother, who came to this country from Czechoslovakia as a young girl. They're not a convenience food by any means, but they're worth the time it takes to make them. Try them and some other (simpler) recipes that follow to rescue the plum from obscurity.

Photographed by C. THOMAS HARDIN

## Chinese Plum Chutney

4 pounds fresh plums, halved and pitted
2 quarts vinegar
1 1/2 pounds brown sugar
1 pound granulated sugar
1/4 pound ginger root, soaked well in water, drained and chopped
1/4 pound salt
1/4 pound mustard seed, crushed
1 7-ounce can green chili peppers, seeded and diced
2 4-ounce cans red pimientos, seeded and diced
1 small onion, chopped
2 cloves garlic, peeled and chopped

Cook the plums in one quart of the vinegar until soft. Make syrup of the other quart of vinegar and the sugars in another kettle. Bring to boil and cook until syrupy. Add the plum-mixture and other ingredients. Simmer for 1 1/2 hours; stir frequently until sauce is thick as jam and most of liquid has cooked away. Seal in sterilized jars. Makes about 8 cups.

## Plum and Grape Catsup

3 pounds fresh plums
3 pounds fresh seedless grapes
3 cups water
Sugar
1 1/2 pints white vinegar
1 tablespoon ground cinnamon
1 tablespoon ground allspice
2 tablespoons ground cloves
1 1/2 teaspoons ground nutmeg

Cook fruit in water until very soft, about 30 minutes. Press

through fine sieve, discarding pits and skins. Measure pulp, add half that amount of sugar and other ingredients and mix in heavy kettle. Cook, stirring frequently, about 1 hour and 20 minutes until mixture is very thick. Skim. Pour into sterilized jars and seal tightly. Makes about 4 half-pints.

Continued

Food and Fashion (originals in color). Food and fashion photographs are important in the production of the *Louisville Courier-Journal* and the *Louisville Times*. A photographer who specializes in food and fashion illustration does much of his work in a studio. He is a member of the *Courier-Journal* and *Louisville Times* photographic team, but makes pictures only for the departments which use his specialized type of pictures.

tions scouted, or the studio prepared, and any special props that will be needed must be obtained.

The fashion editor makes a preliminary selection of clothes in New York, Chicago, Houston, or elsewhere and has them flown to Louisville to be photographed. When the clothes arrive, the fashion editor and photographer make a final selection of the outfits to be photographed, and then the shooting session begins.

Many styles of fashion photography are used, as well as many different photographic approaches. The proper approach, as well as good rapport between photographer and model, is very important in obtaining the mood that will best explain and display the clothes.

Fashion photography sessions are usually scheduled over several days to take advantage of different locations or different models.

# Illustrations

Photographic illustrations are playing an increasingly important role in our papers as well as in all publications. An illustration is used when we are not reporting, but are making a statement (either the photographer's or the papers') or are expressing a story idea or point. To be completely fair to our

# The Courier-Journal & Times
# MAGAZINE
SUNDAY, MARCH 4, 1973

# Beautiful
# dreamers

*The new nightwear is*
*for daydreaming, too.*

"I wish all the rich people could see how it is to be poor."

"For the white and black man to get along together."

"For people that need love to feel like they are going to get it."

# What I want for Christmas . . .

By JUDY ROSENFIELD
Louisville Times Staff Writer

Once upon a time, it seemed every child's Christmas dream was a blank check in a toy store or a pet shop, a candy store or a sporting goods store.

It was a matter of the more gifts the merrier.

Last week some Louisville youngsters made out their Christmas lists in their school classes.

Some of them, to be sure, chalked up lengthy catalogues of toys and games and clothes.

But what others wanted for Christmas isn't advertised on Saturday morning TV, can't be bought on sale or stuffed in a stocking or gift wrapped and piled under the tree.

The youngest children, first graders at Stivers Elementary School, chose relatively simple pleasures—books, pets, bikes, dolls.

"I want a football suit," wrote Jimmy Welch, "because my Dad wants me to have muscles."

Cindy Deimier said, "I want one of those film deals. It's a square box and you see movies in it."

"We decided to let Santa pick me a dolly," said Valerie Young, who added, "Then I can pretend to be a Mommy."

Chris Starr, another Stivers first-grader, wrote, "I would like a puppy dog 'cause I just want one."

At Goldsmith Elementary, third grader Tom Merta wished that "the war would come to an end. So the army men that fight for us could rest and have peace. If the war stopped, I'd be the happiest boy on earth."

"I would like to give to Good Will," wrote Jeff Lowe, another student in the third grade there. "Why? Well, some people don't have Christmas and I'd like for them to have one."

His classmate, Kevin Meredith, said he'd like a table-tennis set most of all.

"It is something that the whole family can play. And my family is more im-

tion. I would like for the war to stop and their world be peace all the time. Inner-war on," said Don Lamar, another Wellersith grader.

She said, "I'd like for my parents to go on a vacation for two weeks and have my sister and I everything that we would need. I don't think my parents trust me. For one thing, I'm the oldest and they probably think that I just might get into some kind of devilment."

"If I could only prove to them that I can be TRUSTED."

"I wish I had the feeling that I was never scared of anything or anybody," wrote Sica Bridgewater. "I wish I could be very good at singing or acting and become a star on television never being nervous at all."

"I would like a movie studio so I could make millions of scary movies and Rock & Roll movies and a drum set so I could be in the Rock & Roll movies."

"I would like some brown leather boots with fringe hanging from the top so I could look Western on my horse. I would like a motorcycle, a blue one with saddle bags, so I could show it off."

Betty Roederer's holiday wish was "for my future brother-in-law to be able to come home from Vietnam. He's only been away for about two months," she conceded, "but it seems like centuries. The reason I want him home is so he can share the fun we have at Christmas."

Some eighth-graders at Shawnee Junior High wondered if they weren't a little old to be making out Christmas lists. They seemed to have no trouble.

Cars, dresses, an end to war and being with their families were their Christmas wishes.

Mike Reed's list was most specific. "If I could have anything I wanted I would want some snake skins (socks), a whole indoor basketball court, a dune and a quarter, an Li Dog, and a big crazy,

start my Christmas savings for next year."

Linda Thomas, another Shawnee eighth grader, explained that her wish was a little unusual.

love from everybody and for people that need love to feel like they are going to get it."

World peace was Loni White's greatest Christmas hope, only she wasn't very hopeful.

"I think that if we have this great gift, children would grow up in a better world, in this world in which we live, children only learn to fight and hate.

"Race against race, and sometimes people of the same race against each other. It's almost like the Civil War. If the world keeps up like this, the world will end sooner than we think."

Aaron Martin, in the eighth grade at Shawnee, was equally pessimistic.

"If I had all the money in the world—which I don't—I would buy the world state by state," he wrote. "The first thing I would do is stop the wars throughout the world. I would feed the hungry, help the sick, find a home for all unwanted babies.

"I would give the hippies and the drug pushers two states to themselves. After I had tried to solve all the problems of the world I would send man to the moon and all nine planets."

But, he concluded, "After all I have ac-

complished, it would amount to nothing—because the world will be destroyed by now."

His classmate Herron Clark wished for "some clothes and some money—not too much, just enough to get me something."

"I would like for everyone to have a merry Christmas. And I would like for everyone to have food and money that doesn't have them. I would like for everybody's dream to come true."

Finally, he said, "I wish all the rich people could see how it is to be poor and without things you really need."

Another student, in tiny, neat handwriting and green ink, explained:

"I wish I were with my family and with my brothers and sisters. My mother is very sick. I wish she was well and could see.

"I wish I could go home and be with the whole family on Christmas. My biggest brother is in the Army and hardly gets to come home for Christmas. I feel like I am in the Army being so far away from home and I feel sad.

"I miss being with my little brother, helping put his toys together for him, then when all the snow has melted we go out and ride our bikes together. And just have lots of fun."

> 'I would like for everyone to have a merry Christmas, to have food and money, and for everyone's dream to come true . . .'

portant to me than anything else in the world."

From another third-grader there: "I would like a baby sister for Christmas because I like my sister and I want another one." Signed, "Love Jill Henry."

"If I could have anything I wanted," decided Tracy Mulligan, "I would want an angel. If I could have an angel I would be the happiest kid in the world because I think an angel is neat."

Donna Sheets, one of Tracy's third-grade classmates, said, "What I would really and truly want is for pollution to be stopped. It's something that is poisoning our air and water and other things. I think that if we all worked together we could stop it."

Pets and bicycles were tops on the lists of sixth-graders at Waller Elementary.

Robert Gosling wanted not only a bike, but games, a race car set, and fishing, basketball, football, volleyball, ice skating and roller skating equipment.

And, he concluded, "A basement to put all this stuff in."

"If I could have anything for Christ-

stereo and some more silk T shirts, some halfton-sleeved shirts, some more open door bellbottoms, a pair of alligator stick-ems (shoes).

"A mansion with butlers and maids all over the place and a good table," he continued. "Peace all over the world. No more crimes, no wars. A house and more money. Lots of money."

His classmate, Robert Ewing, also was pitching for new clothes, "like five or eight pairs of shoes and 10 or 12 pairs of pants and about 20 knits."

He explained: "I want these clothes so the girls can go crazy over me like they always do.

"I want to get my nephew some clothes, too, so the girls can go crazy over him, too. I like my nephew very much."

A pool table was eighth-grader Kenneth Colgate's choice. "This way," he said "We can have fun for nothing. I mean $159. Maybe we'll gamble a little, and a quarter every ball we knock in the hole.

"If I won," he concluded, "I think I'll

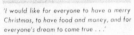
"I wish that the war would come to an end. So that the Army men that fight for us and die for us . . . could rest and have peace."

An advertising photographer—a specialist trained to do this type of work—is shown making pictures of small items in an advertising studio.

The Louisville newspapers are careful to distinguish pictures which illustrate from pictures photographed to report a happening. *Left*, these pictures were made specifically as illustrations to go with a written story about what first grade children want for Christmas.

readers, each illustration is labeled as an illustration by a cutline or by some other means. The studio, special lighting, rear projection, and complicated location set ups are all used extensively in our photographic illustrations.

Both story illustrations and editorial illustrations give the photographer a great opportunity to think and create.

Advertising Photography

There is a strong policy on our newspapers to make sure there is no conflict of interest between the editorial and advertising departments.

In keeping with this policy, and because advertising photography is a very specialized field, we employ two persons whose sole jobs are to do only advertising photography. Even though they are part of the photographic department, they work only for the advertising department.

Much of their work is done in the studio with complex lighting, large format view cameras, and specially designed worktables. Rings, watches, silverware, dishes, and shoes are but a few of the products photographed for the local advertisers. For the photographer's services, the advertiser pays an appropriate fee.

# Kentucky Derby

The Kentucky Derby lasts two minutes. But our planning for photographing the Derby requires three weeks. Fifty-eight photographers using 70 cameras and 400 rolls of film are used to record the event.

For the *Courier-Journal & Times* photographic staff, the Kentucky Derby is the busiest day of each year and the most extensively covered event.

It all starts a year in advance when we critique our work of the Derby just photographed and make changes and plans for the next year.

Two different sets of photographs are taken at the Derby. One group is made up of those photographs that change very little from year to year. These include standard coverage photographs like "around the track," which is a series of photographs taken at specific places showing the horses at various times of the race. Another is an overall of the finish. We also have photographers stationed so that we can cover the entire track in case a jockey is thrown or a horse falls.

These pictures are critiqued each year for importance, impact, camera position, sharpness, and lens coverage. If any one of these can be improved, even if it means moving just 10 feet or changing from a 28-mm. to a 24-mm. lens, we will make the change for next year.

In the other type of coverage we try for the unusual photograph such as a photograph that tells the story of this particular Derby or a photographic angle that has never been seen before. Each year we try very hard to produce different photographs. But after 101 runnings of the Derby, it becomes harder and harder.

Picture stories and specific people stories are planned for the human aspect of the race.

After conferences with the staff photographers, each person is assigned particular subjects to photograph. Often the photographer will make tests with his lens and position days before the race. Assignments covered before the race include features such as celebrities, jockies, and spectators.

During the race each photographer does a specific job. For example: six photographers photograph the start, each from a different angle for a specific reason. The 1974 finish was photographed by thirteen photographers using twenty-one cameras.

Specific owners, trainers, and jockies also were photographed during the race. Each photographer shoots with a particular picture or story in mind, and each is trying to out photograph the other photographers.

After the race the coverage includes the winners circle, jockey, trophy presentation, bettors, winning horse, and much more.

What makes each Derby exciting and challenging to us is that none of the races are ever the same. No matter how much planning goes into the preparation for photographic coverage, one never knows how a race will be run. One year the winning horse may finish far in front of the other horses. The next year the horses may finish close together or the horses may run wide on the track. Each type of race should be photographed differently, so we have to be prepared to have good photographs whichever way it is run.

Staff photographers are asked for specific ideas weeks before the Derby and are usually given the opportunity to photograph their ideas. These can be picture stories or specific Derby race pictures. This gives the photographer the opportunity to photograph what he wants and gives the paper the advantage of their thinking as journalists. By following this procedure, we have a better opportunity to produce that different picture each year and a fresh look at the race. Competition among the staff photographers is great and produces some fine results.

In addition to the photographers who come up with their own ideas, we have roving photographers whose assignment is to photograph Derby Day as they see it. They have no specific assignment before the race so they are free to be creative photojournalists.

The entire photographic staff works Derby Day, and in addition we hire free-lance photographers to cover specific jobs. Staff photographers have helpers who carry cameras, record cutline information, and occasionally trip remote cameras.

The final planning takes place Derby Week, and changes continue with the developments of the news of the Derby. But by the day before the race each photographer knows exactly what he will be doing, where he will be standing, and exactly what lens he will use.

Pictures are coordinated with stories from the city desk and the picture editors, so specific stories often are covered by reporter as well as by photographer.

For unexpected happenings we rely upon the professional judgment of the photographers for the coverage. We have never been let down.

As much planning and work is done with the photographic laboratory personnel for Derby Day as is done with the photographers.

Our laboratory staff develops more than 400 rolls of film and makes around 350 prints on Derby Day. So developing, editing, printing, and proper identification procedures must be perfect.

Each roll of film coming to the laboratory is identified with the photographer's name and roll number and is accompanied with cutline material in specially marked packages. The film is delivered to the laboratory on scheduled runs throughout the day. All film is rated at the same American Standards Association (ASA) exposure index so that developing in the automatic processing machines can be standardized.

Some photographs such as the around-the-track photographs are printed a designated size, but most are printed 8 by 10 inches with the best being printed 11 by 14 inches. After a picture editor makes initial selections, the photographers may print additional photographs if they think something has been missed.

The photographs are published in a special derby section of the papers in which photographs are used extensively.

# The 99th: A Derby of records

## Secretariat sets a new mark . . . and so do the bettors and the crowd

Secretariat, left, and Sham duel in the stretch. Staff Photo by Bill Strode

**By BOB ADAIR**
Courier-Journal & Times Staff Writer

Records are made to be broken, the saying goes, and it was only fitting that on Secretariat's day of redemption—Kentucky Derby day of 1973—the biggest record of all was shattered by the sleek champion himself.

Secretariat's time of 1 minute, 59 2-5 seconds for the gruelling mile and a quarter of the world's most famous horse race eclipsed the mark of 2 minutes flat, set by Northern Dancer in 1964.

Whatever the superlatives bestowed on the striking Meadow Stable champion beforehand, none could do justice to the heart-pounding performance to which Secretariat and jockey Ron Turcotte treated the multitudes in the 99th Run for the Roses yesterday at Churchill Downs.

Charging from last to earn the $155,050 plum from the $198,900 purse in the richest Derby ever, the favored chestnut son of the late champion sire Bold Ruler vindicated himself—at the direct expense of Sham—for his only loss of the season.

The latter, pegged as his main contender, led into the long homestretch, known as "Heartbreak Highway," only to fall victim to the fastest final quarter in the classic's history.

Aided by a bright, sunshiny day that still managed to be comfortably cool, the Derby attracted a record crowd of 134,476 as millions more watched on television. The betting also set a record, the fans pouring $3,284,962 into the Derby's pari-mutuel pool and wagering $7,627,965 for the day.

The embattled top pair left others among the 13 starters far behind as they dueled to the wire. Third-place Our Native finished eight additional lengths back, a half-length in front of fourth-place Forego.

Secretariat, breezing under the wire with a 2½-length margin ran the last quarter in :23 1/5. Only two previous winners—Whirlaway, with :23 3/5 in 1941, and Proud Clarion, with a clocking of :23 4/5 in 1967—had ever negotiated the concluding quarter of a mile in less than 24 seconds.

Unique in having become the only juvenile ever to be acclaimed Horse of the Year, in 1972, then syndicated for a future stud career at a record value of $6.08 million, Secretariat did exactly what the Canadian team of trainer Lucien Laurin and jockey Turcotte predicted he would do.

That was to follow in the victorious footsteps of last year's winner, Riva Ridge, also from the Meadow Stable of Mrs. John Tweedy, and to do so faster and in a more convincing manner. Not since Iron Liege triumphed in 1957 and Tim Tam won in 1958 for Calumet Farm had any stable managed to put together consecutive Derby victories. And never before had the same owner, trainer and jockey won two in a row.

The entry of Secretariat and Angle Light, sent off at odds of exactly 3-2, returned $5, $3.20 and $3 across the board. Sham, with regular jockey Laffit Pincay Jr. restored to the saddle, was the 5-2 second choice. He paid $3.20 to place and $3 to show. Our Native, piloted by Kentuckian Don Brumfield, was the 10-1 fifth choice and rewarded his show backers with $4.20.

The race was run almost precisely to a pattern many experts had anticipated. Possibly the main exception was that Angle Light, who led all the way to beat Sham by a head and Secretariat by four additional lengths in the Wood Memorial two weeks ago, was never a contender.

The role of pacemaker, as most predicted, was played by the fleet Shecky Greene, winner of the seven-furlong Stepping Stone Purse at the Downs a week earlier. The colt named for the TV and night-club comedian took the field the first three-quarters before giving up the lead to Sham, then held no better than some expected and wound up sixth.

Restless Jet was fifth, and after Shecky Greene, in order, came Navajo, Royal and Regal, My Gallant, Angle Light, Gold Bag, Twice a Prince and Warbucks.

Shecky Greene and My Gallant also formed an entry—for trainer Lou Goldfine. They were rated as the crowd's third choice at 5-1 and the disappointing Warbucks as the fourth most popular contestant at 7-1.

All carried the Derby weight of 126 pounds.

Secretariat, praised by some observers as potentially the greatest thoroughbred runner since the immortal Man o' War, undoubtedly will go from the Derby to the Preakness Stakes at Pimlico on May 19 in pursuit of the Triple Crown, last won by Citation in 1948. The concluding step, the 1 1-2-mile Belmont Stakes, will be contested June 9 at Belmont Park.

Last year, it was the 1 3-16-mile Preakness that spoiled the bid of Riva Ridge to become only the ninth Triple Crown champion in racing history. After failing there, he won the Belmont Stakes.

"There are two races to go," said Turcotte, referring to Laurin's announced schedule which calls for Secretariat to run in the Preakness and Belmont and then take a break before contesting other important events in late summer. "I'll take them one at a time."

Turcotte said he went to the whip twice in the Derby—once leaving the 1st turn, when Secretariat raced strongly to the leaders, and in the upper stretch, where the winner briefly lost a little of his momentum.

From there to the wire, Turcotte merely flashed his whip at Secretariat from the left side and the champion responded willingly.

At the start, only Warbucks and Twice

See SECRETARIAT
Back page, col. 1, this section

## Derby Day Index

**This Section:**

The color of Derby Day . . . A day to dress up, see the celebrities and rub elbows with the masses, picnic and play in the greenery of Churchill Downs infield, gamble on the long shots, limp home in traffic jams and drown your sorrows — or celebrate — in a round of parties.

**Sports Section:**

Nuts and bolts of a Derby victory . . . How the winning jockey and trainer saw the race—Section C.

**Today's Living:**

Who's who in the boxes . . . A picture page of the notable guests who give a special flavor to the Derby mix—Section G.

**General News:**

The regular news and feature sections of The Courier-Journal & Times follow this special Derby section.

The Kentucky Derby is very important in Louisville, and the newspapers go all out to cover the event. *Right,* cameramen get ready to photograph the finish of the race. A 4x5 camera and two motorized Nikons were used at this station.

# Color Reproduction

The *Courier-Journal & Times* has been using color photography since the 1930s. In the early days, color photographs were taken on a camera that would separate the color on three different plates. From these plates a carbro print was made, which was then reproduced by rotogravure in the magazine.

Today rotogravure reproduction is still used at the *Courier-Journal & Times*. Standard Gravure—a rotogravure printing plant owned by the same family that owns the newspapers—prints twenty-two Sunday magazines for newspapers around the country, as well as *Parade Magazine*. Spectacolor, a trade name for rotogravure color in the daily newspapers, is also produced at Standard Gravure.

Because of this printing capability and the feeling that newspapers must have good color reproduction to compete with color television and the specialty magazines, the Louisville papers use only rotogravure color.

Spectacolor is used for news and feature pictures on the front page and for picture pages. The cover of *Scene*, the Saturday tabloid entertainment magazine, uses color, and the *Sunday Magazine* uses color throughout.

# The Laboratory

Since photography is changing so rapidly, the *Courier-Journal & Times* designed its photographic laboratory to allow for change. What is effective today may be completely obsolete tomorrow because of silverless image-capturing heat processing, automatic daylight enlarging, laser transmission, electronic visual signals with high reproductive qualities—or by processes at the moment undreamed of.

So the Louisville papers built for the future by preparing for their own destruction. All of our internal walls are easily movable. All permanent fixtures like plumbing are restricted to outside walls. The newspapers are ready to move in whatever direction photography moves. We could quickly dispose of all wet processing. We could pull down walls and install machines of almost any conceivable size. We have the space and the flexibility for change. But for the present the laboratory is very efficient. It works in this manner.

General Concept

The photo area is divided into four zones: (1) a fast zone, (2) a supporting zone, (3) a slow zone, and (4) an administrative zone.

*Fast Zone*

This zone is where everything happens. This is the hub of the operation. It is closest to the entry doors. It has contact with the news department and the picture editors, who remain on the news floor. It is from this zone that photographers start out on assignments and where they return. This is the point from which contact is made with radio-equipped cars. It is where developing, film inspection, information recording, and printing are done.

The *Courier-Journal & Times Magazine* is produced by rotogravure, a process which the administrators believe to be best for the reproduction of color. As a result, the Louisville daily papers use only Spectacolor, which is printed by Standard Gravure. It is not unusual to see a page on the Derby or a feature page such as "Country Life" (*right*) produced by the Spectacolor system and run in a regular edition.

# Country Life

On a visit to her grandparents' home in Austin, Ky., Karen Grabinski takes time out for a late afternoon swing.

Turning the ground over on his farm near Glasgow, Ky. is James Bunch of Barren County.

## *Rural Reverie*

Life in the country has a charm and grace all its own. Though there is always plenty of hard work to go around, there is time too, to enjoy the simple pleasures and the easy moods of country life.

Greg Smith, 6, and his grandfather, Charlie Brooks, of Cave City, enjoy a leisurely afternoon fishing.

*Supporting Zone*

This area supplements the fast area. Here are a copy room, print mounting room, special hand-developing rooms, a room for making large prints, and a chemical mix room. If the fast zone is the center of the operation, the supporting zone geographically surrounds the fast core.

*Slow Zone*

This zone is off to the side, away from the rush. It includes an area for color and magazine photography, a no-rush darkroom and print room, a camera repair shop, and a studio.

*Administrative Zone*

This zone includes administrative offices, a negative file room, storage space, and a photographers' ready room which has cabinets for photographers' personal equipment and cameras, a cabinet of specialized camera equipment, color television receivers, coatracks, reading material, and typewriters. The idea is to keep staff members out of the rush area unless they are needed there. In actual practice, the staff has little time to spend in the ready room. But it provides a point of departure.

The Way It Works

Just inside the entrance door to the fast zone is the control desk manned by a "veteran" who is in actual charge of dispatching photographers to assignments. He also deals with picture editors and has radio control of cars that are out.

Pneumatic tubes nearby put him in almost instant contact with the picture desk on the news floors below. Through these tubes move the orders for pictures from the two photo desks, and back through the tubes go the finished prints at the end of assignments. An intercommunication system puts the control desk operator in instant touch with photographers who may be inside the department but out of his line of sight.

The control operator deals out assignments as they come in from the news floor, and sees photographers when they return from assignments.

Once past this control man, the work flow goes in a great circle that ultimately leads back to this position. Photographers who bring in film have a choice of two processing machines reached through a revolving door light trap. One machine is used for Tri-X film rated up to 800. The other machine develops film rated to 1600. Well above 90 percent of our developing is done through these machines, though individual darkrooms are available for special hand developing. These rooms have available to them Acufine, UFG, DK-50, and D-76 developers.

Hand developing is extremely rare in our operation. The key to the success of machine developing—which does produce consistent, predictable, high-caliber negatives—is constant care and maintenance. Two men who divide their duties between regular laboratory work and care of the machines are the reason why it does work for us . . . and well.

On the *Courier-Journal* and *Louisville Time* the control center just inside the lab is a veritable beehive. Here the control operator gives out assignments as they come in from the news floor. He also deals with picture editors and has radio contact with photographers in the field. The control operator, a veteran in the business, is an important link in the Louisville newspaper photo operation.

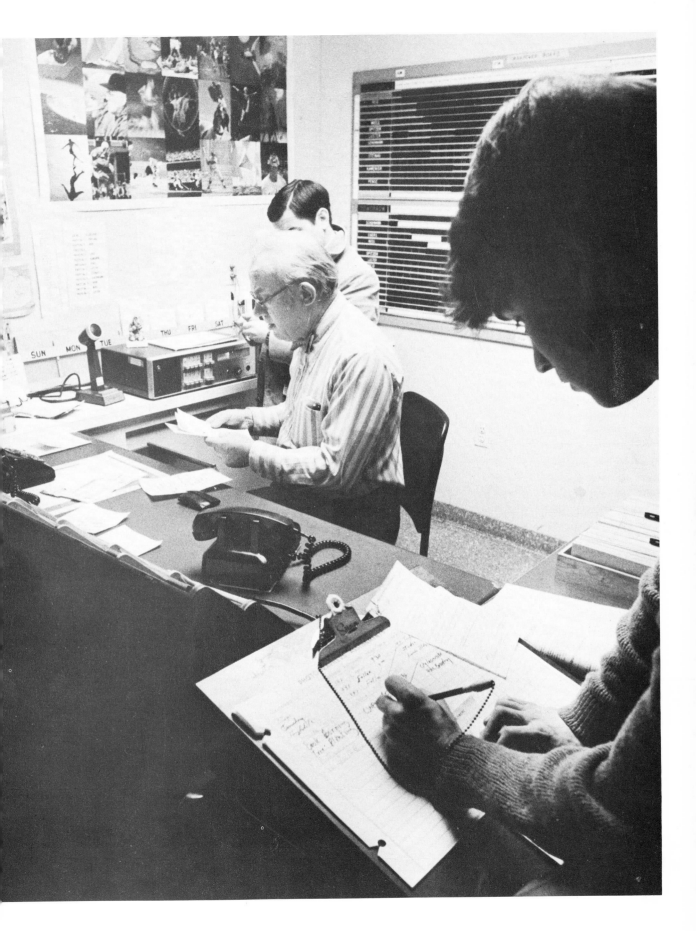

While the machines are developing, fixing, and drying negatives, photographers prepare envelopes for permanent filing of the negatives. Print File Negative Preservers are marked with the date, nature of assignment, and photographer's name. When the negatives emerge from the machines, they are sleeved in the plastic preservers and contact printed on a printer that has rheostat, timer, and special balanced polycontrast filters. The paper used is $8\frac{1}{2} \times 11$ inch Ektamatic, accommodating six negative strips. Two such contact sheets are made, one for the picture desk and the other for the permanent archives. Cutline information is also prepared during this period. This information is typed by the photographer onto a mimeograph sheet which is transferred to the back of each contact sheet and each print that results from the assignment.

Directly adjacent to the place where this information processing goes on is the entrance to the master print room which at present is geared for traditional wet processing. It is possible to bypass wet printing with Ektamatic paper for instant processing, but this procedure is reserved for extreme emergencies. (We have timed it at 13 minutes from photographer's entrance to finished print.) The normal run of printing does not require that speed, and wet printing still accords a higher degree of quality control.

The master print room is 17 by 24 feet. It contains five enlarging booths and two double-sided, temperature-controlled, stainless steel sinks which "work" toward the middle of the room. There, a central sluice transports finished prints through the outer wall to a washer adjacent to the control desk and the pneumatic tubes that will carry them down to the picture desks.

Each enlarging booth is equipped with either a $4 \times 5$-inch variable condenser Omega enlarger or a 35–mm. Leitz enlarger with extralong uprights. The booths were specially designed with light viewers, rheostats, timers, air hoses for blowing dust from negatives, paper bins that hold $8 \times 10$-inch and $11 \times 14$-inch paper in five grades, a drawer for exposed paper, and a space for easels, magnifiers, rulers, and miscellaneous equipment. Each lens on each enlarger has been tested and marked for its own particular optimum aperture.

The master print room also contains other equipment one might expect: a contact printer, cabinet for stock paper storage, and sodium vapor safelights which permit an atmosphere not very different from dim daylight.

The printing chemicals—Ethol, LPD, and Kodak Rapid Fix—are mixed in a remote location and gravity fed to faucets at the central developing sinks. Over each hypo (sodium thiosulfate) tray there is a pinpoint white ceiling light actuated by a floor switch so printers can inspect their work.

Lest men working in the dim confines of the master print room for hours at a time get the feeling they are isolated from the outside, a $2\frac{1}{2} \times 6$-foot window, covered by red safety material, permits them to see what is going on outside around the control desk.

The sluice leads back outside to the control area where everything began. Here there is a $3\frac{1}{2}$-foot circular washer and four old-style flatbed dryers, used because they dry prints faster than anything else we know of. Here, too, are a print straightener, typewriters, cutline information blanks, and the pneumatic tubes.

The entire area—all zones—is under slight, positive air pressure so that when doors are opened air—and dust—flows out, not in.

Since most of our work is 35 mm., cleanliness is imperative. Aside from the outward-flowing air, we fight dirt by forbidding all smoking anywhere except in the lounge and the administrative offices, by a regular cleaning schedule, and by vigilance to avoid pileup of junk on the floors. There is no flak from any of our laboratory technicians or photographers and administrators. They all recognize an imperative when they see one.

The way things operate now, photographers are expected to develop and print their own assignments unless another assignment presses them. In that case, the work can be turned over to laboratory technicians for processing. Laboratory technicians also regularly process film from stringers, bureaus, and reporters and make special prints.

This procedure could be altered. The place is set up so as to operate as a complete lab system with photographers shooting only.

We have a central stockroom for seldom used materials, but paper stocks are kept near each printing station.

### The Supportive Process

Much of what goes on in the other three zones is self-explanatory. Some of it needs amplification. For instance:

#### *Studios*

The main studio is a 25×38-foot room with an 18-foot ceiling. Walls, ceiling, and floors are white. Fluorescent lights in the ceiling are color balanced for daylight shooting. Supplementing them is an Ascor sky bank strobe and Ascor umbrella strobes. A collapsing door makes it possible to divide the studio into one large studio and one smaller one for simultaneous shooting. There is a small adjoining dressing room for models and an overhead balcony for high-vantage-point shooting, plus flats and background paper.

The second studio is located by the food department's kitchen where the food to be photographed is prepared. This is primarily for color, using 3,200 Kelvin lights. It, too, is white, except for one end where floors, ceiling, and walls are painted a flat black. This studio has dimensions of 29 by 54 feet and 18-foot ceilings.

#### *Copying*

One small room is devoted to copying and to dry mounting. Equipment here includes a special horizontal copy stand, 4x5 Calumet camera and process copy lens. Either 4x5 Polaroid film is used, or 4x5 Ektapan is developed in the Versamat.

### Camera Repair

Camera repairs can be costly, and shipment to the factory for repairs can result in many lost weeks of equipment use. With 128 cameras and 312 lenses we cannot afford such losses. So we have established our own factory authorized repair station with all the necessary testing machines, calibrators, tools, and spare parts needed. One man operates this shop, as well as help administer our camera amortization program. This program lets the photographer, if he wants to participate, own his own equipment, with the company paying him

ster print room (*left*) is 17 by 24 feet. ontains five enlarging booths, two double-ed, temperature-controlled stainless steel ks. A central sluice transports prints ugh the outer wall to a print washer acent to the control desk and the pneu-

matic tubes which will carry them to the picture desk.

Washed prints (*top*) are being put on a flatbed dryer. Versamat and Pako developing machines are in the background. Light tables used for the selection of negatives can also be seen.

Each enlarging booth (*bottom*) is equipped with either a 4-by-5-inch variable condenser Omega enlarger or a 35-mm. Leitz with extralong uprights. The booths are designed with light viewers, rheostats, timers, air hoses for blowing dust from negatives, paper bins, and the like.

for its use at a percentage of its value each year. The photographer can obtain all the necessary equipment needed to accomplish his job and can also keep up with the new models and changes in camera equipment.

The Louisville papers save time and money by maintaining their own factory-authorized repair station. Because of a crew which uses 128 cameras and 312 lenses, they canno afford the time usually needed to ship equipment to a factory for repairs.

## Color Laboratory

The color laboratory is equipped with a transparency-processing line and with color enlargers capable of making reproduction or large display prints from 35-mm. up to 8×10-inch negatives. The majority of the newspapers' color reproduction is from transparencies, but sometimes color prints are used.

# Archives

The *Courier-Journal* and the *Louisville Times* have under development—and in the final testing stage—a news-clipping recall system using linked microfilm and computers that will summon from the past an image of any printed story that has appeared in the paper. The system is equally applicable to the recall of photographic images. Contact sheets and their accompanying

One of the extracurricular activities of the Louisville newspapers is book publishing. Presently they are considering publishing a regional photographic yearbook. Author editor, printer, and art director discuss the printing quality as the Barney Cowherd book comes off the press.

cutline information from each current assignment are now being test fed into the computers. Later, this system will be extended to our file of negatives from past years. Ultimately, any image shot in the past and still in existence, whether it was used or not, will be brought within reach.

# New Areas of Material Use

For years we have felt that it was wasteful that the material presented to our newspaper readers was usually thrown away each day. There is a need to preserve much of the material for use in schools and libraries and for use by individuals for reference material or for nostalgic remembrances.

The newspapers are filed, of course, but we felt the need to present the material in a more permanent form for longer retention, so we started a book division. The last two books published have been photographic books, and we are now publishing a regional photographic yearbook.

In the future a more extensive use of books, magazines, and filmstrips is planned, all on a regional basis.

Soon the public will be able to use computers for information retrieval of stories and pictures that have been published in the papers.

Nationally, we are operating a syndication service called Pegasus for Sunday magazines and are publishing an abstract quarterly magazine on specialized information.

All of these areas are designed to provide additional material for our readers, which helps achieve the goal of the *Courier-Journal* and the *Louisville Times,* the goal of serving the public.

In newspapers, photographers have the opportunity to introduce man to his fellow man. By appealing to human compassion they can help in the search for a more meaningful world.

If photographers are to be known as photojournalists, they must portray what is going on with trust and integrity; must see a situation as no one else can see it; must photograph it and come back with understanding, awareness, and information that can be communicated only with a camera. I hope all newspaper photographers will accept the challenge, for serving the public is the greatest responsibility and privilege in the world.

# Student Participation

1. Lewis Hine, who photographed in the early 1900s, said "Photography could light up darkness and expose ignorance." Bring to class three pictures from local newspapers which in your opinion do this very thing.
2. Explain the following statement: "Newspaper photographers must be responsible journalists who follow the advice of Carl Mydans: 'Take your pictures with your mind, heart and a camera.' "
3. Discuss the enterprise system described in the chapter and define a freestanding picture.
4. Discuss the part ethics plays in the Louisville *Courier-Journal* and *Louisville Times* photographic program.
5. Tell what you think Mr. Strode means when he says, "Far too many Sunday magazines have been forever gentle, unprovocative, and sweetly amiable." Bring to class at least one example that proves the statement.

Color and horse racing are big business for the *Courier-Journal* and the *Louisville Times*. Here, in a Spectacolor page for the regular May 4, 1974, issue, the two are combined. Race-minded readers appreciate the treatment given their favorite sport.

# THE LOUISVILLE TIMES

Rhythm and power of a once-in-a-lifetime Thoroughbred captured by Richard Nugent, staff photographer. It's Secretariat, of course, under Ron Turcotte, winning the 1973 Derby leg of the Triple Crown.

### rowd and betting may set records

# Derby outlook: fast track, sort of slow horses

By MARVIN N. GAY JR.
Louisville Times Staff Writer

cords apparently will be falling all
he place at today's 100th running of
Kentucky Derby at Churchill Downs
t one — the track record. The track
ard of 1:59 2-5 for the 1 1-4 mile
t, set last year by the sensational
tariat, isn't likely to be threatened.

— 3-year-olds in this richest Derby
n't been running that fast. In fact,
t of the winners have
—embarrassing — they have been
close in comparison with previous
ises.

ach Supt. Thurman Pangburn said.

"If there is no more rain, the track will
be fast.

If the horses run like slow-pokes it will
be because they are lacking in ability and
not because of the racing surface.

Nevertheless, Downs resident manager
Bob Gorham, who has charge of the tickets, foreseet that a record 142,000 to 145,-
000 spectators will be in the stands and
infield "if we have a good day (weather-
wise).

Princess Margaret of Britain and her
husband, Lord Snowdon, crossed the Atlantic to see this 100th Derby

Last year paid admissions totaled 133,-
881, an all-time high.

Wagering last Derby Day set a record
$7,627,905 and this mark also could
topple today. Gorham isn't sure, though,
because the Derby will be run as the
eighth race. Last year it was the ninth
race. The change was made to accom-
modate television to the Eastern section
of the nation.

A record amount of $228,134 had been
bet through yesterday at the Downs on
the Derby. The board probably was
helped along by a record Derby-eve
crowd of 42,000.

Judger and Cannonade, coupled in the
betting, head a record number of 23 hope-
fuls scheduled to compete about 4:30 p.m.
Central Daylight Time for a purse of

$228,500 with $274,000 to the winner.
Both amounts are records, but the glory
that comes with victory in America's No.
1 horse race possibly weighs as heavily
for the owners. The race will be televised
by CBS (Channel 11 in Louisville).

The cost of trying to win the Derby
went up this year, accounting for the record purse. The nominating fee remained
the same, $100, and 260 colts were named
as possible Derby runners. But the entry
fee was increased from $2,500 to $4,000,
and the starting fee, due before the race
today, went up from $1,500 to $3,500.

W. C. (Woody) Stephens, the trainer
of Judger and Cannonade, is in an envi-
able position with two colts going into

the Derby off smashing triumphs. Judger
in the Blue Grass Stakes at Keeneland
and Cannonade in the Stepping Stone last
Saturday at the Downs.

Some horsemen see a one-two finish
for the Stephens entry (Judger-Cannon-
ade or Cannonade-Judger). The last entry
to run one-two was from Calumet Farm—
Citation and Coaltown, both trained by
Ben Jones. The year was 1948.

The task for Stephens is more formidable because a field of only six went to
the post in the Citation-Coaltown sweep.
Barring a late scratch or scratches, the
Stephens colts will have 21 challengers.
The previous high for a Derby came in
1928 when 22 raced.

The odds against Stephens, a native

Kentuckian, saddling the one-two finish-
ers are astronomical. Still, his charges,
given the breaks in an unwieldy field,
might accomplish the feat.

Judger and Cannonade ran one-two in
the Florida Derby, Judger winning by
three-fourths of a length. Earlier this
week, Stephens said, "Judger and Cannonade are awfully close together."

He noted that Cannonade carried 4
more pounds than Judger in that 1 1-8-
mile race.

"Those colts have been on a set schedule, all winter and spring, coming up to
the Kentucky Derby," as of the 60-year-old

See DERBY
Page A5, col. 1

### Do prices go
### p during
### Derby week?

By FRANK FOX, JOE GAGLIARDI
and LES WHITELEY
Louisville Times Staff Writers

...tors in Louisville during Kentucky
...festivities do pay more for lodging
...transportation than at other times of
...year.

...t, contrary to popular belief, they
...rently do not — with some ex-
...ons —pay more for their food and
...

...st motels and hotels jack up their
...es for Derby visitors in no secret.
..., usually based on a minimum three-
...t stay (Thursday through Saturday),
...been increased anywhere from $5 to
...per cent this year. Most of these
...es make it quite clear that Derby
...brings higher rates, like the "sea-
...in Florida.

...th Louisville Transit Co. and Yellow
Co., the city's two major public trans-
...ers, candidly admit they increase
...s for caregoers.

...ere has also been a widespread be-
...that restaurants and nightclubs jack
...heir prices to take advantage of the
...es attracted by the Derby.

...owever, telephone interviews with 2
...en restaurant owners and visits to
...al restaurants and 10 nightclubs and
...pes — prior to the start of Derby
...k and again last night — by Louis-
...Times reporters would indicate that

See ARE PRICES
Page A1, col. 1

THE LOUISVILLE TIMES
FINAL HOME—64 PAGES
SATURDAY EVENING
MAY 4, 1974
Copyright © 1974, The Louisville Times
VOL. CLXXXI—No. 4
TEN CENTS

Sunshine warmed a throng of Derby fans outside the Central Avenue Churchill Downs gate an hour before the 8 a.m. opening time.

# Legal Aspects of Photography

# 14

*Dale R. Spencer*

The newspaper, magazine, or television cameraman, whether staff or free lance, leads a complex, demanding, and sometimes dangerous life. Often we read how a member of this important reportorial group is injured or how his equipment is smashed while covering a riot, shoot-out, protest march, prison break, or other news event. The news photographer is a marked person. He or she is subject not only to physical threats, but also to legal harassment. It is important, therefore, that the modern photojournalist know how to protect himself physically, and more than that, that he have a knowledge of the legal problems.

The photojournalist, indeed, does have legal problems. There are legal problems in the broad areas of defamation and invasion of privacy that affect all journalists. In photography there are legal problems in the specific areas of print and negative ownership, releases, copyright, and the like.

Dale R. Spencer, professor of journalism and a member of the Missouri Bar and the American Bar Association, looks at the legal aspects of visual reporting.

# Ownership and Copyright of Prints and Negatives

Two types of ownership are concerned in photography:

First, who owns the prints and/or negatives?

Second, who owns the copyright?

Both of these questions are essentially contract concerns. This means that if a free-lancer gets an assignment and his customer or client asks for a specific job of so many prints at a certain price the law is clear. The customer or client has agreed to purchase that specific number of prints and they are his. As one court said:

> The usual contract between photographer and his customer is one of employment.[1]

---

1. Lumiere v. Robertson-Cole Distributing Corp., 280 F. 550 (2d Cir. 1922). Cert. Denied, 259 U.S. 583 (1922).

This is true in either a written or an oral contract. Once the assignment is made and understood by both parties, the contract is made.

Contracts usually do not mention the negatives, and the law is indefinite as to who should be the owner.[2] Some cases hold that the negatives "belong" to the customer. Other cases say that the photographer in the absence of an agreement to the contrary has the "right to retain the negative." In effect, however, these courts are saying the same thing: This right to retain the negatives has an important qualification. If the photographer does in fact retain the negatives, he may not "make any use of the negatives without the permission of the customer."

Thus, the best principle to work under seems to be that the customer or client has purchased the prints and the negatives, but the photographer can keep the negatives. The logic for the courts is that the assignment was for the prints only and the negatives are simply work materials that the photographer may retain but not use. The negatives are part of the job package the customer bought.

One court said this general rule does not apply where a cameraman takes a photograph gratuitously, for his own benefit and at his own expense, it having been held that under such circumstances he is the owner of the photograph and the negative.[3] If the photographer then sells the print, the negative remains the property of the photographer. He can make and sell additional prints to other clients or customers.

If, however, there is an agreement that this is an exclusive sale to this client, the photographer is not free to make and sell additional prints to others. If the picture is sold for a specific purpose, that is, for use in a single publication without reuse privileges, the client or customer cannot use it for any other purpose. He cannot make and use additional prints from the print he bought.

The situation is clearer and more definite when a photographer is working full time for an employer. Working on a full-time basis means the employer owns and can have possession of the prints and negatives. Problems may arise if the employee moonlights or free-lances for others. These problems can be avoided or solved satisfactorily only if the photographer and his employer enter into a contract as to the duty and off-duty creative effort.

The problem of off-duty creative effort is one which applies to all artists, writers, and the like, as well as to photographers. The contract as to off-duty effort should be as clear and as specific as possible. If the contract says all of the creative efforts of the photographer belong to the employer, there is no legal possibility of free-lancing during the evening or on weekends.

Ownership of copyright presents similar contract problems. Early cases held that a photograph was not a "print or engraving" and was not, therefore, a proper subject of copyright. In 1865, Congress extended copyright protection to negatives and photographs by expressly including them among the articles for which copyright was provided. The express designation of photographs has been continued in all subsequent copyright statutes.

Copyright has been the object of much tinkering but little in the way of substantial change since the present law was passed in 1909. Revisions of this

---

2. Hochstadter v. H. Tarr, Inc., 61 N.Y.S. 2d 762 (1957); Colton v. Jacques Marchais, Inc., 61 N.Y.S. 2d 269 (1946).
3. Press Publishing Co. v. Falk, 59 Fed. 324 (1894).

statute have been discussed by the Congress since 1968. Statutes and court decisions have established that the essential effect of copyright is to give the photographer or his agent or employer the exclusive right to multiplication of copies of his creations for sale.

The courts have held that it is an undeniable fact that a photograph may embody original work and artistic skill and be in fact an artistic production. This is true because it is the result of original intellectual conception on the part of its creator due to the arrangements of lights, groupings, posing, and other details—to produce an artistic, pleasing picture.

The basic purpose of copyright protection is to provide compensation to authors for contributing to the common good by publishing their works and for photographers by publishing their pictures. Copyright however is not primarily for the benefit of the photographer or author, but primarily for the benefit of the public.

The steps in securing a copyright are basic and simple:

First, the photographer must affix the copyright notice to each print. This notice consists of the word *Copyright* or the symbol plus the name of the copyright owner and the date.

Second, two copies of the photograph must be sent to the Register to Copyrights, Library of Congress, Washington, D.C., with Form J and six dollars.

If the photograph is not published, it may be copyrighted by sending only one photograph and six dollars to the Register of Copyright. If the photo is later published, another registration will be necessary along with another fee.

Protection lasts for twenty-eight years and is renewable for twenty-eight more years. A copyright may be sold, assigned, even bequeathed by will, but the agreement or intention must be in writing and signed by the owner of the copyright. This again is contract law, and the new owner or assignee has all of the rights of the original owner. The agreement may specify any limitations on the ownership the parties to the contract may agree upon.

Ordinarily, the photographer who creates the picture is the owner or copyright proprietor. However, as in ownership of prints and negatives, the situation may be different if the photographer is hired to make the picture for a customer or client. In most cases the courts say the customer or client is entitled to the copyright.

# Restraints on Photographers

Recent cases of "prior restraint" concerning photographers and journalists having access to and taking pictures in public places have been decided in favor of the press. In one case, a Duluth, Minnesota, photographer's movie camera was taken from him by a police officer.[4] The photographer had filmed the arrest of suspected burglars from a public boulevard where there was no restriction on the public. The federal district court said the right to use the camera could be restricted only if it interfered with police duties. The court cited the Pentagon Papers case[5] in deciding against the prior restraint of the police and the resulting "chilling effect" on the press.

In another case a federal district court in Indiana gave newsmen a constitutional right to have access to and to make use of public streets, roads, and

4. Channel 10, Inc. v. Gunnarson, 337 F. Supp. 634 (1972).
5. New York Times Co. v. United States, 403 U.S. 713 (1971).

**Ruth Snyder in Electric Chair** by Tom Howard of the *New York Daily News*. This is the famous or infamous "stolen" picture (Curtis D. MacDougall, *News Pictures Fit to Print . . . Or Are They?* [Stillwater, Okla.: Journalistic Services, Inc., 1971], p. 98). The picture was made January 12, 1928, in the death house at Sing Sing Prison. Howard, a Chicagoan and unknown to New York prison authorities, had strapped a subminiature camera to his ankle, with a cable release controlled from his pocket. The illegal picture was certainly a breach of ethics and of journalistic principles. Ruth Snyder and Henry Judd, who also was electrocuted, had been convicted of murdering the woman's husband. Included in 50 Memorable Pictures exhibit.

Legal Aspects of Photography

highways for the purpose of observing and recording in writing and photography the events that occur on these streets, without interference.[6]

The concern is important enough that a bill to make it a crime to interfere with a working journalist was encouraged through the legislature by the Long Island Press Photographers Association in November 1973. The bill would make it a crime to so interfere and punishable by as much as a year in jail and a $1,000 fine.

If property where a photographer wants to take a picture is privately owned and privately used, the owner must give permission to come onto his land. Likewise, in places such as museums and theaters permission usually must be given by the owner of the property. Even when privately owned, the public use of areas such as shopping centers will allow access in many cases for photographers and other members of the press. But if there is doubt, permission should be requested because the property is privately owned.

One interesting case that should concern photographers is *Galella* v. *Onassis*.[7] Under the First Amendment protection of free speech and press Donald Galella, a free-lance photographer, had sought damages and an injunction against former President John F. Kennedy's widow for interfering with his photographing her. The widow, now Mrs. Jacqueline Onassis, and the Secret Service agents in opposition sought an injunction against Galella's interference with the agents' activities protecting the Kennedy children.

After a six-week trial the court dismissed Galella's claim and granted relief to Mrs. Onassis and the Secret Service. The court enjoined Galella (1) from keeping Mrs. Onassis and her children under surveillance or following any of them; (2) from approaching within 100 yards of the home of Mrs. Onassis or her children, or within 100 yards of either child's school, or within 75 yards of either child or 50 yards of Mrs. Onassis; (3) from using the name, portrait, or picture of Mrs. Onassis or her children for advertising; and (4) from attempting to communicate with Mrs. Onassis or her children except through her attorney.

The federal district trial court found Galella guilty of harassment, intentional infliction of emotional distress, assault and battery, commercial exploitation of Mrs. Onassis' personality, and invasion of privacy. The appeals court said that evidence at the trial showed that Galella had on occasion intentionally physically touched Mrs. Onassis and her daughter, "caused fear of physical contact in his frenzied attempts to get their pictures," followed Mrs. Onassis and her children too closely in an automobile, and endangered the safety of the children while they were swimming, water-skiing, and horseback riding.

The appeals court said that Galella had "insinuated himself into the very fabric of Mrs. Onassis' life . . .," and the relief granted Mrs. Onassis was framed in part on the need to prevent further invasion of Mrs. Onassis' privacy. The appeals court was not sure whether Galella's actions "accords with present New York [privacy] law," but the court said there is no doubt that it is "sustainable under New York's proscription of harassment."

Thus the appeals court based its decision on "harassment" and not on invasion of privacy. The court said Galella's actions went far beyond the reasonable bounds of news gathering. The court added:

---

6. Gazette Publishing Co. v. Cox. Unreported decision by Judge Cale J. Holden, U.S District Court Southern District of Indiana. May 2, 1967.

7. Galella v. Onassis, 487 F 2d 986 (1973).

When weighed against the *de minimis* public importance of the daily activities of the defendant, Galella's constant surveillance, his obtrusive and intruding presence, was unwarranted and unreasonable.[8]

However the appeals court did modify the lower court's order to prohibit only (1) any approach within 25 feet of Mrs. Onassis or any touching of the person of Mrs. Onassis, (2) any blocking of her movement in public places and thoroughfares, (3) any act foreseeably or reasonably calculated to place the life and safety of Mrs. Onassis in jeopardy, and (4) any conduct which would reasonably be foreseen to harass, alarm, or frighten Mrs. Onassis.

The court added:

> Any further restriction on Galella's taking and selling pictures of defendant for news coverage is, however, improper and unwarranted by the evidence.[9]

Although the decision in the appellate court was based on harassment and not on invasion of privacy, the possible threat of this interpretation looms large for photographers. The tort of invasion of privacy or the right of a person to be left alone has grown during the past eighty years. It concerns the protection of a person's name, portrait, image, likeness or picture, sketch, signature, coat of arms, and the like, by another but without the person's consent. It can be violated by use of voice, musical, or other style, as well as by print, broadcast, or photographs in story, dialogue, dramatization, fictionalization, testimonial, and the like.

Defamation, an ancient tort, is almost synonymous with invasion of privacy to many persons today. Defamation is concerned with damage to a person's reputation and has nothing to do with the right to be left alone. The camera has been involved in many invasion-of-privacy suits because the camera records the entire scene without selecting individuals or parts as a writer does. So anyone in the news picture may feel his privacy has been invaded. Plaintiffs suing any of the mass media today can file a suit in each area, one for libel and another for invasion of privacy, for the same incident—and collect on each.

Defamation is the broad term that covers both libel and slander. Libel concerns printed defamations. The courts explain this by saying that it is a libel if it has "permanence of form." There is no doubt that negatives and prints have permanence of form. *So photographers are concerned with libel and not with slander.*

Libel, damage to reputation, is a false publication of a story and/or a picture that is capable of a defamatory meaning. This means the person is claiming to have been brought into hatred, contempt, or ridicule to a substantial and respectable group, according to an interesting old case. This case concerned a picture of a nurse in a testimonial advertisement in praise of "Duffy's Pure Malt Whiskey." The catch was that the photograph used was of one person while the name was that of another. A successful libel action resulted. True, the use of the portrait of the nurse in the advertisement may not have been libelous to many persons, but the Supreme Court said this did not matter if the advertisement obviously would hurt this woman in the "estimation of an important and respectable part of the community."[10]

---

8. 487 F.2d 986 (1973).

9. 487 F.2d 986 (1973).

10. Peck v. Tribune, 214 U.S. 185 (1909).

The important area of the law about the statement of a picture being "published" in the legal sense is not of much concern to the photographer. If a picture appears in print or is broadcast—it is published. *The idea in "publication" is that the defamation was communicated to a third person.*

Once it is established to the satisfaction of the court that a person's reputation has been damaged and that a jury would understand the publication in a defamatory sense, the defenses come into play. Libel defenses for the press are simple and basic: *truth and privilege.*

The defense of truth usually is believed to have started with the John Peter Zenger trial in 1735. Andrew Hamilton advanced the novel concept at Zenger's trial, and it became almost impossible to convict a colonial editor who published the truth. Most state statutes say truth is a complete defense to a libel action. The problem of what is truth is more difficult for writers than for photographers. The picture usually speaks for itself—and thus is not libelous.

**Wife Beater Gets Whipping** by Joseph Costa of the *New York Daily News* (*above*) This was another stolen camera shot. This picture is in better taste, perhaps, and not so well known as the preceding picture. This picture was taken in a Baltimore jail as a wife beater received a twenty-one-lash sentence when the court invoked an ancient ruling. Included in 50 Memorable Pictures exhibit.

Legal Aspects of Photography

Optical illusions, however, are sometimes created by the camera, and one such situation resulted in a successful libel suit. The plaintiff appeared in a picture used in a Camel cigarette advertisement holding his saddle in such a way that the stirrup strap appeared to be an obscene and ludicrous deformity.[11] It was also a defamation to print a picture in juxtaposition with an article on evolution and a photograph of a gorilla.[12]

Another defense involves the three branches of government and the idea that certain occasions in the public interest demand protection for individuals to speak freely and fearlessly. Thus an absolute privilege arises for public officials in the legislatures in the course of any of their functions in the legislative chambers. Judicial proceedings also have an absolute privilege attached when in the courtroom. The executive department has this same absolute privilege for the head of state and the major officers of executive departments of the federal and state governments. (This immunity from tort damages should not be confused with executive privilege to testify before judicial and legislative bodies.)

The participants in these three governmental areas thus have an absolute privilege from tort liability while performing their official functions. The press has only a "conditional privilege" to cover these governmental bodies as long as the coverage is full, fair, and accurate.

When coverage of the courts is mentioned the subject of Canon 35 arises. This judicial canon, for many years a concern of news photographers, has to do with use of a camera in courtrooms. It was adopted within two years after the 1935 trial of Bruno Hauptmann for kidnapping the Lindbergh baby. The American Bar Association adopted Canon 35 of its judicial ethics which prohibited the "taking of photographs in the courtroom during sessions of the court or recesses between sessions."

At one time all of the states except Colorado, Oklahoma, and Texas had adopted Canon 35 or some modification of it by statute or some state court rules. Some states allowed the judge to make decisions as to the use of cameras in his courtroom.

Canon 35 was amended in 1963 to include television in its ban against use of cameras in the courtroom. The American Bar Association (ABA) has now adopted Canon 3(A)(7) of the Code of Judicial Conduct. The new code is mainly concerned with television coverage, and still cameras get similar treatment as in the old Canon 35. Cameras are permitted in the courtroom only when they will not distract or impair the dignity of the proceedings.

This canon has to be adopted by the various states in some manner before the Bar Association canon is effective on the courts. However, many court judges adopt ABA canon as operating procedure without waiting for their state courts to take any action.

The use of cameras in legislative bodies is as varied as the many federal, state, and local legislative bodies that are in session over the United States. Some allow unlimited photo coverage, while others are like the Congress and refuse access to their proceedings by cameras of any sort.

The national, state, and local executive department officials are somewhat more open to photo coverage. The conditional privilege of the press to cover

11. Burton v. Crowell Publishing Co., 82 F.2d 154 (1936).
12. Zbyszko v. New York American, 239 N.Y.S. 411 (1930).

these bodies and officials is valuable protection against civil liability in defamation—but full, fair, and accurate coverage is essential.

The defense of fair comment and criticism is also available to photographers but appears to be less important than the primary defenses of truth and privilege.

The traditional libel defenses are not available in invasion of privacy suits. If an event or person is newsworthy, then the person involved cannot invoke the right of privacy if a newspaper or television station uses his name and/or picture in the publication of a matter of legitimate public interest concerning his public life.

The defenses for suits against the press for invasion of privacy are: first, that the person or event is newsworthy and, second, if the picture is used for advertising or "for purposes of trade" then consent is the only protection for the photojournalist and his employer. Consent is a release signed by both parties and thus is a contract between the publication and the subject. Written contracts are required in states that have statutes concerning privacy. So when working in the advertising or "for purposes of trade" areas, a professional photojournalist gets a release from the subject or subjects involved.

# Constitutional Protection in Libel and Privacy

The twin torts of libel and invasion of privacy had separate but simple defenses until 1964. If a suit against a publisher was for libel, he had the defense of truth or if the coverage involved the three basic areas of government the press was conditionally privileged to cover full, fair, and accurate.

If a suit involved invasion of privacy, the publisher or radio or television station owner had a release signed by the individual unless the person or event was newsworthy. In 1964 the Supreme Court decided the landmark *New York Times* v. *Sullivan* case and added a constitutional defense to aid journalists.[13] The court said in this case that a person who was a public official could not collect libel damages unless the publication used "actual malice." That is:

> Knowledge that it [the publication] was false or with reckless disregard of whether it was false or not.[14]

Later cases interpret this "reckless disregard" rule to mean that editors, photographers, or reporters on the publication entertained "serious doubts" as to the truth of the publication. Publishing with such doubts, according to the justices, shows reckless disregard for truth or falsity and demonstrates "actual malice."

Two years later the Supreme Court expanded the *New York Times* actual malice rule to include public figures in addition to public officials. In 1971 a plurality of the court expanded the *New York Times* protection to a defamatory publication about an "individual's involvement in an event of public or general interest."[15] So in less than ten years the Supreme Court took the consti-

13. New York Times v. Sullivan, 376 U.S. 254 (1964).

14. 376 U.S. 254 (1964).

15. Rosenbloom v. Metromedia, 403 U.S. 29 (1971).

tutional protection afforded the press in discussing and photographing public officials and expanded this immunity to discussions or photographs of "events of public or general interest."

While this protection was developing in the libel area, the courts were also involved in protection for invasions of privacy by the media. In 1967 the Supreme Court justices said the First Amendment protects the press against privacy suits for false reports of matters of public interest in the absence of proof that the publisher or the broadcaster published the report "with knowledge of its falsity or in reckless disregard of the truth."[16]

This case concerned the use of photographs with an article about a play of a family trapped by convicts in their home. *Life* had photographed the actors during tryouts of the play in Philadelphia. The photographs were taken in the James Hill home where the real incident had taken place. The Hill family had moved prior to the filming. The magazine article included photos of the son being roughed up by the convicts and the daughter biting the hand of a convict to make him drop a gun.

The James Hill family referred to in the article and shown in the pictures had been released unharmed. They even said they had been treated courteously by the convicts. After the pictures and article appeared in *Life*, the Hills sued because they said the article gave the impression that the play mirrored the Hill family's experience which Hill said *Life* knew was "false and untrue."

*Life* used the traditional defense that the article was "a subject of legitimate news interest," meaning it was "newsworthy." The court discussed the possibility that the article was published "for trade purposes," but added this did not remove the constitutional protection afforded *Life*. Thus *Life* received constitutional protection against having to pay damages for invasion of privacy. This case moved the "actual malice" test into the privacy area.

Despite this added protection for photojournalists given in the Time, Inc. versus Hill case, the importance of consent or releases should not be overlooked. A release is a contract signed by both parties and requires the three elements of any contract: offer, acceptance, and consideration. Thus a photographer offers a subject a certain sum for the right to use his or her picture "for purposes of trade"—use it, that is, for an advertisement, to illustrate an article, and the like. The subject *accepts* the *offer* of the photographer and the sum of money agreed upon, and use of the subject's likeness is the *consideration* to make a contract.

Since releases do involve contract law, it is important to have the contract cover the uses of the photo intended by the parties. In a recent case concerning *Newsweek* magazine the court said it simply:[17]

> It is true that if the plaintiff consented to the use of his photograph in connections with this article he would have waived his right of action for invasion of privacy.

However, if the court found that he had consented to the photo's use in a daily newspaper and not in a weekly newsmagazine, the plaintiff's right to be left alone would have been invaded, and the newsmagazine would have had to pay damages.

---

16. Time, Inc. v. Hill, 385 U.S. 374 (1967).
17. Raible v. Newsweek, Inc. 341 F. Supp. 804 (1972).

# RELEASE OR CONSENT FORM

Here is an example of a model photograph release:

Date _____

I, (we) _____ (name) _____ being of legal age and in consideration of One Dollar ($1) and other good valuable consideration, the receipt of which is hereby acknowledged, hereby consent and authorize the __(publication)__ _____ to use and reproduce my name and photograph (or photographs) taken by _____ (name) _____ on ___(date)___ and circulated the same for any and all purposes, including publication and advertising of every description. No further claim of whatsoever nature will be made by me.

(name) _____

(witness) _____     (address) _____

(photographer) _____

(Note: Most publications do have their own release forms. It is important that the form be drafted by an attorney familiar with the law in your state and area.)

# Student Participation

Amendment No. 1 to the United States Constitution states: "Congress shall make no law respecting an establishment of religion, or prohibiting the free exercise thereof; or abridging the freedom of speech, or of the press; or the right of the people peaceably to assemble, and to petition the government for a redress of grievances."

1. Study Amendment No. 1 carefully and thoughtfully use it as the basis for a discussion of this chapter.
2. To better understand our legal system and Mr. Spencer's presentation of the legal aspects of photography, look up at least three cases cited in this chapter. Use either a private or a public law office for your research.

Dale R. Spencer is professor of journalism and member of the American Bar Association and the Missouri Bar. He began his career as a reporter in his hometown, Pocatello, Idaho, before World War II. Professor Spencer graduated from the School of Journalism, University of Missouri, in 1948. After a short time as instructor in journalism at the University, he became sales manager for E. W. Stephens Publishing Company. Spencer worked on the copydesk at the *Buffalo Evening News* in 1952. He served as assistant managing editor of the *Columbia Missourian* and taught copy editing from 1950 until 1973. In 1973 Spencer became acting managing editor of the *Missourian,* a position he held until 1974. In 1958 he began teaching a course in communications law. He has written more than a dozen articles on law, two editions of the book *Law for the Newsman,* and a textbook on copy editing.

# An Introduction to Color

# 15

or many years before it was practical, color reproduction was the goal of the printing industry. Although Currier successfully used the chromolithograph process in the 1840s, the process was slow and expensive, requiring a separate lithograph stone for each of the colors in an illustration. Because of this, most of the color lithographs turned out by Currier & Ives were hand painted. For a number of years, too, fashion plates featured in *Godey's Lady's Book* and in Peterson's *Ladies' National Magazine* were hand colored in an assembly-line operation. One person painted the blue parts of the steel engraving; another the red feather in the perky little hat; and so forth. This method produced very attractive illustrations, but production was slow and, even with the low cost of labor, expensive.

A system was needed which would permit application of color during a regular press run. Because of this need, spot color, a method still used, was developed. Spot color permits the printing of various colored headlines and illustrations in articles and/or advertisements.

If a sheetfed press is used to do the printing, the page must be run through the press as many times as there are colors. Only one color is run at a time. Occasionally the use of spot color calls for good presswork and close register of the various colors used. For example, if the picture were of a three-colored clown, the red used for the bulbous nose must not completely obscure the tan used for the skin. Color printing requires that each color be kept under control. The job of registration is even more critical in the printing of halftone color.

French Impressionist painters developed realism in color in the 1860s–1880s. Some of the Impressionists used tiny dots of color put down with a finely pointed brush, and in so doing they provided a lesson in color reproduction which is still valid and in use today. Pressmen use the halftone to lay down complementary colors much as the Impressionists had done. Photo-offset and photogravure have added to the quality of many color pictures in present-day newspapers and magazines.

## Process Color Printing

Color copy, the copy from which the color illustration is made, can be either a negative color film or a positive print or transparency. Regardless of the form in which a picture is turned in for reproduction, separation negatives must be

Printing in color and especially "full color" has always been an expensive process. Researchers have proved, however, that in spite of the additional cost, it is a paying investment.

A preprint color page (Spectacolor) which appeared in the September 20, 1974, *Jackson Citizen Patriot* and in seven other Booth newspapers. The story and photos were done by Ed Lehr, picture editor of the *Citizen Patriot*. The story was about a fashion buyer for a chain of Michigan store

# She chooses for Michigan

Hurrying through New York's garment district

Looking at hundreds of items may turn up one hot accessory that will make a big season.

STORY AND PHOTOS BY ED LEHR

Kathy searches for wares for "her kind of customer"

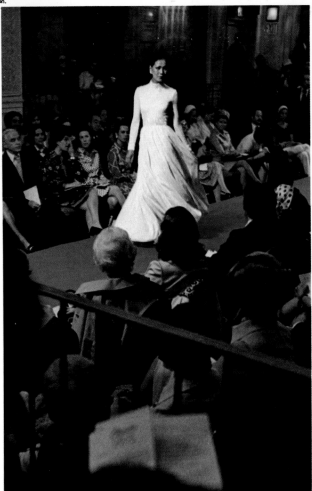

thy tries on a belt. It looks good. She'll take it.

f matches the outfit she saw n the morning. She'll buy it .

thousands of women across .

Althaus of Jackson is buying ions for a chain of Michigan er tastes will have a hand in ning the current autumn 'look'' for women.

as among buyers attending Market'' on New York's Avenue garment district last

's specialty is accessories. ctions complement clothes y her fellow buyers.

g the market four months he fall season, Kathy sees e designers and suppliers, resources'' in the market, this year's look.

offered advice by fulltime k representatives, who are okout for ''hot'' or fast-mov- s.

representatives also know esources have merchandise ompetitively priced — be they rs or suppliers who have fast-moving style.

shion picture nationally is

greatly determined by buying groups such as the one to which Kathy's store belongs. Representatives of several hundred stores across the country pool their efforts and decide collectively what is in and what is not.

Decisions are made on colors, lengths, fabrics, hairdos, makeup and accessories. The latter is Kathy's area and covers shoes, jewelry, handbags, scarves, lingerie and belts. All help to make ''the look''.

If a group decides a certain color is not ''in,'' it will be rare indeed to find it in any store during the season. But the choice, which the consumer ultimately is offered, is the result of careful consideration.

Kathy, for instance, attends shows by the designers whose clothes will be pushed in her stores. She knows what the ready-to-wear market is. When she buys, her resources give her tips on the merchandise that is moving well.

The resource and buyer are on a first-name basis, often embracing like long-lost relatives when they greet each other as the new buying session begins.

Kathy sips a Coke and chatters with the seller about his family. Then come stacks of attractive belts, the samples from which she chooses.

"How has this been going?" Kathy asks a representative of Christian Dior, who is showing her belts and handbags.

'Very well,'' the man confirms. ''Coins and medallions are going to be very big this year. I think you should make these into an ad,'' he says as he holds two styles of belts for her to inspect.

''I think I should make an ad for each,'' Kathy responds. ''Can you help me with it?''

''Yes, we can go 5 per cent,'' he replies without hesitation.

She has just purchased his goods and received a promise of cooperative advertising money. The ads will carry his brand name as well as the signature of Kathy's store.

Throughout most of her week in New York, Kathy is on the move up and down the garment district. She visits by phone nearly a hundred resources and makes appointments with those she feesl have something new to offer.

Her day may include return visits, such as one to Vera, a scarf and accessory designer, where she checks the merchandise she ordered during an earlier trip. At Vera ''they are high-pressure,'' she says.

Continued on next page

For the total ''look,'' Kathy matches accessories a designer shows with each dress. Buyers attending the Claudia Collection opening by designer Halley at the Gotham

This picture of Premier Chou En Lai of the Peoples Republic of China (*left*) is one in the portfolio of pictures which earned the Nikon World Understanding Award for Giorgio Lotti of *Epoca Magazine* in 1973. The World Understanding Award is one of the major prizes given in the Pictures of the Year competition. This picture, made in only the few minutes allotted him, is one of Lotti's favorites. "The carriage of this man —and especially the position of his hands," Giorgio says, "portray great dignity." Mr. Lotti has worked in many parts of the world: Russia, Japan, the Holy Land, Sicily, and China. He has published several books, and his photographs are in collections at the National Library of Paris, as well as at the University of Parma, Italy. (Photo courtesy of Giorgio Lotti.)

Asked to produce a laser beam photograph for an article to appear in a *School Bulletin,* a *National Geographic* photo crew headed by Arlan Wiker took the assignment in stride. The brief caption for the cover picture (*left*) of the *National Geographic School Bulletin* read: "Highly concentrated laser beam flashes across the Potomac River from the Washington Monument." Laser is an acronym formed from the first letters of *l*ight *a*mplification by *s*timulated *e*mission of radiation (see chapter 20, p. 277).

This EPA-Documerica photo by Bob W. Smith dramatically shows the expressway approaching downtown Dallas, Texas. "The assignment," says Gifford Hampshire, Documerica director (see p. 00), "was to show what happens to a modern city without a definite land-use plan." Hampshire had no objections to the extreme wide-angle lens used in taking the picture, asserting that it has provided an acceptable "documentary distortion." In his opinion the wide-angle lens provides emphasis which "makes more real the scene it portrays." (Photo courtesy of EPA-Documerica.)

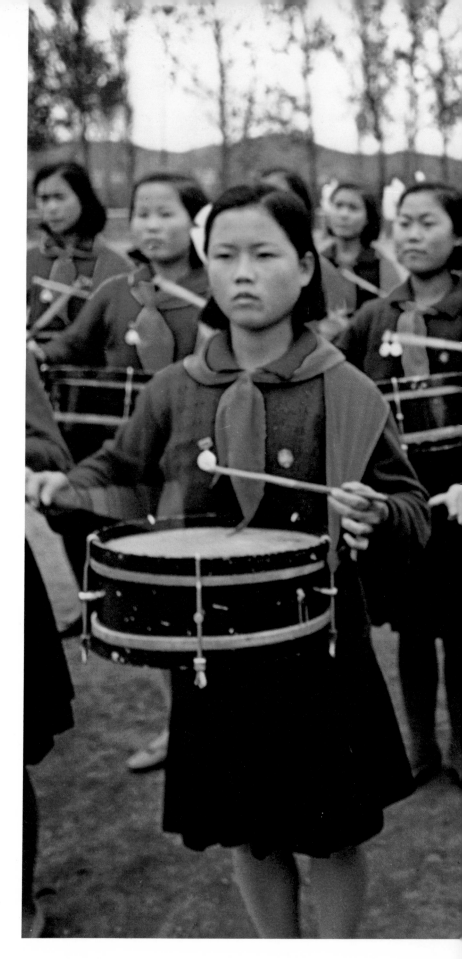

**A Rare Look at North Korea** by
H. Edward Kim. Vast changes have come to
China and North Korea in two decades; yet
political barriers have kept Americans from
getting the facts firsthand. When restrictions
eased in 1972, *National Geographic* began
efforts to send in staff members. Finally,
North Korean officials agreed to admit
*Geographic's* layout editor, H. Edward Kim,
the first American photojournalist allowed
inside Korea in twenty-five years. His word-
and-picture report appeared in the August
1974 issue of the *Geographic* and won an
Overseas Press Club award in 1975. The
picture portrays children of a new order. The
red neckerchiefs identify them as members
of the Young Pioneers, a Communist Youth
Corps. The group wear achievement medals
and badges portraying North Korean President Kim Il Sung. (Photograph by H.
Edward Kim © National Geographic
Society.)

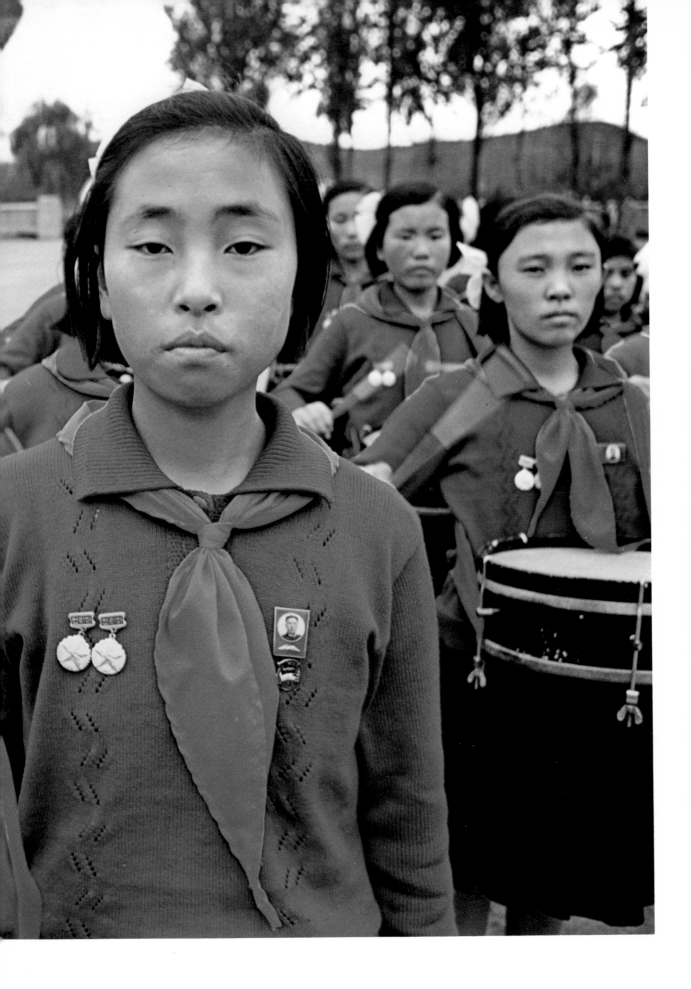

134, NO. 6     DECEMBER, 1968

# NATIONAL GEOGRAPHIC

SEE "REPTILES AND AMPHIBIANS," TUESDAY, DEC. 3, ON CBS TV (page 875A) made. Whether a negative or a transparency is used, the process is the same. The proper filters are used to separate the copy into the complementary colors. Each color is printed in black and white on special paper. From these black-and-white separations are shot the screened negatives from which eventually come the color plates: the magenta or red plate, the yellow plate, and blue plate. Some newspapers require an additional black plate as a stabilizer.

To emphasize: Newspaper color pictures may be shot on either negative or positive color film. Regardless of how it is shot and regardless of whether one uses a positive color print or a color transparency—or for that matter the color negative—the first requirement is a color separation job. If the copy is a print, it may be color separated, using the proper filters, on a process or copying camera. The negative and positive color transparencies are placed in enlarging machines (now often computerized). Here the various colors are printed in black and white on a special nonshrink, nonstretch sensitized paper. These prints, representing the various separation colors, are screened on the process camera. The negatives so produced are converted into color printing plates, all of which are printed in close register to produce the final color reproduction for the newspaper or magazine. The whole process is almost a miracle. To watch the red, yellow, and blue plates, with perhaps a black plate, turn into pretty, colorful pictures is a pleasure, indeed.

The separation process—the system that breaks the copy into its complementary colors—is one part of the color-printing process which for many years delayed full, complete acceptance of color reproduction. Another factor that hindered wide use of color engravings is the cost. Three or four black-and-white pages can be produced in the same press space required to produce one color picture. Color requires considerable extra work, and it is far more expensive than black and white. Why, then, is color used at all?

## Importance of Color

Surveys have proved that color pages are more popular, that editorial and advertising matter bolstered by color illustrations has far greater readership than pages which offer only black-and-white pictures.

An advertisement in the *Monroe City News,* a Missouri weekly newspaper, recently pointed out that "surveys, like the one conducted by the *Independent Press-Telegram,* Long Beach, California, have shown 50 percent, 70 percent, and 80 percent greater dollar sales for a color ad over the same ad in black."[1]

## Run-of-Press Color

Color in a newspaper that is produced by the publication itself is usually referred to as ROP or run-of-press color. Sometimes in an effort to give its readers more and better color, publications use a process known as preprinting. Spectacolor and Hi-Fi are trade names used to identify the products of two business concerns which produce halftone color preprints.

When ordering preprint material, the customer submits pictures and/or transparencies properly scaled, and an accurate layout is submitted with the

Marking the twenty-third anniversary of the ...om bombing of Japan, South Vietnamese ...ildren pray for peace on an island in the ...ekong River. The photograph (*left*) by ... E. Garrett (author of chapter 16) ...ppeared on the cover of the December 1968 ...sue of *National Geographic* magazine. ...Original in color.)

1. *Monroe City News,* May 2, 1974, p. 14.

picture material to show exactly how it is to run. Type matter can also be provided for use with the color plate. The printer carefully follows instructions. Part of the color side of the sheet and all of the opposite side are left blank, permitting the customer to use type or halftones to fill in with local and timely material.

After the color pictures have been printed, the paper is rerolled and shipped to the user. The roll with the color pictures in place is printed by the customer who inserts it in his publication for distribution to his readers. The page is marked in the margin outside the printed surface. On the customer's press an electric eye scans this mark which thus acts as a cutoff and adds to the accuracy of the register as the page goes through the press.

The *Jackson Citizen Patriot* has had considerable success with Spectacolor (see p. 205). The managing editor of that publication explains his operation:

"As far as can be determined, the Booth newspapers of Michigan Spectacolor program, which began in 1970, is the only one of its kind.

"Four times each year, all eight Booth papers—at Saginaw, Bay City, Flint, Ann Arbor, Jackson, Kalamazoo, Grand Rapids, and Muskegon—present the same eight Spectacolor pages on the same day.

"Total circulation is 520,000.

"Spectacolor runs as wraparounds of four sections. Content is split fifty-fifty between editorial matter and advertising. Ads and full-color photos are preprinted by Standard Gravure of Louisville. Rerolled, the Spectacolor color pages are shipped to all eight Booth plants."[2]

Booth's national sales office in Southfield, Michigan, handles the advertising. All photographic work and writing are done by Booth staff people on assignment from their managing editors through requests from the managing editor of the *Jackson Citizen Patriot*.

The effort centers on good color photography and well-written feature stories, both of which offer considerable impact. Examples of Booth Spectacolor work are given on page 000.

# Student Participation

1. Color television produces a wide range of colors by blending the three primary colors: red, green, and blue. Use an encyclopedia to find what is meant by color by addition or subtraction. Be prepared to explain your findings.

2. Why must a painting or a color photograph go through a process of separation before it can be printed in a newspaper or magazine?

---

2. Thomas A. Riordan, January 16, 1974: personal communication.

An Introduction to Color

# 16 National Geographic

## The Magazine That Taught Us How to Use Pictures... and Color

*W. E. Garrett*

The magazine that taught us how to use pictures... and color, by W. E. (Bill) Garrett, senior assistant editor.

As it has done for eighty-six years, the little magazine with the yellow-bordered cover still moves quietly and politely through the publishing world—creating little fuss as it gathers records for endurance and popularity.

Nearly one of every five Americans sees the *National Geographic* magazine every month; yet it can be found on no newsstand. And, furthermore, you don't subscribe, you join the National Geographic Society and receive its journal.

The Society, chartered under the laws of the District of Columbia in January 1888 "to increase and diffuse Geographic knowledge" began the irregular publication of its journal in late 1888.

In the two decades between 1885 and 1905 more than 7,500 magazines began publication in the United States. Today only seven of any significance remain: *Vogue, McCalls, Ladies Home Journal, Cosmopolitan, Argosy, The Journal of the American Medical Association,* and the *National Geographic.* Like the dog wagged by its tail the Society became the world's largest membership educational organization. As a result of the magazine's success, the Society yearly grants more than one million dollars for research and exploration.

The only consistent complaint from faithful members who annually renew, at a near ninety percent rate, concerns problems of storage. Rare is the member so callous as to throw away a single copy.

In nearly a thousand issues to date the magazine has published an unparalleled photographic chronicle of our universe—indexed and available to hundreds of millions of people through libraries and sagging home bookshelves worldwide. Like wine of a good vintage its paper, ink, binding, and contents age well. Browsing through old issues distracts many a person bent on cleaning the attic.

The *Geographic* has scored hundreds of journalistic firsts and collected more photojournalism prizes in media competition than any other publication. Yet it makes no pretense to being a news magazine. Although not an aviation or space publication, it has won ten Aviation/Space Writers awards; while not a science magazine, in recent years its writers received five of the top science-writing prizes.

Throughout the world the yellow-bordered cover ranks as an institution with the wasp-waisted Coca-Cola bottle. Apropos of such shapes, the magazine has earned a certain notoriety for publishing photographs of bare-breasted women beginning with an 1896 wedding picture of a Zulu bride and bridegroom. Yet the *Geographic* has seldom been accused of vulgarity or sensationalism and is generally considered a family magazine.

Partly because of the lack of newsstand sales, the small format, and its universal popularity, it not-so-happily ranks as the most stolen magazine in history. Postal clerks worldwide seem to be the first to spot a story on their area. Occasionally members receive their copies—after they have been well read.

As other magazines weakened and died, frenziedly competing for circulation and advertising, the *National Geographic* has continued to enjoy a steady five-to-eight percent growth rate. As of January 1975, the circulation reached nine million. One month's issue would form an impressive—if unwieldy—stack forty-five miles high; equal to eight Mt. Everests.

This phenomenal success must be credited largely to the early, extensive, and continuing publication of the best in color photography. As a bee and his flowers enjoy a profitable relationship, the *Geographic* and color photography developed together in a symbiotic dependence nearly as inseparable as nectar and honey. From the first pale stone engravings of views of Nicaragua published in its fourth issue in May 1889, the magazine's pioneer utilization of color illustrations expanded until 1961 when high-speed web presses made possible excellent color reproduction on every page.

In addition, the *Geographic* contributed to the present success and popularity of color. Its photographers and technicians made significant contributions to equipment and techniques basic to color photography.

The first underwater color photograph of a coral reef fish was made in 1924 with equipment built by the *Geographic*. Today Bob Sisson shoots action candids of microscopic creatures on equipment he designed that gives a 25-diameter magnification.

But the magazine's most important contribution may have been its continuing development of a public awareness of color aided by the practice of crediting on every color picture published not only the photographer, but also the type of film he used. From the first Lumière Autochrome of a flower garden in Ghent, Belgium, published in 1914, through Finlay Color, Dufaycolor, Agfacolor, etc., these by-lines traced the development and use of new emulsions.

In the Autochrome process, developed in France in 1907, tiny particles of potato starch dyed red, green, and violet blue were spread on a glass plate and coated with a sensitive photographic emulsion. The plate was exposed with its uncoated side facing the camera lens so that light passed through the colored grains before reaching the emulsion. Developing the plate in reverse produced a positive color transparency.

Autochrome was used by *National Geographic* until the early 1930s, but at one time and another the magazine also used most of the other early color processes.

The Finlay color screen mosaic plate of the 1920s had 175 lines to the inch and was a refinement of the earlier Paget plates. A panchromatic glass plate was exposed in the camera behind a so-called taking screen, then pro-

E. (Bill) Garrett is Senior Assistant
tor of *National Geographic* magazine in
rge of layout. In addition, he is responsi-
for planning future articles and for the
ting and photography of many special
cles on his own. He has contributed
pters to several of the Society's books, and
coproducer-narrator for the television
cial *Alaska!* which earned the 1967 Ciné
den Eagle Award. While he has used
ords and pictures," to produce articles
m Canada, Alaska, and Mexico, his chief
rest is in Southeast Asia where he has
ered eleven major assignments.
Much in demand as a lecturer, Mr. Garrett
appeared at seminars and special journal-
programs at the universities of Alaska,
ton, Harvard, Maryland, Miami, Minne-
a, Missouri, North Carolina, Southern
nois, and Syracuse. He also has lectured to
Cosmos Club in Washington, D.C., and
he Asia Society of New York. A frequent
f member of the University of Missouri
to Workshop, Garrett was also a staff
mber of the National Press Photographers
ng short course in 1966, 1972, and 1973.
Among the many honors he has won is
Magazine Photographer of the Year
ard in 1968. Garrett has had several
otographic exhibits at the Smithsonian
titution, Washington, D.C., and at the
orge Eastman House, Rochester,
w York.

a result of his world travels Garrett has
ends in many remote areas of the globe. In
s photograph (*right*), taken in 1973,
rrett says hello to a youngster in Regan,
ntral Burma. He had visited the baby's
rents in 1971, and they were proud indeed
introduce Bill to their new offspring.
Original picture in color.)

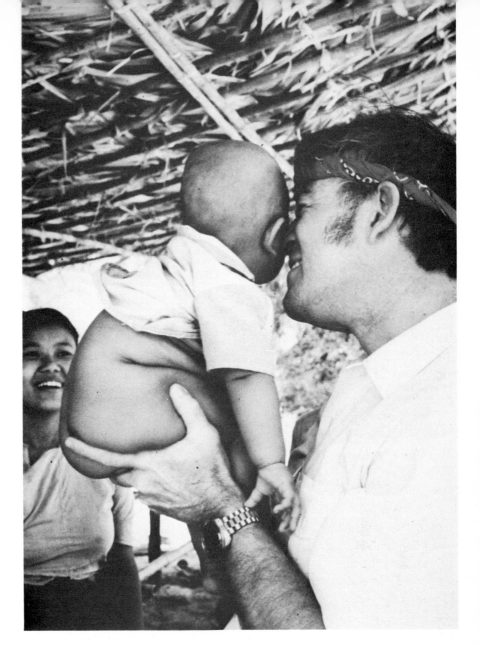

cessed to a negative and contacted onto a high-contrast emulsion. After further
processing, this was registered with the viewing screen to produce a color
transparency.

The Finlay system required special holders, and was not quite as fine-grained
as the Autochrome plates, but it was faster, permitting photography of people
moving though not too quickly.

Agfacolor, a German process, substituted dyed resin for the dyed potato
starch used in Autochrome plates, and permitted photographers to record action
at twice the speed of Finlay plates.

Dufaycolor, developed in the early 1930s, was the first to use film instead of
glass plates. The mosaic screen on Dufay film had parallel lines of blue and
green crossed with lines of red and gave excellent color rendition.

The big breakthrough in color photography came with the introduction of
Kodachrome in the 1930s. Film packs were smaller and lighter than glass
mosaic plates and had the virtue of not breaking when jounced for hours along
backwoods trails or down river rapids.

Beginning in 1938 the monotonous regularity with which photographic credit lines started with the words "Kodachrome by . . ." made Eastman's remarkable roll film a household word and speeded acceptance of 35-mm. color photography by professionals and amateurs. Film credits were discontinued in the January 1972 issue, but the magazine still receives letters pleading, sometimes demanding, that they be reinstated.

Throughout its history the *Geographic* has been subject to praise, criticism, and spoofing.

Frank Luther Mott in his Pulitzer Prizewinning *History of American Magazines* (1957) was complimentary:

> There is really nothing like it in the world. For more than half a century the *National Geographic* has not published a single monthly number that has not been interesting and informative, with some measure of permanent value. If it has seemed to some critics too much of a picture book, even they have to admit that in this it is in harmony with its times, and that its pictures are educational in a high degree. By the middle of the twentieth century it had attained the largest monthly circulation in the world at its price, and it had an assured position among the top ten monthly circulations at any price. This is a fabulous record of success, especially since the magazine is founded upon the editorial conviction that rates the intelligence of the popular audience fairly high. The NGM has long represented an achievement in editorship and management outstanding in the history of periodicals.[1]

Sophisticated publications enjoy painting a pith-helmet-and-puttee image of the *Geographic,* while they marvel at its mystifying success. The magazine treats the occasional condescending satire with the disdain of a St. Bernard for the yapping of a toy poodle.

One of the most ingenious and amusing lampoons appeared in the September 1958 issue of *Mad* magazine. The spoof was titled "The National Osographic Magazine," and it aped the archaic, gingerbread makeup and, with devastating effect, mocked the ingenious titles then in vogue. It featured articles on "Shooting Mau Maus for Fun and Profit" by Trigger Castalni and "Hootchie-Koo Women Don't Wear Clothes" by Lemuel T. Lecher. So brilliantly did the picture captions mirror *Geographic* text style that the editor considered hiring the author.

In February of 1973 NBC's "Today" show devoted five valuable minutes to a complimentary discussion of the *National Geographic* magazine on its seventy-fifth birthday. Fortunately, or unfortunately, they had not checked their copy with the *Geographic's* meticulous research department. NBC missed the birthday by ten years.

In the third edition (1971) of *Collector's Guide to the National Geographic* Edwin Buxbaum, a friend and unabashed admirer of the magazine, felt obliged to note, "Others have been critical. They complain about the text . . . the style has been described, by them, as old-fashioned, archaic, Pollyannaish, or 'Dear Aunt Sally.'"

Traditionally, the magazine has attempted to be accurate and objective, but in recent years under the editorship of Gilbert M. Grosvenor the rose-colored glasses have come off, occasionally to the displeasure of politicians and pressure

---

1. Frank L. Mott, *History of American Magazines* (Cambridge, Mass.: Harvard University Press, 1957).

groups. In the April 1974 issue, for example, an article on Damascus stirred the Syrians to ban the *Geographic* from further entry into their country. The same article prompted the American Jewish Congress to picket Society offices in Washington, D.C., claiming the magazine had been unfair to Syrian Jewry. Editor Grosvenor remarked, "Today there's no middle ground in the Middle East."

*Geographic* members still look to their magazine for vicarious, even escapist, experiences with the world. But as events and controversies of the past two decades stripped away much of the American public's naiveté, they have demanded and received objectively and accurately more of the unsweetened facts of life.

Possibly with some exaggeration for effect, President Harry S. Truman once said, "The only thing new is the history we don't know." To understand the success of today's *Geographic* we must consider its history.

A distinguished group of thirty-three men formed the National Geographic Society in January 1888 and began publication of its journal in October. Gardiner Green Hubbard served as first president and was succeeded by his son-in-law, Alexander Graham Bell, in 1898. Ten years later, the one thousand-member Society verged on bankruptcy.

Bell hired, at his own expense, a young man who had just graduated *magna cum laude* from Amherst and who happened to be courting his daughter to try to save the journal.

This first full-time employee of the magazine, Gilbert Hovey Grosvenor, reported for duty as an assistant editor on April Fools Day, 1899, and the *Geographic* success began to unfold. Although only twenty-three years old, the young man immediately exercised strong leadership. He overshadowed and eventually abolished the awkward committee that had guided the affairs of the fledgling publication. Within the year he rejected all the suggestions of the Society's consultant, the famous publisher S. S. McClure, that "the magazine move to New York, change its name, go to newsstand circulation, and never again mention the Society because people disliked geography." Also, Gilbert Grosvenor married Bell's daughter.

By 1886 Frederick Ives had developed the halftone method for reproducing photographs, but steel engravings were still in vogue. The magazine had already published a few halftones when Grosvenor arrived, but they were generally considered vulgar and less desirable than steel engravings. The young editor found them much cheaper and more satisfying than engravings. Soon, he was using them liberally in *National Geographic*. To obtain photographs he scoured government agencies and telephoned and wrote indefatigably to explorers and travelers. Soon, spending a month's pay to acquire a bulky, 4-A folding Kodak, he began taking pictures himself.

In 1903 he borrowed photoengravings from the Bureau of Education to illustrate an article on reindeer in Alaska. The following year a Russian explorer sent him fifty photographs of the mysterious Tibetan capital of Lhasa: Dr. Grosvenor ran them across eleven pages.

The magazine became a vigorous advocate of the camera, publishing photographs in unprecedented numbers. In 1906 Congressman George Shiras III— a pioneer in the techniques of hunting animals with a camera instead of with a gun—offered *National Geographic* a box filled with unusual flash pictures of wild animals. The magazine ran seventy-four of these photos. Two members of the editorial board resigned in a huff, charging that Dr. Grosvenor was "turning the magazine into a picture book."

Backed firmly by his father-in-law, Bell, young Grosvenor survived not only this crisis, but also several subsequent attacks. His spirit of innovation led to a spectacular sixty-seven-year career as a giant in publishing history.

Possibly Gilbert H. Grosvenor was the United States' first professional picture editor: certainly he was its most successful. His genius made the magazine a success and the magazine made him famous. He edited it for more than half a century while simultaneously serving as president of the Society. In 1954 he resigned these titles to become chairman of the board.

The Hearstian sensationalism and intense muckraking so prevalent throughout the early twentieth century in American journalism apparently never tempted him to nudge the magazine from its conservative course. In developing his editing format he imposed his own cultured background, thoughtful personality, and Victorian courtesy to create a different, but highly successful, form of journalism.

His seven guiding principles in editing were:

1. Insist on absolute accuracy.
2. Use an abundance of instructive and beautiful illustrations.
3. Everything must have permanent value.
4. Avoid trivialities and material of a personal nature.
5. Use nothing partisan or controversial.
6. Use only what is of a kindly nature: nothing unduly critical.
7. Plan each number for maximum timeliness.

How Dr. Grosvenor applied this unique and unlikely policy was best summarized in a eulogy by his longtime associate, Frederick G. Vosburgh:

> Fortunately some of these points, notably numbers five and six, had a certain built-in elasticity and the Editor determined the amount of stretch. There was never any doubt about this, or about his editorial courage . . . This mild-seeming gentleman of courtly manners had the soul and heart of a fighter. Those who challenged his plans and principles struck steel beneath the velvet . . . The Chief, or GHG, as we called him (although nothing but Dr. Grosvenor to his face) was not the kind of editor who would ask writers to conform to his preconceived ideas. "Just make it interesting," he would say to a staff man setting out on an assignment. Two or three generations of *Geographic* men and women owe to him our traditional freedom to report the world as we find it. Our only limitation was summed up in his seven guiding principles.[2]

Mr. Vosburgh applied the principles in his own very successful manner. Under his editorship from 1967 to 1970 the membership grew another million.

Over the years many awards have accrued to the *Geographic* and its editors, but perhaps none so influenced the present magazine as the University of Missouri's School of Journalism Distinguished Service (to journalism) medal presented to Dr. Gilbert H. Grosvenor in 1954. In accepting the medal the editor said, "For fifty years I've practiced honesty in photography, and today

In 1970, Mr. Garrett did a story on Mexico for *National Geographic* magazine. These children (*right*) were some of the friends he met at that time. (Original picture in color.)

---

2. Frederick G. Vosburgh, "To Gilbert Grosvenor: A Monthly Monument 25 Miles High," *National Geographic Magazine* (October 1966) 130:445–87.

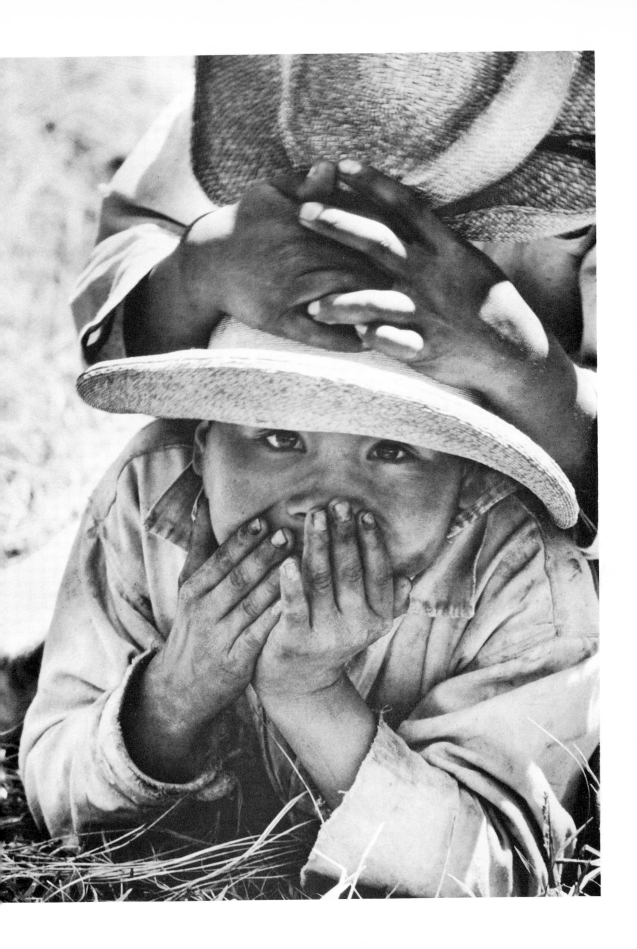

I met a group of young people dedicated to the integrity of the published photograph."

His fascination with techniques and principles taught by the school led to a continuing interaction with the school and its annual one-week Photojournalism Workshop. Over the next decade this special relationship led to the hiring of a flood of young people—many graduates of this university. "Too damn many," complained some of the staff. But the Midwest journalism background provided ideal training for maintaining the honest, unpretentious, and unsophisticated photographic tradition of the magazine.

This flood of young talent soon became a necessity to keep pace with the driving, aggressive leadership of the new editor, Melville Bell Grosvenor. After working for thirty-seven years in the long shadow of his father and his immediate predecessor, John Oliver La Gorce, in 1957 he took over a magazine that had grown stodgy toward the end of the patriarchal reign. MBG, as the staff knew him, burst over the scene like a cluster of Fourth of July rockets on a quiet night. In one decade, with a revitalized magazine as its core, he more than doubled membership from 2,175,000 to 5,500,000, and transformed the Society into a multimedia publishing giant.

*Geographic* books became the most lavishly illustrated bargains in the history of publishing. He launched an atlas and globe program and initiated a television series that immediately set records for both documentary integrity and audience response. Network officials, with the same foresight exhibited by publisher McClure sixty years earlier, had insisted that there was no place in their dynamic new medium for the little geography magazine with the yellow-bordered cover. One wrote of a *Geographic* presentation that surpassed all previous audience ratings for documentaries . . . "It was a fluke, don't expect it to ever happen again." But it did, repeatedly.

In 1963 MBG moved the Society and its magazine into new headquarters, a ten-story building designed by Edward Durrell Stone that stands as an outstanding example of functional modern architecture in Washington, D.C. A similar building twice as large now houses computers, business offices, and correspondence sections required to handle the Society's business.

One of Dr. Grosvenor's first acts as president was to order new high-speed web presses designed and built to replace the sheetfed presses that had become a sentimental luxury.

When he called the staff together to announce that we would drop black-and-white photography and go to all color immediately, a member of the business department moaned, "We'll go broke."

Instead, the membership responded to this daring innovation, and the revitalized annual growth rate of nearly ten percent more than covered all costs.

This year Dr. Grosvenor explained, "If I hadn't made the move, we probably would have folded. We went from sixteen small presses to four large ones. Our paper costs dropped twenty percent immediately with the big rolls instead of the sheets. The quality of the magazine improved dramatically. In publishing, you simply cannot stand still."

More important than any equipment, Melville Grosvenor brought a receptivity, a hunger for new ideas and approaches that stimulated his staff. He edited and led with an enthusiasm described by some as brilliant, by others as childlike and uncontrolled.

At the outset, he formed a planning council to advise him.

"I wanted to hear what all of them had to say—not just the big guy, not just the guy who talked the loudest, but the little guy over in the corner, too. They weren't a committee but a council. I listened to their advice, then went in my office, thought it over, and made the decision myself. You can't run a magazine by committee."

Typical of his faith in color photography is his attitude toward *Life* magazine.

"It was such a great magazine. What a shame they had to fold. You know, I think if they had used more color they might have made it."

At the heart of his system—like the core of a nuclear reactor—he enshrined the magical little $1 \times 1\frac{1}{2}$-inch color slide. Engravers had been encouraged, trained, and assisted in making plates from 35-mm. film for the *Geographic* when most publishers and printers wouldn't touch the "toy" film.

Custom equipment made possible efficient processing, labeling, editing, and filing of masses of the little slides. Every editor and writer concerned with photographs is furnished with light tables and background projection equipment. A layout machine projects transparencies to page size, and black-and-white prints on nonstretch paper are produced and pasted into a master dummy. Copies go to all editors, writers, engravers, and printers involved in the story.

Inevitably at the end of every assignment loomed the dummy approval or projection session. For some staff members these meetings offered all the charm of rowing into a hurricane in a leaky rowboat.

In a carpeted and paneled room the editor, dummy makeup in his lap, sat before a rear-projection screen which resembled a television console. All staff members concerned with the story gathered behind him. Equipment, custom-built to his specifications, permitted the editor to change, focus, enlarge, and reduce and crop 35-mm. slides exactly as he wanted.

As room lights dimmed, all other concerns faded and the editor became part of the story with an enthusiasm that usually kept him on the edge of his chair. His love affair with life was contagious. "Would you look at that," he would marvel. Often he touched the screen as if the act would waft him into the exotic scene before him. Dozens of questions flowed as fast as answers could be found among the staff present. Crops and placements on the page were challenged. His knowledge of geography and astonishing expertise in 35-mm. photography could cower a photographer or picture editor not rock-sure of his story. He loved his photographers, but there was a saying around the office that "you're only as good as your last story." No one wanted his last story to be a bad one.

Every session had its lectures. "I'm sick and tired of goggle-eyed flash pictures." "Can't we use available light?" "We don't have space in our magazine for pictures that don't help tell the story."

The side stitching or stapling essential to make a permanent binding creates a tight, awkward gutter. It bothered him more than anyone. "Keep the pictures out of the gutter," was a recurring order from MBG.

A generous number of rejects were provided for his scrutiny. God help the picture editor if too many were better than the selects. Occasionally he took exception to the story approach and ordered the dummy scrapped or revised.

But a story he liked provoked an effusively scribbled "Congratulations" on the dummy cover—usually addressed to no one in particular, but savored by all who had worked on it.

Another assignment of Bill Garrett's for
his magazine was a story on Southeast
Alaska. Later, he directed a film about that
country, an hour-long CBS special television
program. (Original pictures in color.)

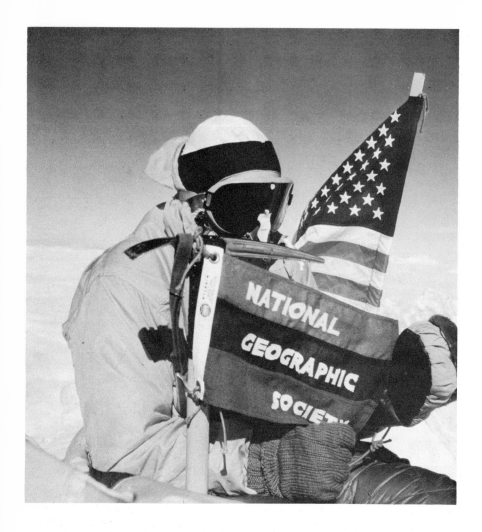

**On Top of the World.** *National Geographic* staffer Barry Bishop holds United States and Society flags that he had carried to the summit of Mount Everest in 1963. (Original in color.)

A picture editor who survived a few years of projection sessions had learned the *Geographic* system. He could look to promotions and a long career in a variety of areas within the organization.

Among the old grads are: Barry Bishop, member of the Society's Committee for Research and Exploration; Robert L. Breeden, Senior Assistant Editor and Chief of the Special Publications and Filmstrip Divisions; Donald Crump, Special Publications Illustrations Editor; Robert Gilka, Director of Photography; Leonard Grant, Editorial Assistant to the President; Joanne Hess, Chief of the Lectures Division; Bryan Hodgson, Senior Editorial Staff; H. Edward Kim, Layout and Production Editor; Michael Long, Editorial Staff; O. Louis Mazzatenta, Layout and Production Editor; Thomas R. Smith, Associate Illustrations Editor; Herbert S. Wilburn, Illustrations Editor; and most important, the present editor, Gilbert Melville Grosvenor.

I have been promoted, too, but after twenty years I still have not graduated. As Senior Assistant Editor responsible for selection and layout of all visuals, I'm still facing the sessions; only now we average six or seven stories a month instead of five, as a few years ago. There have been two new editors since Melville Bell Grosvenor moved to Chairman of the Board in 1967, but projection sessions still determine the fate of every story.

Under editor Gilbert M. Grosvenor, a young, dynamic staff now produces the finest magazine in the Society's eighty-six-year history. In addition the

Society produces five illustrated books a year, a four-title set of children's books, and six public service books with a total sales of some three million copies. Recently, the editor ordered a print run of 550,000 of a large format book on American Indians. The Society produces a filmstrip series that uses more color photographs than the magazine, a separate school magazine, a series of television specials, educational films, globes, maps, atlases, and records.

It originates more color assignments (36,000 rolls shot in 1973) and publishes more color photographs (over 5,000 in 1973) than any other organization in the world.

Prophets of doom would have us believe the day of the still photograph somehow is over—that it died when *Life* folded. Just as Mark Twain responded to a report of his death by quipping, "The reports of my death are greatly exaggerated," so photography can respond by showing more markets today than ever before. And even *Life* seems to be reviving.

After the mirror, the still camera ranks as man's favorite tool of visual communication. This "mirror with a memory" is still a fledging—it has countless places to go and people to see and events to record—perhaps even in worlds undiscovered. The little magazine with the yellow-bordered cover will be around to publish the best of what is photographed.

# A Story from Genesis to Revelation

The germ of a *Geographic* story idea may emanate from the myriad sources available to any publication—editors, readers, field men, and so forth. Most funnel through the Editorial Planning Council to the editor. Upon approval, photographer, writer, and picture editor are assigned. A story conference with the editor precedes field travel. Once on location, the photographer and writer work together or separately, but regularly compare experiences and trade ideas.

With thorough captions, film shipments are made as often as possible. A technical staff reviews all processed film for possible camera trouble before it goes to the picture editor.

He will try to keep in close contact with the photographer, detailing story progress by telephone, cable, or letter. Upon completion of field work, the photographer, picture editor, and layout editor (and the writer when possible) work up a layout taking into consideration any artwork or maps required.

The editor, at his projection session, approves, alters, or kills the package. If approved—a high percentage are—the original transparencies go to the engravers. An elaborate quality control system traces them through production and onto the presses. Every month approximately 106 pages print letterpress (150 line screen) at R. R. Donnelley and Sons Company in Chicago; 40 pages print offset (150 line screen) at Fawcett Printing Corporation in Rockville, Maryland. All of the signatures (printed on 60-pound coated paper) are bound, addressed, and mailed from Chicago. Computer-produced tapes of addresses are sent from Washington to Chicago by bus. They are within hours of being up-to-date with address changes. Seven and one-half million pounds of magazines fill 175 Post Office semitrailers per month and begin the journey to coffee tables of the world.

This capsule story trip compresses to its utmost simplicity the work of dozens of people which may stretch over months or even years.

# The Geographic Photographer

Because he travels far, well, and adventurously, the *Geographic* photographer holds one of the few jobs left in the world that evokes the romantic Richard Halliburton image. In truth, he goes places that would stir a green envy in Halliburton. One of Barry Bishop's assignments took him to the top of Mt. Everest. Tom Abercrombie crossed the Arabian deserts with Moslem pilgrims to the heart of forbidden Mecca. Five years earlier he was the first journalist to reach the South Pole. Dean Conger crossed Inner Mongolia and wintered in Siberia. Luis Marden discovered and photographed the remains of Captain Bligh's H.M.S. *Bounty* off the shores of remote Pitcairn Island.

Today the average *Geographic* staff or free-lance photographer is in his thirties, speaks several languages, has a sensitive eye, and a delicate ego. He must be physically, emotionally, technically, and creatively competent to handle any assignment on short notice anywhere Director of Photography Robert Gilka needs him.

He must be well educated although not necessarily in a formal, degree-oriented system. Once he is hired, the world becomes his campus, and serendipitously the job provides an education no school can match.

Because of their talent, their unique adventures, the demands for thorough research, and on-the-job training that comes from working closely with staff writers and editors, *Geographic* photographers often become writers themselves. A few years ago five of the top ten articles in the annual readership survey were by photographers or were picture essays.

But successful *Geographic* stories and ego-balming adventures exact their tribute. Extended and lonely absences generate a high divorce rate for staff families. Even when wives travel with the photographers, problems arise. A romantic Arab sheik offered Tom Abercrombie fifty camels for his attractive wife.

A photographer must have a taste for exotic food and the guts to digest it. But even the most travel-toughened stomach falls victim to the countless intestinal germs that seem to lurk in every pot. One man quit because his stomach could not handle the job.

I have eaten rat and deadly jungle snakes and sucked the brains from chicken heads as an honored guest. I have drunk the bile of a cobra mixed with Chinese wine, thought by my host to be an aphrodisiac. I have sorted bugs and vermin from cold rice with Asian armies. But by actual count I have suffered more stomach misery from hotel food than from any primitive fare.

At the same time the bugs you swallow work inside, you may be literally eaten alive from the outside by mosquitos, black flies, bloodsucking leeches, or plain bedbugs.

Every field man carries his bottle of pills marked "For Fevers of Undetermined Origin." Still, malaria, hepatitis, and diseases yet unnamed slip past the best defenses.

Insensitivity to a custom official's desire for a bribe can cause hours or days of sweltering and exasperating delays. Aluminum camera cases hold a magnetic attraction for thieves and con men.

While photographing a fire-walking ceremony in Burma—the entranced crowd pushing and jostling—I felt the weight of a spare camera go slack on my shoulder. I spun and grabbed in time to retrieve my departing Leica, its strap neatly sliced through.

Frigid lather of the Antarctic rimes the beard of *Geographic* staffer Thomas J. Abercrombie. When his one-hour visit to the South Pole lengthened into three weeks—his plane blew a gasket—Abercrombie volunteered to help dig a snow mine for water and glacial study. Here his face shows the result. (Original in color.)

To an unruly crowd of two or more a photographer offers an easy target for their anger. Loren McIntyre received an unprovoked beating and kicking in Peru recently at the hands and feet of a mob of gringo haters. Loren keeps in shape by running ten miles a day, so was able to save himself by executing a very hasty retreat—without his cameras.

Melville Grosvenor's helicopter crashed and burned in Australia in 1969. He leapt clear, but his cameras and lenses became molten exhibits for an insurance claim.

Many of us have been shot at, but only two have been hit. Dickey Chapelle, a free-lance journalist, died in Viet Nam while on patrol with the Marines. Although Dickey was not on a *Geographic* assignment at the time, she photographed and wrote often for the *Geographic* and was part of the family.

Emory Kristof received a mortar wound in the right eye while doing a story on the United States Army in Viet Nam. Fortunately, he recovered the use of the eye.

Particularly on nonhazardous jobs where the good photographs come hard, the photographer is often up before dawn breaks. Days have no end and weeks have no Sundays.

Competition for space toughens every year. Excellent young photographers continually appear at Bob Gilka's door, some bringing fully developed stories. Yet the number of pages available remains fixed at about 146. Approximately one-fourth of the photographs are not supplied by professional photographers. They flow in from adventurers, scientists, naturalists, and laymen with stories to tell.

Every astronaut to go to the moon became a *Geographic* photographer, and three provided articles. David Scott wrote the only article ever published on what it is really like to walk on the moon.

Robin Lee Graham, the first teenager to sail around the world alone, photographed his trip and wrote a series of three articles on his experiences.

Many of the magazine's great bird photographs of the past decade have come from Frederick K. Truslow, a former businessman who has spent a large part of his retirement years zipped into a sweltering blind.

Since Gilbert H. Grosvenor served as the first staff photographer and staff writer as well as editor, field work (writing, photography, and often both) has been the rule rather than the exception for *Geographic* editors.

"You've got to shove people out of the office," insisted Melville Bell Grosvenor. "How else will they learn about the world. We don't edit from some ivory tower."

# F8 and Be There

Although I have not been privileged to be on the prestigious photographic staff, I have often worked as a photographer and writer because of this policy of "shoving" editors out of the office.

As a photographer you hope viewers will appreciate and dwell on your photographs' content, but all too often, perhaps for lack of anything else to say, they will ask, "What f-stop did you use?" Such a question is comparable to asking a writer what ribbon he used to type a story. For a while my stock answer to the how-did-you-make-that-picture? type of question, was, "F8 and

The handsome headquarters of the National Geographic Society (*right*) rises ten stories above the heart of Washington, D.C., six blocks from the White House. Since 1964 it has served as home base for the Society's executives, editors, and roving staff men. Designed by renowned architect Edward Durrell Stone, the building is lauded as one of the most beautiful in the nation's capital. (Original in color.)

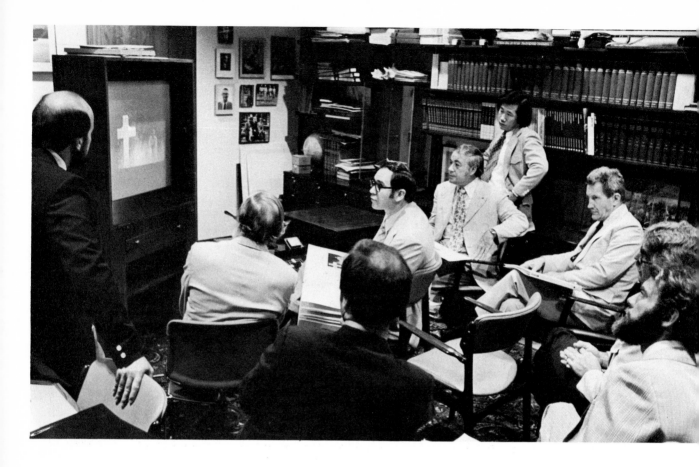

Actively engaged in a projection session about West Australia photographed by James Stanfield (*back row, right*) and written by Kenneth MacLeish senior assistant editor (*second from left*) is this group of *National Geographic* officials. In the center, holding a layout and looking at the screen, is Gilbert M. Grosvenor, editor. Next to him is Bill Garrett, and next to Bill is H. Edward Kim, chief, layout and production. At Garrett's left, with his hand to his mouth, is Robert E. Gilka, director of photography. Next to Gilka is Thomas R. Smith, associate illustrations editor. The two men with their backs to the camera are unidentified. (Photo by Joseph J. Scherschel, original in color.)

be there." The answer may seem snide or secretive, but it was not meant to be. Seldom do I remember what f-stop I used, or the shutter speed for that matter. Technique varies as writers' styles vary, but basically there are no secrets in either profession.

Every imaginable photographic device from the electron microscope to Skylab's orbiting solar telescope may be used to make *Geographic* pictures, but basic equipment for assignments remains the ubiquitous and versatile 35-mm. camera, both range finder and reflex types available to every amateur.

Thorough knowledge of photographic technique compares to a writer's need for good grammar. Among professionals both must be taken for granted. But, to follow the simile: straightforward technique without gimmicks compares to simple declarative sentences as the surest way to communicate with a reader or viewer. Naturally, how creatively basic technique is applied determines a photographer's professional competence.

I do not demean technical skill, but today learning basic camera technique is easier than learning to type. It should not be necessary to deal with it in a university curriculum. For teaching advanced skills photographic schools are generally better equipped and staffed than an academic institution. Also, a good apprenticeship offers excellent training.

Despite my foregoing protests: just a word on technique. In addition to two cameras and several lenses, my gadget bag always contains a small electronic flash, a penlight, and a tabletop tripod that can be braced against any firm support or used as a chest pod. With this equipment most of the photographic problems I have encountered can be handled. Certainly when more elaborate

In the control center where future *Geographic* magazines are planned, Editor Gilbert M. Grosvenor posts deadlines for coming issues. The man in the group who appears to be applauding is Melville Bell Grosvenor, editor-in-chief, and board chairman. (Original in color.)

equipment becomes necessary and is available, it should be mastered and used. But too much equipment can hobble a photographer as much as too little. When a picture situation becomes a production, the pictures can slip away amid all the confusion.

As for the "be there" part of my answer, for the photojournalist there can be no substitute. Portraits cannot be shot by telephone—yet. Wars cannot be covered from bar stools safely away from the action. To photograph a walk on the moon you must be there.

There are different qualities of "being there." Some aspiring photographers would not see a picture if it jumped up and exposed itself. Others seem always to be instinctively into a situation. Like a puppy following its mother, good luck follows photographers who research their assignment and are prepared intellectually and physically to work hard, quickly, and to the point.

No matter how simple the equipment or smooth the photographer, his presence seldom goes unnoticed today. Truly candid photography is rare.

Rapport with the subject may be the single most essential condition to a successful job, yet it becomes increasingly difficult as the power of the camera becomes better recognized. It does not just document and educate—it can also hurt, humiliate, and anger.

A Mexican butcher once chased me through a market waving his cleaver because I "grabbed" a photograph of him at work. I didn't stay to find out why he did not want his picture taken.

Many of us have surrendered our film and occasionally had a camera smashed by self-appointed censors in sensitive areas. George Mobley once fled for his life across rooftops in Beirut while the *Geographic* writer blended with the mob which chased him. According to George the writer joined in screaming "get the photographer."

All of us occasionally, if not regularly, invade the privacy of our subjects to some extent—whether we be photographing a peasant woman hoeing a roadside field or young lovers along the banks of the Seine.

As professionals when we aim a camera at somebody, we want something for our own selfish reasons. One colorful tribal lady in Laos told me of going to town and finding her picture being sold on postcards without her permission. At the very least she felt entitled to some payment. This situation differs little from possible magazine or book use of her picture.

A friendly, open, honest approach to a subject almost always beats the *paparazzi* or grab-shot technique except in a fast-breaking event. Too often we justify our "right" to photograph the world and its people with the same self-righteousness of a missionary in China fifty years ago converting "heathens." Today neither missionaries nor candid photographers find a welcome there. In China as in many other countries photographing a person without his permission is not done. All too soon we may encounter this attitude everywhere.

During demonstrations in the United States crowds suspect us of FBI or police connections. Recently the freedom of all of us to work suffered when it became public knowledge that many accredited journalists—none *Geographic* —work for the CIA full or part-time.

The Soviet daily *Pravda* once accused the National Geographic Society of being a spy organization. It is an easy assumption for a suspicious government to make since *Geographic* fieldwork must be thorough and painstaking.

In fact, we do gather intelligence or information, but for our readers. In striving for honest reporting we must be painstakingly thorough whether as photographers or as writers. On any assignment representatives of special interests hassle and cajole. Truth rarely enjoys the benefit of a public relations agent. And seldom is there a truly noncontroversial subject.

It is impossible to fully comprehend the impact of our work on the public.

Bruce Dale expressed the fear that his nostalgic pictures of isolated mountain life in the United States will contribute to the destruction of that way of life, which he came to love and respect. Their appeal will incite tourism and its commercial caterers.

In a way Dale's concern symbolizes all *Geographic* photographers' awesome sense of responsibility, knowing that their work reaches some forty-five million people each month. Where else today can a photographer operate with so much freedom and entertain, educate, and influence so many people?

# Color Versus Black and White

The all-time champion for boring bull sessions must be the perpetual sophomoric hassle over whether the camera lies. But for me one other old chestnut-ridden session rankles even more. That is when a bunch of the good old boys and photographic "artists" get together and pontificate on how black and white is more "creative" than color, how you cannot "communicate" as well in color as in black and white, how everything looks too pretty in color, how you can't express yourself as well in color. What nonsense!

This picture was taken by Bruce Dale, *National Geographic* photographer who twice won the Magazine Photographer of the Year Award (in 1968 and 1973). Portrayed is a Hungarian child and kitten outside the youngster's shantytown home on the edge of Esztergom, Hungary. (Original picture in color.)

Nearly 250,000 Moslems jam Haram
Mosque in the holy city of Mecca to pay
homage to Allah. Those in the center
(blurred in this time exposure) circle the
black-draped Kaba, the most sacred of
Islamic shrines. Five times each day the
world's 456,000,000 Moslems turn toward
Mecca to pray. This photograph was taken by
Thomas J. Abercrombie, a member of the
*National Geographic* foreign editorial staff.
(Original picture in color.)

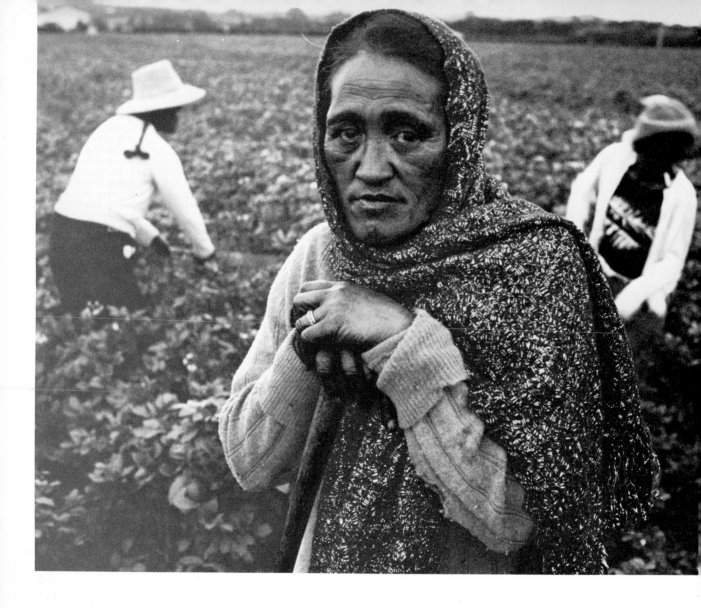

If color is so bad, why did nature use so much so well? If it is so limiting creatively, why have all the great painters used and continue to use it? If it is so bad, we should wear deep-blue glasses to enhance our pleasure at watching a cardinal in the snow or a sunrise over a misty mountain lake or in viewing a Paul Klee painting.

For the first half-century or so of illustrated publications there were very real problems with color—both the film and the means of reproduction were expensive and bad. Presses were not designed for the close tolerances needed for three- or four-plate registration. Some paper soaked up inks like used blotters, then stretched, shrunk, and wobbled through the press until the reproduction looked like a color-blind test card. Color had a bad name, and you cannot blame photographers for avoiding it.

Low film speed of early emulsions and slow lenses combined to make color photography slower than cave painting—and more cumbersome. Volkmar Wentzel of the *Geographic* staff began his career carrying hundreds of pounds of glass plates on overseas assignments that lasted months. Today he can put the equivalent number of 35-mm. exposures in his pocket for a day's shooting.

Until after World War II, most lenses were not apochromatic or "color

This informal picture of a Maori woman hoeing potatoes with other laborers was taken by Gordon Gahan near Pukekohe, New Zealand.

corrected." That is, they focused different colors at different distances from the lens—just as now infrared must be focused differently than the visible light.

Because of the novelty and expense of early color procedures, editors demanded and photographers shot "color" pictures, not necessarily good pictures. The "red shirt" school of photography developed. Film manufacturers hyped up the colors past any reality. Engravers were either unwilling or unable to produce subtle tints. The gaudy results were the same as turning a bunch of hungry kids loose in a candy factory—sickening.

Then why the continuing push for color? Primarily because, unless you are color-blind, the world is in color. Its beauty and its ugliness come equally in color. At the *Geographic* our primary use for photography has always been documentary: to show this universe and its wonders to our readers, to educate and inform.

As far as Dr. Melville Grosvenor was concerned, the only reason for not using color was money and quality. "The people wanted it, and as soon as we could afford to do it right, we gave it to them," he has said.

The present editor says simply, "I take color for granted." But he demands increasingly more interpretive and innovative use of it.

With tougher standards and more freedom to shoot subjectively, *Geographic* photographers find the full chromatic palette as much a necessity as a variety of lenses. Brilliant colors still appear, but the expression "monochromatic" no longer denotes black and white. It may mean blue and black or blue and blue or green and green, but used with taste to better communicate.

The skill with which they now use color speaks for itself. Six of the last seven University of Missouri–National Press Photographers Association Magazine Photographer of the Year Awards went to *Geographic* photographers. In the same period they have collected ninety-five awards in the White House News Photographers Association competition.

As concern for ecology became not only fashionable but also profitable, color portrayals of scenes and creatures, once almost the sole domain of the *Geographic,* proliferated everywhere—from *Audubon* magazine's superslick crusading to corporate me-too advertising.

We have seen that documentation in color of pollution and poverty conveys the full, disgusting reality of these blights; that the impact of the great Weston and Ansel Adams scenics can be matched in color; that war pictures with their red blood and green slime nauseate and repel powerfully—as they should; that color properly used does not romanticize or glorify war, but degrades it. The ills of society as well as the beauty of nature can be communicated more powerfully and creatively in color than in black and white.

Fast, stable emulsions now make exposing color comparable to black and white. Speed and quality of printing no longer mitigate against color. President Nixon returned from China on a Monday night. By Friday morning a 164-page book with 64 pages of color covering his entire trip was being sold in bookstores and on newsstands.

Of course color is harder to handle. Some photographers still do not know how, and it frightens them. But so is a spaceship harder to handle than an automobile, and a four-minute mile is harder to run than a five-minute mile.

Obviously, black and white will continue to be both a creative and a practical tool. Its stark simplicity makes it an important and artistic and communicative medium. Most situations calling for speed and economy can still be handled

Once alerted to the capture of a whale, several hundred Barrow, Alaska, residents dash out to help butcher it. The *Geographic* legend writer colorfully describes the scene: "Falling snow mutes the cries of pleasure and softens the bloody scene as the men quickly slice into the carcass." With the help of their women, who pull away the foot-thick blubber with long-handled hooks, they often reduce an eight-ton whale to a spot in the snow in five to six hours. This photograph was taken by Emory Kristof, of the *National Geographic* photo staff. (Original picture in color.)

best in black and white. Where paper and press cannot handle color well, it is better to trust to a good black-and-white reproduction than risk the unintentional abstractions created by horrible register and haphazard ink flow.

But, as communicators we must be concerned with "how and when," not with "if," color can be used professionally. We must utilize the technology available, press for better tools, and be prepared to experiment and gamble.

As older photographers fade away, their passionate arguments against color photography will go with them. New generations come on relentlessly like waves on a beach. They will be comfortable with color—whether in publications or exhibits, on television, on the videotape unit, or in mediums not yet envisioned. And naturally they will learn to use it more creatively, profitably, and fearlessly to communicate events and ideas.

# Student Participation

No publication has had a greater influence on photojournalism and on the use of color photography as a means of communication than has the *National Geographic* magazine. It is probable, too, that no publication has earned such an honored place on the shelves of private and public libraries than this magazine.

It should be an easy matter to borrow a dozen or so copies of *National Geographic* to bring to class. If your selections of magazines are spread out over a period of twenty years, you will be surprised at the transitions the *Geographic* has made in its philosophy of photojournalism.

Howard Chapnick (*left*) is president of Black Star Publishing Company, one of the leading photographic agencies in the world. His association with Black Star for over thirty years has involved him in every aspect of photojournalism.

He has participated for the past ten years as a staff member of the University of Missouri Photo Workshop. He currently teaches an Urban Photojournalistic Workshop course at the New School for Social Research. He often is a guest lecturer before various professional groups.

Mr. Chapnick has produced two books that combine photography with poetry or prose— *The Illustrated Leaves of Grass* and *The Illustrated World of Thoreau*. (Photo by Leo Choplin, Black Star.)

# 17

# The Free-Lancer and the Picture Syndicate

*by Howard Chapnick*

Howard Chapnick, president of Black Star—a large picture agency in New York—talks about the free-lance photographer and the picture agencies.

The vision evoked by the word *syndicate* is that of a "Mafia" of the picture business sitting in concert making decisions which affect the world's free-lance photographers. In fact, there is no more chaotic, undisciplined, and unstructured group of individual entrepreneurs than "picture agencies," those purveyors of pictures and photographic talent without whom the growth of photographic journalism would have been impeded.

Only the Associated Press (AP) and United Press International (UPI), among worldwide distributors of journalistic material, qualify under the definition of "syndicates" producing, purchasing, and distributing photographs for simultaneous publication in a number of newspapers and periodicals in different localities. Their impact is all-pervasive. Their news-gathering facilities are overwhelming, their offices and photographers ubiquitous, their knowledge of events taking place unmatchable, and their means of transmission via wire-photo and radiophoto unbeatable. Added to their own substantial resources, their contracts with individual newspapers throughout the United States enable Associated Press and United Press International to distribute worldwide the photographic production of the staff photographers who work for these newspapers. Withal, both of these giants of journalistic photography are compelled to use the services of free-lance photographers to supplement the barrage of images which inundate their central offices from the far corners of the world. Contact with either the central photographic offices or local bureaus of Associated Press or United Press International will elicit for the free-lance photographer answers to questions of when they assign photographers, how much they pay for assignments, what rights they procure, and all the other pragmatic bread-and-butter questions that relate to any business relationship.

I come from a different photographic world than the high-powered press services. My world is the world of the comparatively small picture agencies whose contributions to the development of photojournalism have been overwhelming. It has been the picture agencies which have been the traditional home for many of the great free-lance photographers and source of the most powerful and creative photographic essays of our time. It was to the picture agencies that the early photojournalistic mass media publications turned for photographic talent when the game was just beginning back in the late thirties. So it is indeed relevant and important that any book on photojournalism should examine the contemporary role of the picture agencies and their relations to the many thousands of free-lance photographers who have developed in the short history of the profession. As in many other fields, the educational institutions in photography are turning out enthusiastic, creative, committed photographers who have something to say about the world, without real insight into how they can most intelligently achieve their ends with a minimum of pain and disenchantment. Perhaps becoming a great artist or a great anything requires pain, difficulty, and suffering. This chapter will hopefully be a practical guide for those free-lancers who want to take the picture agency route.

# The Picture Agent—Man in the Middle

A picture agent is a man surrounded by millions of pictures, dozens of photographers, countless editors, researchers, art directors, and users of photographs clamoring for just the right images. His is a business fraught with overwhelming detail. He is caught between the legendary "limited budgets" of potential clients and the rising expectations of photographers. He is required to be businessman, negotiator, and creative innovator. His mom-and-pop-candy-store approach is one of the last of the small, highly personalized businesses to survive in this technological, highly computerized age. His business resists computerization by virtue of limited capital and anachronistic pricing which has not kept pace with rising costs. He is responsible to the photographer for the successful placement of his material, responsible to the editor to satisfy his needs for honest imagery, and responsible to the public as another communications arm in their search for information and truth. He lives by his wits (as does the free-lance photographer) in one of the toughest businesses man has yet devised. He has no secret markets. The success he has is in direct proportion to the amount of hard work and creativity he brings to his work. He sometimes succeeds with mediocre photographers and fails with gifted artistic photographers. He responds to and anticipates the news.

# Meeting the Picture Agent

I have often been accused of being tough on the work of photographers who come to see me. There is no closed-door policy. I try to see every photographer that comes up the pike, not because I am a nice guy, but because the future of the agency is dependent on the replenishment of talent and the enhancement of our picture files. You never know which appointment is going to produce a salable set of photographs.

We shake hands. The photographer pulls out his portfolio, and I look at his pictures. I then ask if the photographer has come to see me for my charm or for the straight dope regarding his work and its applicability to the field as I understand it. If it's the straight dope he wants, it's the straight dope he gets, painful as it might be. I consider it a disservice to any creative person to give less than a constructive, honest evaluation of his work. It is, after all, only a personal opinion which may be wrong, but my thirty years in the business have produced some wisdom in evaluating the type of work that photographers bring to me.

A portfolio should be ruthlessly edited. It should tolerate nothing but the best images. It is the free-lancer's creative calling card. It is your opening shot to say to the guy behind the desk that you are a great photographer. He knows that every picture you take is not on that level, but if he sees only the best, he also knows that you make no compromise with quality. Never dilute the impact of the portfolio by including too many photographs. Diversity enhances it. So give that portfolio the tender loving care it deserves and use it to knock out the viewer who may be an agent or an art director who has the power of life and death over who gets what assignment.

# A Photographer's View of the Picture Agency

Harry Redl is a free-lance photographer currently working out of Phoenix, Arizona. He has been a free-lancer in San Francisco, Hong Kong, and Vienna. What follows is his personal view of the picture agency.

> It is important to one who is working thousands of miles from the main markets for photography. The picture agencies benefit the photographer particularly in the preservation of subsidiary reproduction rights which may in turn generate large amounts of money in the future.
>
> To a busy free-lance photographer, an agency can mean the difference between success and failure.
>
> Most important is choosing the right agency for one's own needs. If distribution worldwide is your problem, find an agency that specializes in that area.
>
> Some photographers are incapable of functioning without the ministrations of an agency to sell their pictures, handle their finances, soothe their egos, and find them work.
>
> Laymen shudder at the high cost of representation picture agencies charge the photographer and sometimes they are right.
>
> However, an agent often will negotiate a level of pay the photographer would never have dared to propose. The agent will insist on conditions that benefit the photographer, and when reproduction rights are involved, it can mean large amounts of money for the photographer he would otherwise not have received.
>
> For the photographer who has difficulty facing clients or haggling over money or who just lives too far away from the markets, an agent is an absolute necessity.
>
> Perhaps most important, an agent makes it possible for a photographer to spend his time on photography rather than on selling his product.

# An Interview with a Picture Agent

If I were a free-lancer in search of information, I would put some questions to Howard Chapnick which I would evaluate with a jaundiced eye because he is a picture agent who has an axe to grind in behalf of the picture agency business. So, for the purpose of gaining as much information as possible, let us conduct a mythical interview between Howard Chapnick, mythical free-lancer, and Howard Chapnick, picture agent of thirty years experience.

Question: Is an agent indispensable to the success of the photographic free-lancer?

Answer: No. Many free-lancers have been more successful without agents. Others have found agents very valuable, particularly in the early years of trying to get established. There are no absolutes to "making it" since we are all unique individuals with varying degrees of aggressiveness, different levels of creativity, and diverse needs to operate alone or as part of an organization. There is, I suggest, no substitute for personal contact and the direct articulation of ideas and presentation of your work. Who knows your work better than yourself? No one! Can a third person digest and regurgitate your ideas better than you can present them yourself? Obviously not.

Question: If a free-lancer does not need an agent, why go on with the chapter? Is there any justification for his existence?

Answer: An agent can be of tremendous help to a free-lancer, opening doors and providing access to clients who might otherwise not be receptive to seeing the work of the photographer. This is particularly true when the photographer is unknown. If the agent is reputable and is known for "not pushing a dead horse," the entrée the agent provides is invaluable. He can also be helpful in portfolio development, in stimulation of editorial ideas, and particularly for "stock agencies" can serve as a repository for file material and generation of other than assignment income.

Question: Do agents exploit photographers?

Answer: Probably no more often than photographers exploit agents. I would like to think that human beings never exploit other human beings. But that is not realistic. Instead of *exploitation,* perhaps we should discuss the relative roles of the ideal principal-agent relationship where each party can achieve some measure of creative satisfaction and financial benefit. Some agents serve as editorial sounding boards, bringing vast experience to what makes for a viable and salable editorial idea. Some agents are financial counselors, financial backers, marriage counselors, psychiatrists, psychologists, casting directors, equipment carriers, and general assistants.

Question: How has the role of the picture agency changed with the demise of the big picture magazine?

Answer: I cannot speak for all picture agencies, but at Black Star the loss of first *Collier's* in the early fifties and subsequently the *Saturday Evening Post, Look,* and *Life* in quick succession have forced us to reevaluate many facets of our operation. The greatest impact, psychologically and financially, for the free-lancer and the assignment picture agencies came from the loss of *Life* magazine. *Look* and *Post,* even though important markets, depended strongly on their respective photographic staffs to fill the majority of their picture pages. *Life,* during the golden era of the mass magazine circulation race, served as the major source of income for the editorially committed free-lancer. Many photographers could count on contracts, page rates, or free-lance day rate assignments from *Life* which were sufficient to maintain them without additional work. Publication in these magazines provided instant prestige, access to work for advertising agencies and industrial companies, development of a valuable file of residual images for future stock sales, procurement of material which had secondary sales possibilities in foreign countries, and perhaps equally important ego and creative satisfactions. Free-lancers and agencies, faced with the reality of the disappearance of *Life,* were suddenly forced to come to grips with a new set of economics and the search for replacement markets. The Black Star staff, which once numbered twenty-five photographers, has been reduced forty percent by attrition, placing a greater reliance on stringers. All of us, photographers and agencies alike, are forced to work harder, be more energetic in the generation of ideas and markets. The loss of *Life, Look,* and *Post* may ultimately prove to be one of the greatest boons to photojournalism in transition and the new economics of magazine publishing in which the advertising tail does not wag the editorial dog. It is now recognized that a magazine is predicated on whether the consumer is willing to plunk down his money at the newsstand for the publication. Advertising revenues are important but peripheral to the magazines' financial health. The economically unsound madness of selling magazines at a subscription rate loss in ever higher numbers was recognized when advertisers turned to television as the medium providing "bigger bang for the advertising buck." This philosophical change in magazine publishing can ultimately serve to bring greater stability to the future of photojournalistic publications and consequently to the free-lance photographers and agencies with whom they deal.

Question: Why do photographer-agency relationships go sour?

Answer: Probably for the same reasons that any relationship between human beings declines. But there are very special elements to the photographer-agency relationship. For one thing, the agent is dealing with a creative individual, whose process of creative maturation and values is constantly changing. The picture agent realizes that losing a photographer is a natural hazard of the business—that often the needs the agency has served in the past have been outlived. The photographer may have evolved a new philosophy about his work, or his financial needs may have increased to a point where he reevaluates the relationship. His financial requirements may have diminished by virtue of new alternative life-style philosophies, or any number of human factors may dictate new options to be explored. From the agency viewpoint, the interest is to maintain relationships for long periods to compensate the agency during the photographer's most productive years for the time, energy, and money invested during the lean development years. The agent should, therefore, try to be responsive to the changing financial and ego needs of the photographer within the context of good business policies.

Keeping the lines of communication clear is of optimum importance. The photographer must articulate his changing attitudes and assure agency responsiveness in order for the relationship to endure.

It is perhaps too obvious to suggest that some relationships fall apart because the agent does not work hard enough in representing the photographer, the photographer gets lazy and does not stimulate the agent with ideas, the photographer develops personal problems which distort all his relationships, the agent may get slipshod in accounting procedures or the photographer unprofessional in rendering of accounts, or the photographer overstates expense accounts or begins to turn in work for which the agent has to apologize. The free-lancer is only as good as the last job he has done and cannot afford a letdown in quality on any assignment.

Question: What factors are most important in selecting an agent?

Answer: Choosing an agent is like choosing a wife or husband. Except for the question of sexual compatibility, which might also be a consideration in some cases, the factors of temperament, mutual goals in photography, efficiency, and reputation take second place to the most important factor of all—how do you, the photographer, relate to the agent who may represent you? Is this the person you will be proud to have working in your behalf? Does he have the understanding to discuss your work, and if he has the understanding, does he have the articulation to express what you are trying to communicate? Does the agent, despite his good intentions (the road to hell is plastered with good intentions), have the time to represent you as fully as you would like?

Putting aside the question of temperamental compatibility, one must come to grips with the mutual interests of the photographer as they relate to those of the agency. A photographer interested in annual report assignments should not associate with an agency with magazine photojournalistic predilections. Although such roles are not always easily defined, an effort should be made to find the closest accommodation for your personalized needs.

# The Picture Agency — Types and Specialties

Each photographic agency is unique in its operation. Some are purely "stock agencies" or photographic libraries. Some handle only color transparencies; some, a combination of black-and-white photographs and color transparencies. Some are photojournalistically oriented—others lean to industrial or public relations photography. Some syndicate picture stories and single pictures in the United States—others distribute material in foreign countries. For the sake of logic and organization, we will attempt to categorize the kinds of agencies that exist and the general methods of operation.


Assignment Agencies

These agencies are the photographer's representatives or agents who try to generate assignment work from magazines, industrial companies (annual reports, brochures, company magazines, internal and external), advertising agencies, and other users of photography. At Black Star, we represent two categories of photographers—staffers and stringers. The staff photographers are those who work and bill exclusively through Black Star. Stringers are generally hinterland photographers in geographically diversified areas who do occasional assignments to supplement their work from locally developed clients.

Individual personalized representation is obviously most desirable, but at an agency such as Black Star, it is impossible. The economics of the business do not allow it; the photographer cannot expect it. He is entitled to efficient, conscientious handling of his material and ideas, but he should dispel the idea that he is the *only* photographer to whom the agency is obligated.

Assignment agencies are limited in number, but are constantly on the lookout for new talent. Globe Photos, Camera 5, Nancy Palmer, Transworld, Photo Media, Ltd., Monkmeyer, Gamma, Sygma, Magnum Photos, and Woodfin

Camp Associates are among the chief agencies in assignment photography. All except Magnum Photos are privately owned. Magnum is a cooperative agency owned and supervised by the photographer members. In recent years, Magnum has opened its doors to nonmembers, but rarely do assignments go to other than members or close "associates." Lee Jones, project supervisor at Magnum, has this to say about the development of relations with new photographers: "We are delighted to look at the work of any photographer . . . often the more 'hinterlands' the better, providing: he or she has something to say, he or she is not coming to us to learn how to make money, he or she is prepared to wait for an answer, and perhaps a not very comforting one. And providing he or she has already decided to be a photographer and has spent a good deal of time producing visible proof of that decision. I, for one, am not interested in talking to people who are in the process of making 'life-style decisions.' I am interested in seeing the results of a lot of introspective hard work."

Agencies want to see the work of photographers, for photographers are the lifeblood of agencies. Dilettantes and people uncommitted to hard work need not apply. Nor should anyone approach an agency without full realization that picture agencies are not charitable institutions, that agency services cost money.

### Stock Agencies

By far the largest category among picture agencies is the stock agency. New York is the heart of the stock picture business. There you will find small personalized agencies, specialized agencies, and large repositories of color and black-and-white images. There may be other listings in this constantly changing business, but we have referred to the 1974 New York Yellow Pages telephone directory for a definitive listing of the stock agencies.

# Photographic Agencies

| Name | Address | Specialty |
|---|---|---|
| Animals Animals | 161 East 82nd Street<br>New York, New York 10028 | Wild Life |
| Black Star Publishing Co., Inc. | 450 Park Avenue South<br>New York, New York 10016 | All Subjects |
| Camera Clix | 404 Park Avenue South<br>New York, New York 10016 | Art |
| College Newsphoto Alliance | 342 Madison Avenue<br>New York, New York 10017 | Feature Stories on Social Problems |
| Contemporary Color | 18 West 30th Street<br>New York, New York 10001 | All Subjects |
| DPI, Inc. | 521 Madison Avenue<br>New York, New York 10022 | All Subjects |
| A. Devaney, Inc. | 40 East 49th Street<br>New York, New York 10017 | All Subjects |
| Dewys, Inc. | 60 East 42nd Street<br>New York, New York 10017 | All Subjects |
| Eastern Photo Service | 60 East 42nd Street<br>New York, New York 10017 | Africa & Asia |
| Editorial Photocolor Archives | 342 Madison Avenue<br>New York, New York 10017 | All Subjects |

| | | |
|---|---|---|
| Four by Five, Inc. | 342 Madison Avenue<br>New York, New York 10017 | All Subjects |
| Freelance Photographers<br>Guild, Inc. | 251 Park Avenue South<br>New York, New York 10010 | All Subjects |
| Ewing Galloway | 420 Lexington Avenue<br>New York, New York 10017 | All Subjects |
| Globe Photos Inc. | 404 Park Avenue South<br>New York, New York 10016 | All Subjects |
| Keystone Press Agency Inc. | 170 Fifth Avenue<br>New York, New York 10010 | All Subjects |
| Frederick Lewis, Inc. | 35 East 35th Street<br>New York, New York 10016 | All Subjects |
| Magnum Photos, Inc. | 15 West 46th Street<br>New York, New York 10036 | All Subjects |
| Nancy Palmer Photo<br>Agency | 129 Lexington Avenue<br>New York, New York 10016 | All Subjects |
| Photo Media Ltd. | 5 West 20th Street<br>New York, New York 10011 | All Subjects |
| Picture Concepts Inc. | 57 West 56th Street<br>New York, New York 10019 | Environmental |
| Rapho/Photo Researchers | 60 East 56th Street<br>New York, New York 10022 | All Subjects |
| H. Armstrong Roberts | 420 Lexington Avenue<br>New York, New York 10017 | All Subjects |
| Shostal Assoc., Inc. | 60 East 42nd Street<br>New York, New York 10017 | All Subjects |
| Sygma Photo News | 322 West 72nd Street<br>New York, New York 10023 | News and Feature Stories |
| Tarius Photos | 25 West 45th Street<br>New York, New York 10036 | All Subjects |
| Underwood & Underwood | 3 West 46th Street<br>New York, New York 10036 | All Subjects |
| Woodfin Camp Inc. | 50 Rockefeller Plaza<br>New York, New York 10020 | All Subjects |

There is no pot of gold at the end of the stock picture rainbow. Conversely, pictures stagnating in a photographer's collection in Albuquerque, New Mexico, have no value or prospect of generating income for the free-lancer. Stock picture files for the free-lancer are like buying equities. It is an investment for the future which can continue to pay dividends for years to come. In the case of many Black Star photographers, the residual sales from material originally shot on assignments have generated revenues many times the fee received for the original assignment. Never in the short history of photojournalism have the opportunities for sale of existing material been more salutary. Why?

1. The simplicity and immediacy of visual communication has increased the use of photographs in a multiplicity of media.

2. Users of photographs have found that in lieu of costly assignments, it is often possible to find just the right image to satisfy their needs.

3. Contemporary graphic sophistication has forced publishers to revise and update existing volumes to compete for the visual attention of the reader. This is particularly true in educational books for young people who have been weaned on the visual and respond to visual stimuli as opposed to linear word constructions.

4. There is a greater understanding by communicators of the special con-

sciousness and power of the still image with its concomitant isolation of the moment and enhancement of meaning and impact.

5. The advent of color photography and the sale of color transparencies have generated at least three times the per-picture price of black-and-white photographs.

Most stock agencies work on a consignment basis. They do not purchase photographs outright from contributing photographers. The prevailing split is on a fifty-fifty percent basis, payment being made to the photographer on payment by the client. Some agencies insist on large-format transparencies, 4 by 5 inches or larger. Recent years have seen greater acceptance of 35-mm. transparencies, and the large-format transparency requirement is much less evident.

No stock agency can anticipate salable subject matter. The requests are infinite in their diversity. Scenics, sports, industry, animals, family life, science, agriculture, construction, traffic—these are a few of the categories in constant demand. A photographer with a large number of photographs reflecting the life, customs, industry, agriculture, and people of countries of the world must enjoy stock picture success over the long haul. The photographer should recognize that this is a business for the long haul—that patience is the name of the game. Today's dormant picture is tomorrow's sale.

Discussions and correspondence with some of the leading stock picture agencies have elicited tips for more effective dealing with the agencies and handling of material. Dave Wilson of Globe Photos says, "The sole reason for the existence of the agency is to take the sale burden from the photographer's shoulders and therefore the nitty-gritty aspects of sales are the exclusive business of the agency. The incipient photojournalist when he first approaches an agency should realize that he is not going to get free information about the sale of photos."

The agencies are in constant need of photographs—black-and-white prints and color transparencies. They are not doing you a favor by dealing with you. They are only as good as the photographs they have, and they require a constantly expanding file of relevant and outstanding images.

*Captions*

Captions are a necessity! Agents, picture researchers, and editors are constantly frustrated by the sloppy unprofessionalism of some photographers. Caption-less pictures are useless unless they are symbolic and nonspecific. Simple good sense dictates that sales should not be lost for lack of caption information.

*Releases*

The highest payments for photographs are those sold to advertising agencies. No release, no sale! Then answer your own question as to whether releases are required for successful stock sales. For editorial noncommercial purposes releases are not generally required unless the individual picture is being held up to ridicule or otherwise being defamed. If the opportunity presents itself in any situation to procure a model release, get it. The release expands the potential horizon for that particular image.

The pictures belong to the photographer. Most agencies will not accept responsibility or liability for loss or damage to transparencies, prints, and negatives. Many agencies require that prints and transparencies remain on file for minimum periods. Those minimum periods vary. A. Devaney, Inc., requires a minimum of three years; Globe Photos, Inc., five years.

Simplistic but true is that good pictures sell better than mediocre pictures.

The much maligned editors and art directors are professionals. They know their jobs and can generally be counted on to select the best photograph technically and compositionally with the greatest content. When you send pictures to an agency, remember that your pictures are competing with those produced by some of the best image makers of the world. So do not settle for second best when you make the photograph. Take that extra time for the elements to be in the right place, for the light to be moody and dramatic, to use foreground, middle ground, and background most effectively in the frame, and to make sure that the message of the picture is direct and unconfused.

# Ideas

The successful photojournalist, like the successful salesman, like the successful writer, like the successful anything, must be a person with ideas. Anyone can learn to use a camera, but an empty head can't do a damn thing with a camera. A free-lance photographer, working with or without an agency, must be a well-rounded individual with more than superficial interest in every aspect of the world in which he lives. A college education is not a prerequisite, but thorough training in the arts, philosophy, history, literature, and the other disciplines that make for a perceptive mind should be encouraged. The image of the cigar-chomping, rough-hewn, agggressive, insensitive photographer of yesteryear has been replaced by the picture of thoughtful chroniclers of the times using the camera to make more penetrating and sensitive photographs interpreting events in more meaningful terms. Those whose formal education or self-education has been neglected will find that they cannot be equally at home with kings, scientists, and beggars and therefore are not capable of relating to the subjects with the depth that is required.

There are those who will argue that the question of *ideas* may range far afield from a discussion of free-lance photographers and picture agencies. I disagree. At the heart of the relationship is the quotient of idea productivity. Some photographers will never have an idea—others will walk ten feet and have ten ideas. The most valuable photojournalist to the picture agencies is the person who can give the agencies the tools with which to work—*ideas*. There is no dearth of great image makers among the photographers of America. But there certainly is no great plethora of photographers who have something to say about the world or have the capability of refining their ideas into cohesive well-articulated subjects.

The young photographer seems to have an excessive fear of the possible theft of his ideas. I am sure there are many instances where a magazine or agency has appropriated ideas for their own benefit without respect for the inherent rights of the originator of the idea. After thirty years of dealing with ideas, my experience has been that most people in this creative business recognize that ideas are a commodity—the most important commodity the free-lancer has in his arsenal of assets. The ethics are on the highest level. There are few comparable businesses where transactions are negotiated on trust, commitments made without written purchase orders, obligations fulfilled on the basis of a telephone call or a handshake.

Photojournalism may be dead for those who refuse to think. I would guess that more than half of the so-called photojournalists, free-lance or otherwise, have nothing to say. Saying nothing with a camera is as negative as saying nothing in conversation, in the written word, in art, sculpture, and architecture, or in any field of creative endeavor. For that category of photographer, the best advice this chapter can render is to suggest giving up photojournalism as a career. For the others, read on!

Where do photographic ideas come from? From reading newspapers, from watching television, from living and observing people, from anger and rage that one wants to express about inequities in society, from the desire to celebrate what is beautiful in people and in nature. From curiosity and caring and restlessness and adventure and getting involved and the desire to peel off the skin of our mores and culture and have a visual look at the reality. From not taking things at face value and giving yourself the opportunity to find out that things are not what they seem, that preconceptions and stereotypes do not prove out. From simple everyday existence. The one great controvertible myth in the photojournalistic business is that to be a salable, palatable, acceptable idea for publication requires that it be bizarre and unusual. The only requirement, I suggest, is that it be visual and well defined. The simplest idea photographed with understanding, compassion, and love can sometimes prove to be the most compelling. Think back to some of the great photographic essays in the short life of photojournalism and contemplate the simplicity of the ideas. Ideas are there for the taking. It was Brian Brake who recognized that "Monsoon" was indigenous to and had great impact on the lives of hundreds of millions of people. It was W. Eugene Smith who found a "Nurse Midwife" to reflect her personal affirmation of life or a "Spanish Village" to show some of the eternal truths of man's existence. It was the sheer force and power of the David Douglas Duncan personality and intellect which enabled him to convince Picasso to allow the camera to present every aspect of his humanity and artistry. The Pulitzer-Prize-winning photographic essay by Brian Lanker of the *Topeka Capital-Journal* on the birth of a child (see page 141) was related to the most commonplace of all events—birth. Nothing cataclysmic, nothing spectacular, not the biggest, the smallest, or the most beautiful—just the most real, the most honest, and the most straightforward.

Each community is a microcosm of the world containing people, albeit of different ethnicity, values, attitudes, and cultures. Where there are people, there are ideas for stories to be written about and photographed—stories related to the gut issues of life—work, survival, emotions (happiness, sadness, love, hate, etc.). It matters not if the photojournalist is working for a general interest or special interest magazine or for an industrial publication. The criteria and opportunities are the same; the issues and concerns are the same. The variables lie in the special approaches of the journalist to the subject, the selectivity of the idea, the perceptiveness of the photographer, the depth with which he treats it, and the bias and point of view he brings to the subject.

**Homeward Bound** by Talmadge Morgan of *Cocoa Today*. This silhouette, from a feature point of view, illustrates the chill experienced in 1973 by the people of Rye, New York, during the worst ice storm in a decade. (Photo courtesy of Talmadge Morgan.)

There is one nonsense which we should dispel immediately. Photographers sometimes say that they should be given the opportunity to go to the more exotic corners of the earth because their home bases do not produce stories or ideas. It may be that a change of scenery would be a temporary stimulant, but the probability exists that equal sterility will accompany the photographer in Shangri-La.

Locale is no detriment just as it is no panacea to success. I recall the days of Cal Bernstein who mined the territories of the West Coast, Denver, New York, and Salt Lake City for their photojournalistic lodes. Everybody said that Salt Lake was a dead end for a photographer, that nobody could generate work in such a sterile area. But it was in Ogden, Utah, that Cal Bernstein found a "High School Married Couple" that became an extensive essay for *Cosmopolitan* magazine or "The Rebirth of Loren Peck," a *Pageant* magazine essay which treated the rehabilitation of an automobile accident victim.

To give substance and specifics to how ideas are developed, we might perhaps play what I call the Idea Game. Take any subject in which you have an abiding interest. Old Age? Industry? Sports? Weather? Then try to develop as many editorial visually translatable ideas within the limitations of the subject as your mind can generate. I have selected the general subject of Winter for the purpose of this exercise and have come up with the following partial list of story possibilities:

The Free-Lancer and the Picture Syndicate

Winter on the farm

Winter nights

Aftermath of a blizzard

Winter in the city

Winter sports

The abstract beauty of winter

The joys of winter (for children)

Winter in Yellowstone or other national park

Life at 40 below

Winter holidays

Ice

Snow removal

Zoo in winter

Winter carnivals

Winter on the beach

Winter folklore

Winter transportation

Maine winter

These are only points of departure for your fertile mind. See how many you can add.

I leave this subject with a special plea to photographers to open their collective eyes, break the stereotypes, develop a style of personalized photojournalism, and suggest ideas you care about and want to do. You will find that the success of your relationship with the picture agency will be enhanced by your active stimulation of ideas with which the agency can work in your behalf.

During the heyday of *Life, Look,* and *Post,* they were the principal backers for interesting long-term expensive depth photojournalistic projects. As this resource declined, some agencies undertook to fill the void. The history of Black Star is replete with instances where the financial and creative resources of the agency have helped photojournalists realize well-conceived projects. At the height of the civil rights struggle in the United States, Black Star underwrote a "Southern Documentary Project" by a group of committed photojournalists intent on bringing their personalized perspectives of the struggle to the magazines of the world. These involvements are not always altruistic—the agency recognized that its greatest resource is in the quality of the journalistic material it develops.

# How Agencies Generate New Uses for Old Material

Pictures have perpetual value. The value of any individual image is impossible to ascertain. Its value is determined by being in the right place at the right time for the right use. Residual sales are primarily based on fortuitous accident, but either the free-lancer alone or in concert with the agency can

generate sales by thoughtful, intelligent handling of existing material. Charles Rado of Rapho Guillumette may hold the world's record for getting the most mileage out of a photographer's work. Besides sales of Ylla's famous photographs of animals to magazines, book publishers, encyclopedias, advertising agencies, and the like, he also systematically put together a series of children's photo books on many of the wild animals she photographed.

As the diversity of media uses of photography have expanded, the dynamic picture agency has been forced to consider peripheral uses of the material even as the photography is being accomplished for primary use. The agency becomes more than a picture peddler, but rather creative packagers of concepts designed to get maximum financial return from the material. A classic example of a free-lance photographer who has endeavored to exploit this principle in combination with Black Star is Flip Schulke, Miami-based specialist in underwater photography. The Tektite project was a combined effort of the Department of Interior and the National Aeronautics and Space Administration (NASA) to allow scientist–aquanauts to live in underwater habitats for longer periods of time while performing scientific experiments. After completing magazine commitments for United States and foreign magazines, Schulke led the final Tektite scientific expedition in an evaluation of films, cameras, and lenses under underwater conditions. A half-hour documentary film resulted from that effort. The still pictures have been incorporated in a trade book on Tektite for the adult market, as part of a *Man in the Sea* series for the young people's book market, for use in a contemplated filmstrip series on man's exploration of inner space, and for subsidiary illustrative purposes in educational books, encyclopedia, advertising, and magazine illustrations. Every editorial idea does not lend itself to this saturation treatment. The thinking free-lancer can enhance his income and satisfactions by trying to generate ideas which allow for this approach.

Some years ago, I had the opportunity to be involved in preparing an idea for a magazine in which the photographer was asked to illustrate poetry passages from Walt Whitman's *Leaves of Grass*. Some years later we were able to produce a book completely with existing pictures from stock files on the same subject. Without the catalyst of the book idea, those pictures would have continued to sit in the files gathering dust instead of generating income. The use of photography in audiovisual and electronic media, greeting cards, posters, record covers, annual reports, house organs, brochures, and myriad other outlets provide creative opportunities for new uses of picture material never contemplated in the early days of journalistic illustrative photography.

# Foreign Markets

The world of photojournalism does not begin and end with the magazines of the United States. There is a great big wonderful world out there in Germany, France, England, Scandinavia, Spain, Japan, Brazil, Italy, and other countries whose price structures are on the rise. It is possible to put together simultaneous assignments on the same subject through careful exploration and exploitation of those markets. The picture agency is uniquely qualified to bring these markets to photographers through direct contacts and subagents. It sure beats not reaching them at all.

Many times commonplace subjects make interesting pictures. This pattern photograph of a lunar moth on a screen door, taken by 13-year-old Teri Smith of Alexandria, Virginia in May of 1967, was a first place winner in a nationwide contest sponsored by Scholastic Magazines, Inc., and Eastman Kodak Company. Courtesy of Teri Smith, 1967 Scholastic/Kodak Photography Awards. First place award.

# The Free-Lancer, the Picture Agency, and the Future

The market for photography has never been better. Think back a short forty years when *Life* and *Look* came into existence and recall how few markets for creative photography existed. We are using the camera less and less for the documentary photo essay and more and more for commercial purposes. The competition is keener, there are more photographers scrounging for every job, and the times are changing. Photojournalism and the photojournalist will adapt and change with contemporary needs. The limitations of the printed page will be replaced by the use of hundreds of still images telling cohesive stories on television, in filmstrips, in motion-picture theaters, and for home viewing through the medium of cassettes. Already we are seeing photojournalists adapting the picture essay form in combination with text to produce meaningful full-length books. Photojournalism does not need journals to disseminate its message. It needs dedicated creative people who do not sit around whining about their condition and the loss of what once existed. It needs people who face up to today and who are responsive to the needs of today. The role of the picture agency in this chaotic period of change is to bridge the gap between the creative free-lancer and the new markets.

# Student Participation

Like many other chapters in this book, chapter 17 is comprehensive. To get full benefit from it requires that students refer to it time and again. A once-over lightly is unfair to the photographs, to the student, and to the author who has worked hard to provide new insights into the free-lance business and into picture syndicates.

The first thing which comes to mind in studying this chapter is that the successful free-lancer is a special type of person. He is a business man, an artist, an illustrator, a reporter. Many are writers as well as photographers, and further, more times than not, they are as much at home with movie or videotape equipment as they are with a battery of lights and still cameras.

This situation points up the complexity of our times and emphasizes the numerous demands placed upon present-day photojournalists.

1. Elaborate on this statement of Howard Chapnick: "Only the Associated Press and United Press International, among worldwide distributors of journalistic material, qualify under the definition of 'syndicates' producing, purchasing, and distributing photographs for simultaneous publication in a number of newspapers and periodicals in different localities."

2. Describe the duties and responsibilities of the picture agent—the man in the middle.

3. What single event caused the greatest impact, psychologically and financially, for the free-lancer and the assignment picture agencies?

4. What is the difference between an assignment agency and a stock agency?

5. How has the advent of color photography and the sale of color transparencies affected the price of black-and-white photographs?

6. Write a paragraph explaining the importance of each of the following subjects touched on by Mr.

Chapnick: (a) captions, (b) releases, (c) rights.
7. Do you agree with the following statement of Mr. Chapnick? ". . . more than half of the so-called photojournalists, free-lance or otherwise, have nothing to say."
8. List at least five sources of profitable photographic ideas.

9. Does Mr. Chapnick believe that in photojournalism "to be a salable, palatable, acceptable idea for publication requires that a [picture or pictures] be bizarre and unusual"?
10. Write a paragraph explaining how an agency can generate new uses for old material.

# Innovation Is a Must

# 18

L ife is a competitive situation. Publishers, editors, writers, news photographers—all work hard to capture a fair share of the readership and profits circulating in their respective communities.

Today's newspaper competes with radio and television—and with the other publications which circulate in its trade territory. To hold its own in such circumstances, it is imperative that each newspaper try to outdo its competitors; each tries hard to give its readers something they cannot get elsewhere.

One way to outdo one's rivals is to inaugurate a picture program which outdistances all competition. By hiring more and better photographers and picture editors, by advocating extensive use of color photography, and perhaps by changing to cold type or photo-offset production means a newspaper is going all out to take advantage of its word-and-picture offerings.

A few thoughtful and innovative publications gain extra mileage from picture programs at the end of the year by producing a slide-tape presentation of events in the community during the year. Available in December, the slide-tape shows are shown at schools, churches, and service clubs under the auspices of the newspapers. This is an inexpensive project, and one which builds mountains of goodwill. If the slides are also set to music (something most modern photojournalists can easily do), an interesting program becomes an easy, economical matter.

## An In-Plant Photojournalism Workshop

Changing pace, let us look at a project conceived and carried out by Ed Lehr, picture editor of the *Jackson Citizen Patriot*.[1] Mr. Lehr is one picture specialist who qualifies as an innovator.

To give a new dimension to and a new respect for visual reportage, Ed recently held the first four-day workshop for members of the *Citizen Patriot* staff. Patterned as closely as possible after University of Missouri photo work-

---

1. Ed Lehr majored in photojournalism at and has a master's degree in journalism from the University of Missouri.

Editors and photographers on the *Citizen Patriot,* Jackson, Michigan, believe that these are the times when publications must be innovative when it comes to using pictures.

Ed Lehr, picture editor of the *Jackson Citizen Patriot* (*right*) inspects the final pages of the *Citizen Patriot* book *People, Times, Places, and Pride.* The foreword of the experimental publication was written by Tom Riordan, managing editor of the *Citizen Patriot.*

# About this book

Today's daily newspaper is a conversation piece today.

Tomorrow, it is a piece of scrap.

However, in nearly every issue there are stories and pictures which literally cry out to be read and looked at again and again.

That's the idea which prompted this book — to preserve many of the memorable words and photos from issues of the Jackson Citizen Patriot during 1973. This material carries the mark of journalistic excellence.

It was conceived by Ed Lehr, 30-year-old Jackson Citizen Patriot picture editor. Ed undertook the task of making the selections for this 80-page volume.

The result: an absorbing collection of events and people who helped make news during a 12-month period. It's not all-inclusive, of course, but an interesting cross-section from the life of one midwestern community. There are major and minor happenings, the charming and the pathetic, the joyful and the heartrending.

Praise for this book goes to the entire news and photographic staff of the Jackson Citizen Patriot and to the paper's production department.

Although primarily aimed toward regular Citizen Patriot readers, the book also should be of interest to other newspapers and journalism schools.

It is printed by lithography on 70-pound enamel stock with a 10-point Kromekote cover.

We welcome your thoughts on this publication.

Tom Riordan
Managing Editor
Jackson Citizen Patriot

Lehr and the book's ending pages. (Citizen Patriot photo by Ron Mann)

# people
# times
# places
# pride

Jackson Citizen Patriot

JACKSON, MICH. 49204

shops, Mr. Lehr's goal was to "set a tone for a deeper kind of photography" than is usually found on newspapers. We believe he has succeeded.

On the first day the workshop participant developed preliminary ideas for several stories. After additional research and polishing, he presented the story idea he considered the best at the evening session. Once he had earned staff approval, the participant was ready on the second day to begin shooting. No contrived pictures, no setups, were allowed, and the two rolls of film allotted were turned in that same evening.

Contact prints were made and turned over—one set to the photographer who had made them and another set to the staff. The staff consisted of Tom Riordan, managing editor, Lehr, and other local people. Barry Edmonds of the *Flint Journal* was visiting photo expert. The second night the staff reviewed slides made from pictures taken that day and spent considerable time discussing story line and direction.

One more day was given to shooting and critiquing the individual stories. On the fourth (and last) day each photographer chose his opener and all other selects that comprised his story. That evening, under staff direction and using $8 \times 10$-inch prints, the group scaled and laid out the final story.

Lehr believes that *Citizen Patriot* photography rapidly improved as a result of this project of concentrated thinking and seeing.

# A Newspaper Book

After the workshop, to encourage better pictures—and especially to spark a sustained effort to provide a better day-by-day record of his community—Ed made an even more startling suggestion: He proposed a newspaper book, *People, Places, Times, Pride.*[2] The proposal, made nearly a year after he had suggested the workshop, was written as an interoffice memorandum and distributed to staff members and co-workers in December 1973.

After posing such questions as What is news? What are good pictures? and What pictures should be used in the *Citizen Patriot?,* Mr. Lehr told his story of "quality photojournalism, and how it came about."

> An early photojournalistic effort that sustained broad coverage [Lehr began] was that made by Roy Stryker and the Farm Security Administration photographers.
>
> Purpose of this effort [the picture editor continued] was to document the depression areas of the country, and then through releases to newspapers let everyone know that the whole country was working to end hard times.
>
> Stryker insisted that his photographers be thorough and honest in their research prior to going on a picture assignment. If they could not answer questions about the things they were going to photograph, they would need to dig deeper.
>
> A project built along lines similar to FSA [Lehr explained] was the Missouri Photo Workshop. Stryker, of Pittsburgh, Stan Kalish, picture editor of the *Milwaukee Journal,* John Morris, picture editor of the *Ladies Home Journal,* and Cliff Edom, University of Missouri, organized the first Workshop in May 1949. Others on that first staff were Harold Corsini, then working with Stryker on "The Pittsburgh Story," and Russ Arnold, then a Chicago free-lance photographer.
>
> One of the important lessons, from the Workshop [Lehr told his co-workers] was that every story approved was a legitimate story idea.

over of *People, Times, Places, and Pride left*) which was released for newsstand ale in Jackson, Michigan, during the ummer of 1974.

2. *People, Places, Times, Pride.* Copyright 1974 by Booth Newspapers, Inc.

The photographer on a newspaper wears
many hats. Sometimes he is an illustrator,
rather than a photo-reporter. Whatever his
job he competes for attention and strives to
make a picture that is different. This abstract
of a man in a bedsprings factory was made
by Kenneth Heinen during a week-long
University of Missouri Photo Workshop.
Heinen is on the pictures staff of the
*Washington Star Sunday Magazine.* (Photo
courtesy of Kenneth Heinen.)

That was what Ed Lehr was seeking for his newspaper—a source of valid picture story ideas. He wanted a list of stories which needed to be told and enough competent, sensitive photojournalists to do the job.

In considering his major goals, Lehr conceived the idea of producing a book about the city of Jackson, Michigan—a book in which nothing but the best of photography would be used. One subject to be covered, Ed's memorandum pointed out, was the major changes in the town. Other suggested subjects included industry, labor, buying, selling, churches and schools, all a part of the town's personality.

Stepping back to examine what he had written, Lehr concluded, "I find that I have described what I would like to cover with our newspapers."

"Only a newspaper staff," he reasoned, "can be on top of such changes and record them as they happen in a permanent manner. Only a newspaper staff can be familiar enough with a town to understand why it works," Ed decided. And "only a newspaper would have the continuity necessary to put a town in its proper perspective."

That is the kind of reasoning which induced Ed Lehr to start thinking about publishing the book. Here is how he thought the production problems could be managed: the book would be a tabloid-size publication printed on quality offset paper, only previously published material would be eligible for publication in the book, and only the best material which had appeared in the *Citizen Patriot* would be presented. The following guidelines were set forth.

First, the book would be a measuring device, a check, to determine whether all of the city of Jackson was properly covered.

Second, the book would be a quality product, a permanent, compact quality publication which would enable persons to remember the very best photos and stories.

Third, production would be relatively simple. The page negatives would be the source material; page Veloxes would be shot down to the desired size for direct platemaking. All negative work would be handled in the shop.

Fourth, since it was an unusual and different kind of publication, the book would have an incredible sales potential, provided that the product was good enough.

Fifth, such a book (in Ed's mind) would assist in the evaluation of editorial material and would help the publisher determine whether or not the newspaper, offerings were strong enough to sell. The book was to contain "no advertising," and "no entertainment material." It would thus provide a dollars-and-cents evaluation of the *Citizen Patriot* editorial package.

Sixth, the book would serve as a sustained and continuing report for the citizens of the Jackson trade territory.

Seventh, the book would offer a standard with which to measure assignments. If an assignment was good enough for the book, then it most certainly was good enough for the newspaper where it originally appeared.

Eighth, and final reason for publishing a book was that careful perusal and evaluation of its contents would ensure, in Ed Lehr's words, "that we cover material in the *Citizen Patriot* trade territory which up to this time has regularly been overlooked."

As this book was being written, the first issue of the newspaper book rolled off the press. To make a valid and definitive check on its value will require considerable time and several issues. Certainly an innovative and different program, Lehr believes the book, which has gone beyond the financial break-even point, is a complete success. Future books, which will be done within the plant itself, will have a better opportunity to make money than the first one, which was published commercially. But the most important thing, Lehr believes, is that a book like this performs a community service by spotlighting and preserving many interesting and important stories in a way that a "here today, gone tomorrow" newspaper would not. Lehr believes that the book has made it possible to provide a more comprehensive, more innovative picture package than the *Citizen Patriot* has previously produced.

Other publications have also felt that the *Citizen Patriot* experiment was worthwhile and Bill Strode of the Louisville *Courier-Journal* and *Louisville Times* credited the Booth newspaper's book as the inspiration for the production of a similar book by the Louisville newspapers, which was printed in the spring of 1975.

# Student Participation

1. In your opinion, how can a person be innovative with a camera?
2. From local publications select five examples of innovative photography.
3. Granted that you were made director of photography on your school paper or your hometown paper, what innovation would you suggest to improve the picture coverage?
4. Do you advise newspapers in your area to reuse the best word and picture stories from their publications to produce a periodic commercial picture book? Why or why not?

# Careers in Photojournalism

# 19

**M**any persons reading this book intend to be photojournalists. With this thought in mind, let us take a closer look at the field which challenges us.

An interesting book by Arville Schaleben, for many years a managing editor of the *Milwaukee Journal,* provides some valuable information. Schaleben opened the chapter on "The Picture Field" by pointing out, "Photojournalists are in strong demand . . . People who take pictures or people who handle pictures are in a fast-growing and exciting field."[1]

With the demise of *Life* and *Look* and the death of some of the larger metropolitan dailies, the picture field, some believe, is not as bright as it once was. There are still many jobs for the picture specialist, and probably more pictures are being used today than at any time in history. Trade journals, small weekly and daily publications—among these and other groups one can find many publications which believe wholeheartedly in the words-pictures team. Each day they seek the services of picture experts, and they do not discriminate against race, creed, or sex.

A good camera reporter, well trained in his profession, is capable of holding a job on a magazine or newspaper, or for that matter on television. This chapter helps him evaluate himself before applying for a job.

## Qualifications

In Schaleben's book James Godbold, once president and publisher of *The Daily Courier,* Conroe, Texas, had some thoughts about photojournalists. Mr. Godbold was for many years chairman of the educational program of the National Press Photographers Association and at one time was director of photography at *National Geographic* magazine. A frequent staff member of the University of Missouri annual Photo Workshop, Godbold's experience gives him much authority to comment on photo reportage. "A photographer," he said, "must have the same background and qualifications as any other reporter. I refuse to recognize the man who uses a notebook and typewriter as a reporter and the man with a camera as a photographer. I call them both reporters—both newsmen."[2] Another important bit of information from

---

1. Arville Schaleben, *A Definitive Study of Your Future in Journalism* (New York: Richards Rosen Press, Inc., 1961).

2. Schaleben, *Definitive Study.*

Schaleben's book is the report on Earl Seubert, chief photographer of the *Minneapolis Tribune*. Seubert, like Godbold, has extensive experience and the credentials to back up his opinions. Seubert has frequently been on the staff of the Missouri photo workshops and has earned the national Newspaper Photographer of the Year Award—has, in fact, earned the title several times. Consider these words of his:

> . . . One thing that helps me is that I think pictures all the time. I shoot a lot of pictures. I even "shoot pictures" when I don't have a camera in my hand; wherever I see people responding to life—anywhere, everywhere, on my way to work, in the backyard, going to and from assignments. Spring, summer, fall, winter, inside, outside . . . wherever I find people responding to the people around them, I find pictures.[3]

In the foregoing, we have touched upon two important precepts, two factors which should constantly be part of the thinking of budding photojournalists.

### Precept 1

A good photographer is dependable and responsible. He is intelligent and alert. The news photographer is also a reporter, just as much as any word reporter.

### Precept 2

The photojournalist is a complex person. Knowledgeable about all that is going on—and fully abreast of the times—he knows and likes people.

As Earl Seubert discovered early in his career, and as many great photographers before him had learned, "where people are interacting, there one finds material—great material—for his camera."

"News is of the essence," Frank Luther Mott often expounded for the benefit of his students. And so it is. Any news photographer worth his salt will be on hand to cover spot news events: fires, wrecks, tornadoes, and the like. It is necessary that such occurrences be recorded. But, since hard news is only a small portion of the matter which eventually finds its way into print, and since photographing the obvious is only a small part of the work done by a news photographer, it is imperative that he be trained to do much more. Let him learn that "photography is a language," as pointed out by John Whiting.[4] Let him master the sentence structure, the syntax, the compositional elements of the language of pictures; let him learn that in visual communication, just as in verbal communication, one must follow the rules of unity, conciseness, and coherence. Above all, let him never forget that *picture content is his first consideration.*

As a young person studies to become a photojournalist, let that person learn how to research a story and how to write it. Let that person, too, learn something about the humanities, something of political science, and something of philosophy—of aesthetics and ethics. All of these disciplines will help him (or her) to become a more understanding, more perceptive person.

Once the budding photojournalist has completed his college education, he faces the awesome task of getting a job. Just where will he go? And what will

---

3. Ibid.
4. John R. Whiting, *Photography Is a Language* (Chicago: Ziff-Davis Publishing Co., 1946).

First Award, General News Class, in the
30th Annual Pictures of the Year competition, this shocker titled **Cease Fire** was
made by Mike Zerby of the *Minneapolis
Tribune*. (Photo courtesy of Mike Zerby.)

he do to get that first job? All photographers do not begin work on a large newspaper, magazine, or television station. They might break in as a cameraman-writer-picture editor and jack-of-all-trades on a house organ, a trade journal, or some other kind of specialized publication. In fact, some veteran photojournalists recommend this kind of start, not only because there are not enough *National Geographics* and Louisville *Courier-Journals* to utilize all the help which is available, but also because one usually can learn more and develop faster on a trade journal or smaller publication.

# Assembling a Portfolio

At this juncture, logic dictates that a prospective photojournalist carefully study his negatives, prints, and contact sheets and that he work hard and conscientiously to print the best portfolio he possibly can. The pictures need not all be full 16 × 20-inch or 11 × 14-inch prints. An occasional change of size can be helpful. Bleed some of the pictures, that is, make them flush on all sides with the mount. This arrangement provides a change of pace and suggests a bit of professionalism. A portfolio representing the best pictures you have ever made will do much to tell a prospective employer about the kind of photographer you are now and the kind you will be ten years hence.

Your portfolio should have (1) good picture content and (2) craftsmanship beyond reproach. Your pictures should have more than passing interest to the observer. While an employer does not select members of his staff solely on the revelation of a handful of photographs, a reasonable number of good pictures properly presented can be of great value to the job seeker.

In making up your portfolio, be sure that it has variety and that it represents the full range of your versatility. It would be foolish, indeed, if your portfolio consisted only of pretty pictures, or only of portraits, or only of one type of camera work. Among other things, your portfolio should give proof of your all-around ability. It should honestly portray examples of your best camera work, your best cropping, your best craftsmanship.

### Divisions in Picture Competitions

To help you decide the types of pictures your portfolio should contain, check the divisions featured in current newspaper and/or magazine photographic contests. In the Pictures of the Year[5] competition, one of the oldest and largest of its kind, you will find the following divisions:

### Spot news

These pictures because of their spontaneity prohibit advance planning. Spot news pictures are usually grab shots and sometimes they can be attributed to luck. "The photographer was in the right place at the right time." True, luck sometimes plays a part in the making of a great picture. More times than not, however, the winning picture is the result of years of experience, self-discipline, and well-trained reflexes.

---

5. The Pictures of the Year competition, held annually since 1943, is jointly sponsored by the School of Journalism, University of Missouri, National Press Photographers Association, and Nikon, Inc.

### General news and documentary

The term *documentary* is included here as a concession to non-news magazines which, although they do not cover hard news as do newspapers and television, they do produce a number of documentary pictures which closely parallel what has come to be known as general news. The general news picture, unlike the spot news photograph, may be planned. Knowing the route of a parade, for example, a photographer can place his camera on a tripod to photograph the mayor in the reviewing stand. Should a dignitary in the parade be assassinated by a sniper, that would provide a spot news picture. No photographer could prepare himself for that contingency. It, like most spot news pictures, would have been a "shot from the hip," a grab shot. If the resulting picture were reportorially and technically good, a portion of that goodness could be attributed to luck and a portion to experience—quick seeing and quick responses.

### Feature picture

A feature picture is a human-interest shot presenting an unusual situation. The feature shot often is humorous. Too many times feature pictures are trite and contrived. A seven-foot basketball player being guarded by a midget five-footer might make a sports feature, but the photographer would have to work hard to come up with something different. A feature picture, generally speaking, presents something different from the norm.

### Sports picture

The sports picture offers no classification problem. But the photographer who plans to have one or more sports pictures in his portfolio should make sure that he avoids clichés and stereotypes. Some of the best sports pictures are those taken of spectators, showing audience reaction to a particular situation. Jubilation or tears at the end of a hard-fought game are typical examples.

### Pictorial picture

The pictorial picture is a pretty picture, one that a person likes because of its aesthetic appeal. It may be an abstract, a pattern, or a portrayal of something as common as a sunset and still fall within the pictorial picture class.

### Portrait/personality picture

This type of picture indicates much more than the photograph often referred to as a mug shot. The portrait/personality picture should be of fine technical quality and should be an interpretation of the character of the subject.

### Home and family interest picture

This classification was created to release women's pages from the tyranny of fashion and society pictures. While the latter type of pictures may still be found on women's pages in prizewinning publications, they seldom are placed there to the exclusion of all others. Present-day women are interested in politics, science, and many other subjects. Pictures which portray the broad variety of women's interests are fair game for the women's interest division.

Careers in Photojournalism

## Other Picture Divisions

All successful pictures communicate. The single picture makes a statement. Many pictures, properly organized and properly displayed, usually tell a more complete story. The picture series, in its strictest definition, is a story in cinematic style. The picture series or sequence, as it sometimes is called, shows progressive action—the passing of time or the changing of space.

*News picture stories, feature picture stories,* and *sports picture stories* are all found in the Pictures of the Year competition. Usually they follow the traditional format and have a beginning, a middle, and an end.

Some picture groups are merely collections of pictures, although they may be loosely bound together with a common subject. A picture of a group of hats would not have a beginning, a middle, and an end, nor would it have much in common with a picture series or sequence shot on a racetrack taken with a motor-driven camera.

### Picture essay

The last form of layout is the picture essay (see pages 000). More sophisticated than the others, the essay makes no attempt to have a beginning, a middle, and an end, nor does it show a series of progressive action. The pictures in a photo essay have a considerably deeper purpose. Words are usually important also, and each photo makes a point, reporting one facet of the entire word-and-picture combination. At its beginning *Life* magazine featured traditional picture stories. Later, when the magazine became more sophisticated, many picture essays were featured, not a few of which were brilliantly done.

# Beginning a Photojournalism Career

The young college graduate fully prepared to enter photojournalism and/or allied fields has many opportunities for employment.

He can, of course, be a free-lance photographer and work for himself (see chapter 17). To be a successful free-lancer one must have many accomplishments. He must understand the publishing business, must have many contacts among picture buyers, and must be a businessman as well as a photojournalist.

The newly graduated photojournalist could start his career as a photographer or as a combination photographer-reporter on a weekly or small daily publication or on a house organ. The pay on a house organ is surprisingly good, and the experience is broad. Many professional journalists advise this type of start, and some consider it to be the real market, the real opportunity for budding photojournalists.

If one's first try is with a big, long-established publication, the going may be tough. Even here, however, an internship or beginning job is not an impossibility. Internships are important during one's college days. The National Press Photographers Association, in conjunction with many schools of journalism, sponsor intern programs each year in cooperation with newspapers and television stations. Through its intern chairman, the photographers' association makes a big, one-shot effort to place college-trained personnel in summer jobs. The program works in two ways. It helps newspapers and television

GRACEFUL RETREAT by Fred Comegys of the *Wilmington News Journal*. This picture earned third place, Pictorial Class, in the 30th Annual Pictures of the Year competition. Taking such a picture required that the photographer have an observant eye and finely tuned reflexes. (Photo courtesy of Fred Comegys.)

stations fill the gaps during vacation months, and lets students have a firsthand taste of the real thing.

Television networks and local stations have need of still and motion-picture photographers. They must turn out an untold number of prints for publicity releases to newspapers, shoppers, and the like. The television station also needs transparencies and/or stills for newscasts and commercials.

A research specialist, the person whose job it is to find the right man or woman for a given position, once told me that photojournalists, generally speaking, are not interested in administrative work. After placing a student as art director on a large daily newspaper, the specialist complained that photojournalists prefer to shoot pictures rather than to train for the more lucrative position of picture editor, art director, director of graphics, or what have you. The jobs he mentioned are important, good paying, and influential. Student photographers should accept a staff job if that is what they want. They should, however, look to the future and to the time when covering fires, wrecks, and so forth, will have lost much of its appeal.

And here is another thought for the qualified job seeker.

Why not buy or start your own picture publication? We know a college student who did. Upon graduation, he borrowed money and became part owner of a weekly newspaper. With the deal he became the editor and manager. This young man, now a successful publisher of a Missouri weekly newspaper, made much more money his first year out of college than he would have had he hired out as a photographer—or for that matter, as a picture editor. Moreover, he greatly enjoyed his role as a country editor, being an important man in his community.

Do not overlook the picture networks, Associated Press and United Press International, nor the picture agencies such as Magnum Photos, Pix Inc., Black Star, and the like (see chapter 17). A director of an agency once told me that "not nearly enough young people are learning the agency business." He believes an agency can provide a much higher income and as much satisfaction as shooting pictures if given the chance.

# Final Thoughts

As Mr. Schaleben said, "People who take pictures or people who handle pictures are in a fast-growing and exciting field." Good luck. Make the most of it.

# Student Participation

1. Write a letter to a friend who, like yourself, has been studying for a career in photojournalism. In your letter submit an outline telling your friend how and where he should apply for his first job.
2. From all the pictures you have taken and enlarged, carefully select five for a class display which you believe provide an effective nucleus for your portfolio.
3. Would you recommend that the friend in ex. 1 try first for a job on: (a) a large daily newspaper? (b) a large magazine? (c) a weekly newspaper or small journal? (d) a specialized trade journal? Give reasons for your answer in each instance.
4. As a photojournalist, what type of job do you hope to have in ten years?

# 20 A Look at the Future

Photojournalism, in its brief history, has come a long, long way. Despite the fact that publications such as *Life* and *Look* have fallen by the wayside, there remain many opportunities for the photojournalist of the future. The main requisites for tomorrow's successful camera reporter are that he be well educated, like people, and be aware of all the things going on about him.

Photojournalism has undergone many changes since the 1930s. Faster, more sensitive, better-quality film has done much to upgrade photography and photo reporting. Among the many important changes through the years was the shift from 5x7 and 4x5 press cameras to 2¼x3¼ twin-lens reflex cameras and then to 35-mm. cameras. And the end is not yet in sight.

Motivated by threats of a silver shortage, and by the spectacular success of the 35-mm. camera in the 1930s, some persons today are considering the use of film about half the size of the 35-mm. frame (Eastman's 110).

With our better lenses and better equipment, some authorities believe the day is close at hand when the news camera will be a subminiature camera loaded with film closely akin to videotape. If and when that happens, completely new technology will also be needed. As photojournalists, we must have our fingers on the pulse of a changing photojournalism at all times.

Before we will know what has happened, ecological demands and technological changes could force newspapers and magazines to adopt completely different formats. Conceivably, tomorrow's newspaper could be delivered on a closed-circuit television network.

Film manufacturers, however, do not fear the future. In a recent magazine article Anthony Frothingham, an Eastman Kodak specialist, wrote: "In a society which is turned on by the prospects of technological advance and tuned in to the notion of rapid obsolesence, the impression created in some people's minds is that film has outlived its usefulness, that nothing new can happen in film, that there is room for only one visual medium in the days ahead. In short, that film is dead."[1]

Taking issue with that opinion, Mr. Frothingham expressed the belief that "the emergence of video technologies has already stimulated the film industry to look for new ways to improve its own capabilities. The end result of this cross-fertilization will be to make film and tape more than alternative agents for communications . . . it will make them compatible partners in getting the job done."[2]

---

1. Anthony Frothingham, "Film Industry; That Is the Future," *Audio Visual Communication* 7, no. 1 (December 1973): p. 24.

2. Ibid., p. 24.

Using the Super 8 camera as the cornerstone, Kodak has recently introduced a practical sound system. A cartridge similar to the standard silent Super 8, is used, and the film has a sound track which is automatically recorded in the camera during the filming. After processing, the film is shown on any standard Super 8 sound projector or on a tape deck projector, also a Kodak product.

The Eastman Company also offers a video player for Super 8 film. Primarily intended for educational use, the player may soon have commercial application for any closed-circuit television system. The big advantage is that one day Super 8 cameras may generally replace more bulky television equipment. Such an arrangement would be more versatile and less expensive. In addition, a broad utilization of the subminiature system would permit the use of vast libraries of existing Super 8 educational film.

Norman D. Lang, of Massachusetts Institute of Technology, lends credence to this thinking in a recent article in which he states:

> The time has come when almost anyone can produce a video program from the beginning to the end without a room full of sophisticated instruments, a degree in electronics, and a refresher course in calculus.
>
> Portable video taping in particular has come a long way. Today you can grab a deck or two; can shoot a program in the morning and have a completely edited tape by late afternoon . . . incorporating different camera angles of two Porta-pack tapes.[3]

# The Laser Beam and Picture Production

To explore another facet of tomorrow's photojournalism, let us take a look at the laser beam: a dictionary defines laser (or lazer) as "*l*ight *a*mplification by *s*timulated *e*mission of *r*adiation. A device, usually containing a crystal such as a synthetic ruby in which atoms, when stimulated by focused light waves, then emit them in a narrow, very intense beam; also called an optical maser."[4]

A *National Geographic School Bulletin* describes the laser beam in more romantic terms:

> Unlike the turban-wearing giant that puffs from Aladdin's lamp, the laser's genie bursts forth in the shape of the sharpest, purest, most intense light ever seen by man . . . when focused it is billions of times brighter than sunlight . . .[5]

Invented in 1960, the laser "has just begun to shed light on its many uses." In essence Geographic's writer said:

> Laser light (one wavelength, one color) is coherent. The waves are "in phase," and each step reinforces the other, producing a strong, concentrated beam which can travel for long distances without "fanning out and growing weak." It is this coherence on the part of the laser beam which enables it to perform such miracles.[6]

---

3. Norman D. Lang, "Videography—Portapack World . . . It's Getting Better All the Time," *Industrial Photography* 23, no. 8 (August 1974): pp. 32–33.

4. *Webster's New World Dictionary,* College Edition, 1957 s.v. "laser," p. 824.

5. National Geographic School Bulletin 46, no. 7 (23 October 1967), p. 98.

6. Ibid, p.

A Look at the Future

The equipment to send and receive pictures by wire is considerably improved over that in service twenty years ago. The illustration on the opposite page (*top, left*) shows the Associated Press Laserphoto machine. "It is here, says Robert Gilka, photo director of *National Geographic* magazine, "that the laser beam is being used to best advantage." (Photo courtesy of Associated Press.)

*Below,* Unifax II, United Press International receiver. *Top right,* shows the excellent skin texture and minute detail which can be obtained from Unifax II. The device through which the laboratory technician looks is part of an infrared sensor assembly to be used in a Skylab space vehicle. (Photos courtesy of United Press International.)

Discovery of the laser beam has had and will continue to have great impact on mankind. It has made possible bloodless surgery. In the field of communication, as in medicine and other sciences, it has created miracles. Important in televising man's first step on the moon, the laser first gained attention in photography when it was used (in the hologram) to experiment in the production of three-dimensional pictures. Another laser beam breakthrough in photography occurred in 1966 when Arlan Wiker, assisted by other members of the *National Geographic* staff, took a magnificent night-time color picture in Washington, D.C.

Recently the Gannett Newspapers announced the development of "a new laser-plate process which eliminates normal engraving and stereotyping procedures in letterpress printing." The Gannett management enthusiastically reported that the process "promises much for the future." So does the dry plate maker (for offset printing) which was described in *Editor and Publisher* (9 February 1974).[7]

The Associated Press (AP) has also long been concerned with picture quality. In 1973 in a brochure, AP had this to say:

> More than two and one-half years ago, the Associated Press Board of Directors commissioned the AP research team and the Massachusetts Institute of Technology to develop "a complete new system, embracing completely new concepts" of transmitting pictures by wire . . .
>
> Improvements have been made in Wirephoto over the past 38 years, but with more than 800 members moving into offset and improved printing processes, it was apparent higher quality wire pictures were needed than were possible by electrolytic or electrostatic processes.
>
> With the help of Dr. William F. Schreiber and his staff in the electronic laboratory at MIT, two years of research have produced a revolutionary photo system.
>
> We call this breakthrough "Laserphoto."[8]

The brochure elaborated on the advantages of Laserphoto:

> The laser beam, used to penetrate outer space, now is harnessed by Massachusetts Institute of Technology scientists and AP's Research and Development team to propel AP members into a new era of photojournalism.
>
> Laserphoto's application of modern electronics and new principles of photo reproduction and photo transmission offer a quantum leap forward for AP members! Pure photographic quality for outstanding reproduction.
>
> *The Achievement:* Picture editors at AP papers will receive at their elbows individually cut and stacked glossy photographs—not facsimiles—of unmatched sharpness and clarity, all done automatically.
>
> *The Next Step:* The "electronic darkroom" with computer editing and transmission of AP photos.[9]

The three-phase timetable, as revealed in the brochure, is a busy one, indeed. The brochure concludes:

> *Phase I*—In 1974 AP begins an approximately 24-month program of replacing all photo receivers and transmitters. Photofax and Automatic Wirephoto receivers are replaced as new Laserphoto machines become available.
>
> *Phase II*—With all new receivers and transmitters in place, improvement in

---

7. Made by Burgess Newspaper Products Div., 3M Company.

8. Wesley Gallagher, Associated Press brochure, 1973.

9. Ibid.

A Look at the Future

picture quality is accomplished by an overnight change in the AP system's "scanning structure," producing a picture closer in quality to the original.

*Phase III*—As AT&T expands digital transmission lines connecting larger cities, AP gradually introduces computer handling of pictures on regional desks, offering high-speed, high-quality service to members in cities served by digital facilities.

At its hubs, AP stores network picture transmissions in computers. AP edits pictures on video screens and selects pictures for relay on state networks.

This phase is to be completed probably by the end of the 1970s.[10]

In an issue of the *Wall Street Journal,* we find these words:

The Associated Press announced the award of a $6.1 million contract to the Radiation Division of Harris-Intertype Corp., Cleveland, to manufacture receivers and transmitters for AP's new Laserphoto news picture system.

Wes Gallagher, AP president and general manager, said the contract covers production of 900 receivers and 600 transmitters for installation in newspapers, television stations, magazines, and AP bureaus throughout the country.

The Laserphoto system transmits photographs by wire using a laser beam and dry-silver photographic paper. It is designed to meet the high-quality standards of modern printing processes by delivering photographic, rather than facsimile, reproduction quality.

Pilot production of Laserphoto equipment will begin in June and full production is scheduled to begin in the fall, Mr. Gallahger said.

Full replacement of the present AP receiving and transmitting photo units in the U.S. will take about two years.

The initial production of Laserphoto machines will be at Radiation's plant in Miami, which will turn out 60 machines monthly.

AP also has signed an agreement with Minnesota Mining and Manufacturing Co., St. Paul, to guarantee the availability of the dry-silver photographic paper to be used in Laserphoto, it announced.[11]

# Computerized Photography

Pictures by wire, which did so much to stimulate wider use of photojournalism in the 1930s, will continue to contribute greatly. In a letter from Jerry Umehara, a foreign picture editor for United Press International (UPI) in New York, we learn something of the function of UPI's new "scan-converter."

"The computer," he wrote, "can, upon command, convert a picture being sent on the United States domestic network into either the European mode [network] or the South American mode [network] . . . a picture coming from South America or Europe can also be converted into the United States mode. When it is not convenient to transmit from one network to another, the pictures are stored on tape and played later."[12]

F. W. Lyon, United Press International vice-president for newspictures, elaborates on Umehara's information: "The computer [scan-converter ] has [as of February, 1974] been in service for nearly eighteen months. It allows us to convert the domestic network to the international net, or vice versa, on a near real-time basis, with no attendant loss of quality. Instructions are given to

---

10. Associated Press brochure, 1973.

11. *Wall Street Journal,* 4 March 1974.

12. Jerry Umehara: personal communication, January, 1974 (paraphrased in this text).

the computer by typing a message on a teletype machine. The computer responds by telling the operator what it is doing."[13]

Pleased as he is with the scan-converter, Mr. Lyon is equally enthusiastic about Unifax II, UPI's new picture receiver introduced in 1974. Unifax II uses an electrostatic recording process and has the following advantages over existing (1974) electrolytic systems:

> *Dimensional stability:* The paper remains dry throughout the process. There is no stretching or shrinking . . . no problem in maintaining register on color separations.
> *Permanence:* Unifax II electrostatic copies are archival in quality . . . as permanent as the paper base itself.
> *Definition:* Unifax II improves definition and gives a picture of unusual sharpness and clarity.[14]

# Summing Up

In the future, newspaper color will be of better quality and will be commonplace. Thanks to sensitive, computerized color-separation machines, newspapers and other publications will photograph fast-breaking news stories in the morning and have color layouts in afternoon issues. Film will continue to increase in quality and sensitivity and may eventually disappear in favor of processes which will enable the cameraman, with the click of a shutter, to record the scene and immediately transmit pictures to the newsroom or picture desk. Here they will be edited. With captions attached, they will be sent to the layout department to be prepared for immediate printing, or will be stored in a complex retrieval system for future use.

Yes, we are living in an exciting age, and more exciting times are just around the corner. No scientific contrivance, however, and no invention in the foreseeable future will eliminate the need for alert, perceptive human beings.

One important influence on photojournalism of tomorrow are the people who depend upon words and pictures for their news, information, and entertainment. Born in a visual age and nurtured on television and on picture newspapers and magazines, they are demanding. Not satisfied with just any "click of the shutter," they demand much of today's photojournalist and in the future will demand even more. Photojournalism of the future must be perceptive and must have integrity and believability.

Does photocommunication conform to the new journalism? That question leads to another: What is this thing called the new journalism?

In a recent monograph James Murphy pointed out that, though Truman Capote disagreed, critics hailed his book *In Cold Blood* as a "classical example of the new journalism."[15]

In their approach, today's photojournalist and the photojournalist of the future are not unlike Capote. Both are sensitive and honest. Both are subjective rather than objective.

Tomorrow's photojournalist will be a special type of person. An artist at heart, he will have all of the earmarks of a well-trained reporter. Most young

---

13. F. W. Lyon (1974): personal communication.
14. F. W. Lyon (1974): personal communication.
15. James Murphy, "The New Journalism: A Critical Perspective," *AEJ Monograph,* May 1974.

A Look at the Future

men and women who enter the field will be college graduates. Many will be specialists with degrees. Present-day newspaper and magazine readers are more critical, more demanding than ever before. Many are college trained, and the product they buy must be good.

In review, tomorrow's photojournalist will have mastered the ABCs of visual communication. He will know the sentence structure and the syntax of photography. He will know layout and design and its many ramifications. Tomorrow's photojournalist will know how to select pictures, how to crop pictures, and how to present the single picture and know how to combine it with other single pictures and picture strips to produce a picture layout or picture page. Yes, the photojournalist of tomorrow will be an expert in research and will know how to write display lines, captions, and, if need be, the word story, itself. Yes, the photojournalist of the future is a person who believes in pictures and the picture language. Above all, he must remember the precept learned early in his schooling: It is not a matter of words versus pictures or of pictures versus words. Rather, it is a matter of words *and* pictures. Tomorrow's photojournalist will contribute his full part to a winning partnership.

# Student Participation

1. Why are some people thinking of changing to subminiature cameras —about half the size of 35 mm. to produce pictures for publications?
2. What is your reaction to the suggestion that conceivably tomorrow's newspaper will be delivered on a closed-circuit television network?
3. What influence do you think the laser beam will have on photojournalism of the future? Use information from this chapter and from an encyclopedia to answer this question.
4. The Associated Press and United Press International both have a program for production of better photographs for newspapers, magazines, and television. List some of the steps they have taken to keep up with modern trends.
5. As they become better educated, people demand more precise reporting and more precise communications media. What effect will these factors have on the newspapers, magazines, and television programs of tomorrow?

# Appendix

## Principles of Selection of News Pictures

*William Stephenson*

William Stephenson, "Principles of Selection of News Pictures," *Journalism Quarterly* 37 (1960): pp. 61–68. Reprinted by permission.

Is there a defensible and preferable alternative to majority rule, when judges are used to select a roster of outstanding photographs? The research specialist who developed Q-methodology in factor analysis proposes an alternative selection procedure and describes its rationale and use.

News pictures are the daily butter, if not the bread, of newspapers and magazines. The photojournalist is as essential as the reporter. As part of the observance of the 50th anniversary of the University of Missouri School of Journalism, a committee was invited to select 50 memorable news pictures of the past half century (1908–1958), the exhibition of which would constitute a recognition of journalism's pride in the photojournalist's art. The need for suitable principles of selection arose, of course, during the long process of getting together an acceptable panel of judges and worthy pictures for them to judge. The collection of 50 memorable pictures was made under the auspices of the School of Journalism, University of Missouri, the National Press Photographers Association, and Encyclopaedia Britannica.

The problems involved seem, at first glance, to be formidable. Expert judgment, rather than popular voting, was indicated. Looking back over 50 years presents its own difficulties of perspective. Principles of selection are little understood, apart from majority rule. It may be of general interest, therefore, to report what was achieved in the circumstances.

### Selection Conditions

The photographs were limited to those given currency in this country, whether taken here or not, whether by an American citizen or not. Discussion at the outset raised questions, naturally, as to the criteria to be employed: Is a significant news picture to be a literal portrayal of a great historical event, or more a picture of great human interest? Must it show originality and be technically perfect? What is the relative significance of spot news photographs—the unplanned, unexpected happening, caught magically in an instant—and general news, where events are currently in the news or are previously announced? How to judge, too, the literal as distinct from the symbolic?

Faced with similar problems in the selection of *fine art* photographs, a committee responsible for selecting the *Saturday Review* "Portfolio of Great Photographs" (*Saturday Review,* May 16, 1959) decided that it was not necessary to establish for its twelve expert judges any specific criteria for selection. Each judge voted according to his own conception of what was a significant photograph, and the photographs gaining the most *pro* votes were selected. The selection, accordingly, was a "representative choice by majority vote."

The procedure seems fair, and up to a point it is probably sound. Clearly, even if it is nowhere made explicit, in the case of the judges for the 50 memorable *news pictures,* it must be assumed that all the judges would have in mind a kind of general journalism creed that significant photographs are in some sense a true report of what is going on in the country. The photographs would be of interest, presumably, to the nation as a whole. They would be in some way educative, but mainly entertaining, and also a reflection, in some degree, of the charter that all journalists are supposed to have, to "admonish and inform the public."

However, little might be gained by making such factors the bases for selection in any formal or systematic sense, and we conclude, therefore, as was done for the *Saturday Review* jury, that the judges should be left to their own devices. Even so, the procedure of majority voting, so widely employed, is weak from a methodological standpoint. The opportunity is not grasped in such a gross vote to learn how far the judges are alike or different in their selections. No one expects experts to be in complete or even close agreement, but one would like to know the facts of the matter. Some judges may be alike in their selections; others, admittedly, may be idiosyncratic.

Considerations of this kind lead, of course, to voting methods of a more sophisticated kind than that of majority rule. They might lead, indeed, to sound reasons for ignoring, more or less, all but one of several judges, whose selection (for sound reasons) might be far superior to those of all the others put together.

One further point requires consideration. It does not seem sufficient to say, and to leave it at that, that each judge will have his own particular criterion for judging photographs. No doubt some have made up their minds, before they see photographs to be judged, about what they believe to be sound criteria for judging photographs. Thus Frank Baker, Senior Art Director of McCann-Erickson, and one of the judges of the *Saturday Review* "Portfolio," maintains that "wearability" is important in a photograph: the ability of the photograph "to endure, to fascinate and refascinate generations of minds" is held to be essential in any creative art. No doubt Mr. Baker would

evaluate photographs in some such terms.

But more usually, the photographs themselves, either by repute or in the mass as the judge looks at them, are likely to set a frame of reference for their evaluation. Thus, another of the "Portfolio" judges, A. Frankfurter, tells us that he did not begin his selection with any particular doctrine in mind, but *after* the selection he wondered why he had chosen some photographs rather than others, and concluded that he had chosen those which not only seemed best composed and technically the best, but also, above all else, those which "made an instant *live*," that is, they were all "moments which somehow have been made to stay." He knew what he liked most, but only afterwards, upon reflection, was he able to say why he liked them.

It may well be that Mr. Frankfurter's is the more general case, and that only after an expert has made his selections will it be profitable for him, or for others, to consider the reasons for the selections being what they are. Something might be gained, therefore, by examining possible criteria *after* evaluations have been made, rather than the reverse. Discussion after making the selections might make it possible, at least, to consider more pertinent selections than those based on majority rule alone.

These considerations lead to methods which have already been developed to provide additional information about the evaluations of judges, and which require no *a priori* or explicit criteria upon which to base evaluations. Some aspects of the methods are described generally in the work of Cronbach and Glesner[1] and, more particularly, in Stephenson.[2] In the study now to be reported, use was made of Stephenson's methods.

Preliminary Screening

Many hundreds of news photographs were collected, first, under James Colvin's auspices, and then by Professor

---

1. L. J. Cronbach and G. C. Glesner, "Assessing Similarity Between Profiles," *Psychological Bulletin,* 50 (1953): 456–473.

2. William Stephenson. *The Study of Behavior: Q-technique and Its Methodology* (Chicago: University of Chicago Press, 1953).

Edom. The latter searched books, periodicals such as *Editor and Publisher,* and contest material in general. He also had available the photographs of sixteen years of contest sponsorship of the School of Journalism at the University of Missouri. All committeemen were involved in forwarding suggestions. The result was a pool of some 300 pictures. After preliminaries, these were reduced to 165, the eliminations stemming from duplication, non-American photographs, and the like.

Professor Edom now prepared sufficient 3x5-inch photographic copies of the 165 to give a complete set to each member of the committee. Each judged the news photos independently. First he looked through all 165, and was asked to add any other news photos that he thought should be included. From his set of 165 plus the additions so introduced, he was invited to select 60 that, in his opinion, were best (by whatever criteria he wished to use). The preferred 60 were returned to Professor Edom, who composed from these a set of 159 news photos which four or more judges had included in their selections. The procedure, clearly, was not materially reducing the number of news photographs—nearly all of them were receiving support from at least four judges.

### Preliminary Factoring

The more detailed evaluations now began, using factor methods (Stephenson). These consist, basically, of requiring each judge to score each picture; the judges are correlated with one another; their correlations are then factor analyzed. If all are judging on the same basis, with the same criteria, the analysis should provide only one factor. If no judge sees eye to eye with another, there should be no factors. If some see things one way and others another, there would be two or more factors. Such is the rationale of factor analysis. It serves to show what the judges are doing systematically (whatever they may say they are doing).

The 159 photographs were divided randomly into three sets of 53 photographs each (designated A, B, C, respectively). The writer visited each judge in turn and gave instructions in how to score on an 11-point scale, from 0 to 10, from least to most memorable, according to the judge's own criteria or viewpoint. Using the sets of 53 facilitated the scoring and made it possible to measure the consistency of the judges as they judged first one set and then the others. They were judged in order A, B, C.

The results of the three sets were in fact similar, showing that the judges were consistent from set to set. Hence it is sufficient to discuss data for set A, to indicate the results.

Table 1 provides the data for set A, for 9 judges (plus one, No. 8, who took part temporarily in this phase of the selecting). All correlate, although in low amounts. The highest correlation is +.63 between judges 2 and 6, and the lowest is −.02 between judges 5 and 7. The low correlations are not to be explained by the unreliability of the judges, however, so much as by the difficulties in discriminating between pictures of such high caliber, all excellent. The judges were consistent in their selections, as their results from set to set proved.

The factor analysis indicates that the judges differ basically. The analysis (centroid method—Thurstone[3]) yields two factors.

It is one of the virtues of factor analysis that it frequently brings new facts to light that one might have suspected, perhaps, but could not otherwise prove. In the present case, there is an interesting discovery of this kind. When the factor loadings in Table 1 are plotted in graphic form (fig. 1), judges 1, 7, and 9 appear at the extreme left of the graph. These men are photojournalists whose daily work is on a newspaper or magazine. Judges 3, 5, and 6, at the other extreme, are wire-service or photo-service men. The judges in between are the historians and public relations officials, none of whom is di-

---

3. L. L. Thurstone, *Multiple Factor Analysis* (Chicago: University of Chicago Press, 1947).

# Table 1

Correlation Coefficients and Factor Saturation for 10 Judges: News Photographs, Set A

| | | | | Judges | | | | | | | Centroid Factors | | Rotated | |
| | 1 | 2 | 3 | 4 | 5 | 6 | 7 | 8 | 9 | 10 | $f_1$ | $f_2$ | I | II |
|---|---|---|---|---|---|---|---|---|---|---|---|---|---|---|
| 1 | — | .22 | .01 | .23 | .01 | .18 | .34 | .25 | .31 | .29 | .39 | −.39 | .55 | .02 |
| 2 | | — | .53 | .45 | .20 | .63 | .24 | .50 | .20 | .32 | .72 | .20 | .35 | .65 |
| 3 | | | — | .32 | .40 | .46 | .13 | .26 | .15 | .17 | .51 | .46 | .02 | .68 |
| 4 | | | | — | .38 | .37 | .13 | .41 | .54 | .28 | .69 | −.05 | .50 | .47 |
| 5 | | | | | — | .42 | .02 | .17 | .17 | .16 | .40 | .26 | .09 | .47 |
| 6 | | | | | | — | .15 | .29 | .21 | .39 | .67 | .39 | .18 | .75 |
| 7 | | | | | | | — | .18 | .32 | .13 | .32 | −.20 | .38 | .06 |
| 8 | | | | | | | | — | .42 | .37 | .60 | −.14 | .52 | .34 |
| 9 | | | | | | | | | — | .22 | .53 | −.43 | .67 | .08 |
| 10 | | | | | | | | | | — | .49 | −.05 | .37 | .32 |

rectly involved in producing the news. The same result appears in sets B and C. Obviously a rather important fact is at issue: The practicing newspaper or magazine men are in some respect poles apart from the picture- or wire-service men. They do not see the pictures in the same way.

Rotation of the axes in fig. 1 to the position indicated by the dotted lines brings this little discovery into better focus. We shall call the new axes Factors I and II. Factor I thus represents (theoretically, if one likes) how the local newsman thinks about pictures, and Factor II represents how the more hectic wire-service men think of them. All are dealing, of course, with news photographs, all of which are of the highest caliber, all well-known in photojournalism.

The factors need not be taken too literally. They merely indicate that there are systematic differences between different groups of judges. They are congruent, however, with the respective broad functions of the judges. Nor will it matter whether *all* community or local photojournalists fall into line with Factor I, and *all* wire-service men in line with Factor II, and everyone else somewhere else or in between.

Theoretically, it is possible that the historians and others in between represent how *most* people in general would judge the photographs. The factors would be what experts do, rather than

just anyone. For the present, however, it is sufficient to proceed with the experts in mind. What is important is the evidence that the pictures are being regarded systematically in at least these two uncorrelated ways.

## Final Screening

Interesting consequences now appear. If the majority rule is used to select 50 pictures receiving the highest scores by the judges, the effect would be to cancel out the judges representing Factors I and II, leaving the final selection in effect to the in-between judges. This follows because the factors are uncorrelated, so that there is just as much chance of a picture receiving a high mark from the Factor I judges as for it to receive a low one from Factor II judges. In such a tussle, the in-between judges will tend to win out.

It is precisely such a happening that makes the majority rule so suspect amongst scientists (and so acceptable to democratic politicians). In the present case it seems that if anyone should count, it should be the experts, but by majority rule they would be involved in mutual blackout.

Under these circumstances a selection of pictures can be taken *from each group* of judges, the 10 best from Factor I judges, the 10 best from Factor II judges, and 10 also from the in-between judges. Averaging within such

**Table 2**

Correlation Coefficients and Factor Saturations for 10 Judges:
Final Set of 64 News Photographs

| | | | | Judges | | | | | | | Centroid Factors | | | Rotated | | |
|---|---|---|---|---|---|---|---|---|---|---|---|---|---|---|---|---|
| | 1 | 2 | 3 | 4 | 5 | 6 | 7 | 9 | 10 | 11 | $f_1$ | $f_2$ | $f_3$ | I | II | III |
| 1 | — | −.08 | −.08 | .27 | −.10 | .03 | .37 | .45 | .15 | .36 | .34 | −.48 | .17 | .60 | .03 | −.08 |
| 2 | | — | .50 | .32 | .26 | .48 | −.07 | .08 | .15 | .21 | .47 | .31 | −.18 | −.02 | .49 | .35 |
| 3 | | | — | .44 | .23 | .27 | −.09 | .19 | .18 | .23 | .48 | .00 | −.48 | .09 | .67 | −.03 |
| 4 | | | | — | .33 | .31 | .16 | .28 | .24 | .41 | .75 | −.17 | −.12 | .52 | .54 | .18 |
| 5 | | | | | — | .15 | −.08 | −.19 | .26 | .04 | .22 | .39 | .27 | −.05 | .02 | .53 |
| 6 | | | | | | — | .21 | .21 | −.05 | .27 | .48 | .19 | −.29 | .05 | .57 | .22 |
| 7 | | | | | | | — | .17 | .01 | .10 | .21 | −.27 | −.14 | .25 | .21 | −.14 |
| 9 | | | | | | | | — | .28 | .56 | .53 | −.59 | .08 | .76 | .17 | −.12 |
| 10 | | | | | | | | | — | .13 | .34 | .00 | .31 | .32 | .00 | .33 |
| 11 | | | | | | | | | | — | .61 | −.25 | .00 | .51 | .37 | .11 |

groups is valid; averaging *across* them is merely making a muddle of systematic differences.

Sets B and C were dealt with in the same way. In the present study the yield from this procedure, from sets A, B, C, was 62 photographs, all different, to which the three groupings of the judges had contributed equally.

The judges had not, of course, compared all 159 pictures as a group of pictures, but only within sets of 53 at a time. There might have been more they liked in one set than in the others. However, this was minimized by the random distribution of the pictures into the three sets. It has to be assumed, also, that the average score given to the pictures would be the same for all judges on any absolute scale of values, if any such could exist.

The yield, then, is 62 photographs from which to select the memorable 50. At this point judges could add any other photograph if they so wished, and two did so. There were 64 pictures, therefore, for final evaluation.

### Final Factoring and Selection

At this stage judge 8 dropped out and another, 11, took his place. All 10 were given 3x5-inch copies of the 64 photographs, as before, with instructions to score them, again, on an 11-point scale. The data were correlated and factored, as before, with the results shown in Table 2.

The original two factors again appear, defined clearly enough by judges 1 and 9 (and less so by 7) in the case of Factor I, and by judges 3 and 6 as before for Factor II. Judge 5, who had appeared on Factor II previously, now separated himself into a different factor —there is other evidence that he had changed his ideas at this point in the judging, and this is clearly reflected in the data. The remaining judges who earlier constituted the in-betweens appear in the same position here as well, except that they are differently in-between (so to speak).

To select 50 from 64 does not, at this point, raise too many difficulties. The committee could be guided along lines indicated by the factoring. Factors I and II have been most consistent, and remain the most clearly defined. The judges in the in-between category do not, it seems, contribute anything systematically different from what is taken care of, already, by Factors I and II. The third factor in Table 2 could be discounted on the grounds that the judge is in a minority of one.

If, then, the 50 photographs are taken which gain highest scores on Factor I, and the 50 are taken which gain highest scores on Factor II, the following results:

1. Forty of the 64 photographs appear in both sets of 50.
2. Twenty of the 64 appear only once, in the one set of 50 or the other.
3. Four appear in neither set of 50.

The 40 could be recommended to

the committee as acceptable for inclusion in the memorable 50. They give equal weight to Factors I and II, and include many of the photographs scored highly by the in-between judges. The additional 10 photographs can be chosen from the 20 of no. 2 above, by taking those gaining highest scores in either factor. This yielded eight more photographs, leaving two at a doubtful level.

The committee met (as to six members of it) and considered these recommendations. They were quite free, of course, to reject them, or to add any other photographs if it appeared at this point that this should be done. In point of fact a photograph was introduced again (from the earlier sets A, B, C which had been of borderline acceptability at that stage of the screening) because, when the final celebration set was contemplated, it seemed that it should be among them. It was the famous "Lone Flyer" (Charles A. Lindberg in pilot's helmet).

The final 50 were thus agreed upon.

## Discussion

The procedure no doubt seems protracted and difficult to understand except by those familiar with the methods of factor analysis. However, it is essentially straightforward and offers distinct advantages. For the present it is proposed to assume its appropriateness and to look briefly at what it implies.

The factors are arrays of the photographs which are consistently provided by some of the judges. In the present case, two tendencies seem to be quite acceptable, on the grounds that they appear consistently and relate directly to the functions of the judges involved. Thus, in the case of Factor I (for the newspapermen), the judges scored most highly those photographs which valued general news, by way of comment, with the emotions of pity and compassion much in evidence. The other factor (for the photo- and wire-service men) involved spot news more, with the sensational and novel more apparent.

The tendencies in these two directions are quite evident, and in line with what might be expected in the circumstances of the daily work of the respective judges. It is to be supposed that the men getting out the daily newspaper or the magazine feel the need to upgrade their publications by the inclusion of more thought-provoking pictures as well as any more sensational ones. They are more prepared to think of pictures as matters of record and as comment on the community scene.

The wire-service man seems more likely to value the directly entertaining and sensational. His is the more hectic occupation, and he thinks of nationwide popularities rather than of the "good" newspaper in his own community.

It might be thought that the in-between judges should be given the greater weight because they are not so much or so strictly involved in either the one or the other of the two standpoints. However, they are not really as consistent amongst themselves as they should be if we are to suppose that there is a coherent basis for their selections. There is some evidence, indeed, that they represent themselves idiosyncratically—the historian values royalty, and the business editor what is political. The practicing photojournalist is more in touch with the everyday objectives of newspapers and magazines, and this is clearly reflected in his selections.

This is not to say that one of the above factors is more desirable than the other. T. S. Matthews, in *The Sugar Pill,* indicates cleverly how different newspapers are differently motivated, each appropriate to its needs.[4] The

---

4. T. S. Matthews, *The Sugar Pill* (New York: Simon & Schuster, Inc., 1959).

same seems to be true of photojournalism.

## Conclusion

The 50 photographs, by any standards, are great photographs. Without question there are many more as great or greater. But these serve to epitomize the photojournalist's work—they reflect both the wire services' vital emphasis on "spot news" and popularity, and the newspaperman's wider sympathies with more "general news."

What the public likes, needs, or wants is another matter.

The method of selection, in general, serves to bring to light systematic differences of the kind here dealt with. The majority rule must always be suspect. And when systematic differences are found, questions of suitable criteria for future judging can be more seriously entertained. A great deal of work, indeed, needs to be done in all areas of art and photograph judging, to determine the motivations at issue besides aesthetic or other principles.

The author wishes to express his warm thanks to Prof. C. C. Edom, without whom little of the above could have been accomplished.

# Glossary

| | |
|---|---|
| *Advertising Photograph* | A black-and-white or color photograph made in a studio or elsewhere for the sole purpose of creating greater sales appeal for a product or service. Successful advertising photography requires great technical knowledge. The advertising photographer is an illustrator. |
| *Air in a Layout* | A page layout in which adequate space between elements on the page creates an uncluttered, "airy" appearance. Picture pages should not be too solid nor too tight. To be inviting a page should, first, have an interesting content; second, it should use white space and air in combination with the illustrations in such a way as to direct the reader in a logical, cohesive manner. |
| *Airbrush* | A compression device used with watercolor to paint out obnoxious foreground or background or to otherwise increase the reproductive qualities of a photograph. |
| *Art* | "The embodiment of beautiful thought in sensuous forms as in pictures, statues, music, or speech or the works thus provided" (*Britannica World Language Dictionary*). Art is also a slang term for any illustrations used in a newspaper or other publication. |
| *Art Director* | The person responsible for the overall design and layout of a publication. A picture editor, who usually determines the sequence and manner in which pictures are to appear, takes his suggestions, together with the rough layout, to the art director. The latter weighs this material against the word stories, maps, and other illustrative material and finalizes the complete magazine, newspaper, or book layout. |
| *Available Lighting* | Natural light available for taking pictures. Faster film, faster lenses, and smaller cameras made possible informal, more believable news photography. One of the reasons for the almost overnight popularity of the miniature camera was that it permitted the use of available (natural) light to make exposures. Minimizing the use of flash photography added another degree of believability to pictures. |
| *Bas Relief* | A photograph which has sculptural qualities. A bas relief is made by placing together a transparent negative and a positive transparency of the same picture and moving them out of register. |
| *Color Preprinting* | A system in which color pictures are printed on a roll of paper. The paper with the pictures is rewound and shipped to the customer who adds the type matter on his own presses. |
| *Color Separation* | Any of many methods used to separate a color print or transparency into its primary colors. The primary colors printed one at a time in close register give the full-color reproduction of the original. |
| *Cover Picture* | The first picture on a thematic type of page. It acts as an *opener* and sets the stage for the story which is to follow. |
| *Crop* | To cut away the unwanted parts of a picture. Cropping enables one to simplify the picture, to increase its impact value and effectiveness. Overcropping, on the other hand, can harm a picture, can detract from its communicative and aesthetic value. |

| | |
|---|---|
| *Daguerreotype* | An early type of photograph produced on a glass, silver, or silver-covered copper plate. Named after Louis Daguerre who invented the process in 1839, it is recognized as the world's "first practical photographic process." |
| *Director of Photography* | A person in charge of directing an entire photographic operation. Usually he is among the top echelon of publication administrators. |
| *Documentary Pictures* | Still or motion pictures which record some phase of life or custom. They are "similar to a monograph in literature." Generally speaking, documentary pictures point out social evils and many times help lead the way to reform. |
| *Duotone* | A combination of two color plates made from a black-and-white original which provide a form of color printing. Although not comparable in quality to full-color work requiring three or more plates, the duotone (two-plate, two-color picture) can sometimes be effective. |
| *Ecological Photography* | A type of camera work which focuses on ecological problems such as pollution, conservation, and the like. Documerica, a governmental program, takes an ecological approach. |
| *Ethics* | The principles of professional conduct which govern the actions of reporters and other communicators—photojournalists as well as writers. |
| *Free-lance Photographer* | A person who is not a staff member of a newspaper or magazine, but who sells his pictures to any market which desires to buy them. Operating on speculation and sometimes on contract, a free-lancer is not limited by a weekly, monthly, or yearly salary. To be successful, he must be a self-starter, able to sell himself and his pictures. Above all, he must know how and where to sell the pictures he takes. |
| *Freestanding Picture* | A picture which stands alone. It does not accompany either a word or picture story, but with its overlines and underlines is a complete entity itself. |
| *General Assignment Photographer* | A photographer who covers news, feature, sports, family interest, and all other types of photographs for publication. The general assignment cameraman differs from the specialized photo reporter in that the latter concentrates on a single type of picture such as news, feature, or sports. On larger publications specialists work on the Sunday papers, on the Sunday magazines (roto section), or on fashion photography. |
| *Gingerbread* | A term often used to describe a picture or layout containing nonfunctional borders, odd picture shapes, and the like. Gingerbread layouts were especially popular in the early days of photojournalism, especially in the rotogravure sections of newspapers in the United States. |
| *Gravure Printing* | The process of printing from an intaglio plate. In this process, the image to be printed lies below the plate surface in ink-filled depressions, in contrast to letterpress printing. *See also* Letterpress Printing; Offset Printing; Photo-offset Printing. |
| *Halftone* | A photoengraving and photo-offset process used for reproduction of continuous-tone copy; also the name given to a photoengraving made from the process. The name implies a tone halfway between white and black. The halftone screen is either a glass screen which is set the proper distance from the film in a process camera or a contact screen which in the camera is placed in immediate contact with the film before a negative is made. Either type of screen breaks the original copy into highlights, middle tones, and shadow dots. The dots, which range in size from coarse to fine, depending upon the number of dots per inch, give the illusion of tone when the halftone plate is printed in a newspaper. |
| *Illuminated Manuscript* | A manuscript decorated with figures and ornamental colored letters. Many authorities consider pre-Biblical illuminated manuscripts to be "the beginning of the illustrated press." |
| *Intaglio* | *See* Gravure Printing. |
| *Juxtaposition of Photographs* | An arrangement of similar or opposite types of pictures in a layout. When properly done, the combination increases the communicative value of each of the pictures used. "The whole is greater than the sum of its parts." |
| *Letterpress (Relief) Printing* | Printing from raised surfaces. In this process, the paper is pressed against the inked surface to produce the impression. *See also* Gravure Printing; Offset Printing; Photo-offset Printing. |
| *Mondrian Layout* | A type of layout inspired by the Dutch artist Piet Mondrian. Illustration designers who use the Mondrian approach believe that white space in the center of a picture layout can be distracting. To avoid this distraction, they put the white space along the edges, as Mondrian did in many of his neoplastic paintings. In addition to working in strict geometric patterns and crowding the white space to the outside, those who favor the Mondrian layout insist on "internal consistency" of space between the illustrations. Even though one does not adopt a pure Mondrian design, white space and cutlines should usually be at the edges of the layout. |

| | |
|---|---|
| *Mortise* | An area of a photograph or illustration which is cut out to receive a pictorial insert, a caption, or display type. |
| *Negative* | A photographic image on transparent material used for printing positive pictures. When it is processed after exposure, the film in a camera yields a negative, the exact opposite of a positive. When a negative is printed on sensitized paper, film, metal, and the like, the result is a positive. |
| *Offset Printing* | A printing process in which a page (or other image) is photographically reproduced on a thin flexible metal plate curved to fit the cylinders of an offset printing press. The inked impression is first made on the metal plate and then transferred to a rubber blanket. The type or illustration is offset from the blanket to the paper. *See also* Gravure Printing; Letterpress Printing; Photo-offset Printing. |
| *Overprinting* | *See* Surprinting. |
| *Perspective* | The characteristic of a painting, drawing, or photograph which gives the illusion of receding distance. In photography examples of perspective are narrowing of railroad tracks (linear perspective) and the graying-out of blacks (aerial perspective) as they approach the horizon. |
| *Photographic Beat* | A specific area of photographic news coverage: police, wildlife, city hall, farming, and so forth. |
| *Photographic Illustrations* | Photographs which illustrate a story idea or point, rather than report a news event. Photographic illustrations should be labeled as such, and should not go under the guise of news photographs. Illustrations allow a photographer the opportunity to create, something news photographs do not. A studio, special lighting effects, rear-screen projection, and setups are all used to produce photographic illustrations. |
| *Photojournalism* | A combination of words and pictures which together form a stronger, easier understood method of communication than either words or pictures alone can produce. |
| *Photo-offset Printing* | A type of offset printing in which a negative print of the copy is used in the photochemical preparation of the printing plates. The process is more economical than other printing processes, a factor contributing greatly to the continuing viability of small suburban newspapers. It is also more versatile, and fidelity of photograph reproduction is greater. *See also* Gravure Printing; Letterpress Printing; Offset Printing. |
| *Pica Rule* | A straightedge divided into pica units as well as into inches used to measure typographic material. With a pica rule a picture editor can measure the size of an original picture and figure the amount of enlargement or reduction needed for the picture to fit a particular space. |
| *Picture Editor* | One who gives picture assignments, selects pictures for publication, and crops and sizes them to increase their storytelling qualities. He (or she) also plans picture layouts, arranging not only the pictures themselves, but also the space and words so that they unite in a pleasing, comprehensible unit. |
| *Picture Page* | A page composed entirely of words and pictures. Picture pages may be planned around a central theme such as Thanksgiving, Christmas, a community, an interesting character, and the like. A picture page may also be a group of pictures without a unifying theme. The most effective picture pages adhere to a theme, although some newspapers feel that a hodgepodge page (with no theme) attracts more people and has greater general interest. When a picture page is being laid out, it is better to use only a few pictures (not more than five) than to use too many. The pictures should vary in size and shape to increase editorial and visual impact. |
| *Picture Strip* | A series of pictures which usually shows a progression of time or action. A how-to-do-it series or sequence is a good example of a picture strip. Here is another example: picture 1, two airplanes collide in the sky; picture 2, the planes swirl downward; picture 3, the planes crash-land. |
| *Proportion Calculator* | A slide rule, wheel, or similar device which permits one to figure the proportionate enlargement or reduction of a line drawing or photograph. |
| *Register* | Alignment of three-color images on a press when natural color reproductions are printed. |
| *ROP Color* (run of press color) | A system of printing which allows color reproductions to be printed on any page or section of a newspaper. |
| *Sketch Artists* | Before invention of the halftone, sketch artists—those who drew pictures of the news event on paper or on wood (reversed)—were the source of most illustrations which appeared in newspapers and magazines. Even now, as in courtrooms and other places where photography is not allowed, the sketch artist very effectively continues to ply his trade. |

Glossary

| | |
|---|---|
| *Spotting* | Using a pencil or a fine-pointed brush and watercolor to eliminate spots on a print surface before it is displayed to the public or converted to a halftone negative. |
| *Stereoscope* | A device used to project or view two almost similar images to create a third dimension. |
| *Subtractive Color Process* | A process of halftone reproduction of full-color art using one plate for each color, usually magenta, cyan, yellow, and sometimes black. The process is in contrast to the additive process of color printing, which uses red, green, and blue. |
| *Surprinting* | A method whereby something additional is printed over an original picture, and the like. Surprinting is usually done during the plate-making process. A caption, for example, or a display line may be printed (white type in a black area or black type in a light area) on a picture. Surprinting, or overprinting as it is often called, can be effective, but it should not be overdone. |
| *Wire Picture Services* | Commercial enterprises which transmit photographs electronically over telephone wires or other long-distance transmission system. |
| *Wood Engraving* | The art of cutting designs on wood (usually in reverse from left to right) for relief printing. The term *wood engraving* applies to an engraved block or a print. A carry-over from the days of woodcuts is the fact that in England photoengravings even now are referred to as "blocks" and in the United States as "cuts." |

# Bibliography

Like an artist, a lawyer, or a doctor, a photojournalist should begin to build a library early in his study. Although he has a college degree or degrees, he should never stop studying. The minute he does, his career heads downward.

The budding photojournalist should know what great photographers have done and are doing. Through reading books, magazines, and the like, he can know what has taken place and keep abreast of the times. More important, however, is the fact that a thorough knowledge of the past and present will at least give him some idea of what the future holds.

Examine the following bibliography carefully. Some of the older books may not be readily available, but most of these books can be found in public, university, or college libraries. All are interesting and valuable sources of research material.

Agee, James, and Evans, Walker. *Let Us Now Praise Famous Men.* New York: Random House, Ballantine Books, 1966.

Baynes, Ken. *Scoop, Scandal and Strife.* New York: Hastings House, 1971.

Bergin, David F. *Photojournalism Manual: How to Plan, Shoot, Edit and Sell.* New York: Morgan & Morgan, 1967.

Bluem, A. William. *Documentary in American Television.* New York: Hastings House, 1968.

Bourke-White, Margaret. *Shooting the Russian War.* New York: Simon and Schuster, 1942.

————. *Portrait of Myself.* New York: Simon and Schuster, 1963.

Braive, Michel F. *The Photograph: A Social History.* New York: McGraw-Hill Book Co., 1966.

Bresson, Henri Cartier. *The Decisive Moment.* New York: Simon and Schuster, 1952.

Caldwell, Erskine, and Bourke-White, Margaret. *Say, Is This the U.S.A.?* New York: Duell, Sloan & Pearce, 1941.

Callahan, Sean. *The Photographs of Margaret Bourke-White.* New York: New York Graphic Society, 1972.

Capa, Cornell. *The Concerned Photographer.* New York: Grossman Publishers, 1968.

————. *The Concerned Photographer.* 2. New York: Grossman Publishers, 1972.

Capa, Robert. *Slightly Out of Focus.* New York: Henry Holt & Co., 1947.

————. *Images of War.* New York: Grossman Publishers, 1964.

Davis, Phil. *Photography,* 2nd ed. Dubuque: Wm. C. Brown Co., Publishers, 1975.

De Carava, Roy, and Hughes, Langston. *The Sweet Flypaper of Life.* New York: Simon and Schuster, 1955 (an Experimental book since reissued).

Denison, Herbert. *A Treatise on Photogravure.* London: Iliffe and Son., 1892.

Doisneau, Robert. *Paris.* New York: Simon and Schuster, 1956.

Doty, Robert. *Photo Secession: Photography as a Fine Art.* New York: Duell, Sloan & Pearce, 1960, for George Eastman House.

Duncan, David Douglas. *This Is War.* New York: Harper Brothers, 1951.

————. *The Private World of Pablo Picasso.* New York: Ridge Press, 1958.

————. *I Protest.* New York: New American Library, Signet, 1968.

————. *Self Portrait: U.S.A.* New York: Harry N. Abrams, 1969.

————. *War Without Heroes.* New York: Harper & Row, 1970.

Edom, Clifton C. *Careers:* Chicago: The Institute for Research, 1961. "Career as a Newspaper, Magazine and TV News Photographer." Research Number 202.

Eisenstaedt, Alfred. *Witness to Our Time.* New York: Viking Press, 1966.

————. *The Eye of Eisenstaedt.* New York: Viking Press, 1969.

————. *People.* New York: Viking Press, 1973.

Evans, Walker. *American Photographs.* New York: Museum of Modern Art, 1938.

————. *Message from the Interior.* New York: Eakins Press, 1966.

Frank, Robert. *The Americans.* New York: Grossman Publishers, 1969.

Frank, Waldo, Mumford, Lewis, Norman, Dorothy, Rosenfeld, Paul, and Rugg, Harold. *America and Alfred Steiglitz.* New York: Doubleday, Doran & Co., 1934.

Geraci, Philip C. *Making Pictures for Publication.* Dubuque: Kendall/Hunt Publishing Co., 1973.

Gernsheim, Helmut and Allison. *Roger Fenton, Photographer of the Crimean War.* London: Secker and Warburg, 1954.

————. *The Recording Eye: A Hundred Years of Great Events as Seen by the Camera, 1839–1939.* New York: G. P. Putnam's Sons, 1960.

Hall, Norman. *Press Pictures of a Decade.* London: Photography Magazine, Ltd., 1960.

Hicks, Wilson. *Words and Pictures: An Introduction to Photojournalism.* New York: Harper Brothers, 1952: reprint ed., Arno Press, 1973.

Horan, James D. *Timothy O'Sullivan: America's Forgotten Photographer.* New York: Doubleday & Co., 1966.

Hurley, Jack F. *Portrait of a Decade: Roy Stryker and the Department of Documentary Photography in the Thirties.* Baton Rouge: Louisiana State University Press, 1972.

Jackson, Mason. *The Pictorial Press, Its Origin and Progress.* London: Hurst & Blackett, Publishers, 1885.

Karsh, Yousuf. *Portraits of Greatness.* New York: Thomas Nelson & Sons, 1959.

Lartigue, J. H., and Lartigue, S. A. *Boyhood Pictures of J. N. Lartigue.* Switzerland: Ami Guichard, Publisher, 1966.

Lieberman, Archie. *Farm Boy.* New York: Harry N. Abrams, Inc., 1974.

Life Library of Photography. *Photojournalism.* New York: Time-Life Books, 1971.

————. *The Best of Life.* New York: Time-Life Books, 1973.

Lyons, Nathan. *Photographers on Photography.* Englewood Cliffs, N. J.: Prentice-Hall, 1966, for George Eastman House.

McCall, Floyd H., and Rhode, Robert B. *Introduction to Photography.* New York: Macmillan Co., 1971.

McCombe, Leonard. *You Are My Love.* New York: William Sloane Associates, 1952. (A love story, based on a feature which appeared in *Life,* told in the special idiom of a camera.)

McDougall, Angus, and Hurley, Gerald D. *Visual Impact in Print.* Chicago: American Publishers Press, 1971.

MacDougall, Curtis D. *News Pictures Fit to Print: . . . Or Are They?* Stillwater, Okla.: Journalistic Services, Inc., 1971.

McManigal, J. W. *Farm Town.* Brattleboro, Vt.: Stephen Greene Press, 1974.

Mich, Daniel D., and Eberman, Edwin. *The Technique of the Picture Story.* New York: McGraw-Hill Book Co., 1945.

Mott, Frank Luther. *A History of American Magazines, 1885–1905.* Cambridge, Mass.: Harvard University Press, 1957.

National Education Ailiance, Inc. *The Complete Photographer, and Encyclopedia of Photography.* New York: Morgan & Morgan, 1942. (Since updated and reprinted.)

Newhall, Beaumont. *Photography, a Short Critical History.* New York: Museum of Modern Art, 1938.

Pollack, Peter. *The Picture History of Photography.* Revised and enlarged ed. New York: Harry N. Abrams, 1969.

Robinson, Henry Peach. *Pictorial Effect in Photography.* Pawlet, Vt.: Helios Publishing Co., 1971. reprint ed. from 1st ed., 1869.

Rothstein, Arthur. *Photojournalism.* New York: American Photographic Book Publishing Co., 1956.

Rothstein, Arthur, and Saroyan, William. *Look At Us . . .* New York: Cowles Education Corp., 1967.

Salomon, Peter Hunter. *Erich Salomon, Portrait of an Age.* New York: Macmillan Co., 1967.

Schaleben, Arville. *A Definitive Study of Your Future in Journalism.* New York: Richards Rosen Press, 1961.

Schuneman, R. Smith. *Photographic Communication: Principles, Problems and Challenges of Photojournalism.* New York: Hastings House, 1972.

Steichen, Edward. *The Family of Man.* New York: Museum of Modern Art, 1955.

Strode, William H. III. *Barney Cowherd, Photographer.* Louisville: *Courier-Journal & Times,* 1973.

Stryker, Roy Emerson, and Wood, Nancy. *In This Proud Land: America 1935–43, as Seen in FSA Photographs.* Greenwich, Conn.: New York Graphic Society, 1973.

Swedlund, Charles, *Photography.* New York: Holt, Rinehart & Winston, 1973.

Taft, Robert. *Photography and the American Scene.* New York: Macmillan Co., 1938; reprint ed., 1942.

Vitray, Laura, Mills, John, Jr., and Ellard, Roscoe. *Pictorial Journalism.* New York: McGraw-Hill Book Co., 1939.

Weston, Edward. *The Daybooks of Edward Weston.* Mexico, vol. 1. New York: George Wittenborn, 1961, for George Eastman House.

———. *The Daybooks of Edward Weston.* California, vol. 2. New York: Horizon Press (n.d.), for George Eastman House.

Whiting, John R. *Photography Is a Language.* Chicago: Ziff-Davis Publishing Co., 1946.

# Index of Illustrations

# Index

#49